RANDY COUTURE

XTREME TRAINING

with LANCE FREIMUTH AND ERICH KRAUSS

LAS VEGAS

First Published in 2010 by Victory Belt Publishing.

ISBN 10: 0-9825658-2-8

ISBN 13: 978-0-9825658-2-7

This book is for educational purposes. The publisher and authors of this instructional book are not responsible in any manner whatsoever for any adverse effects arising directly or indirectly as a result of the information provided in this book. If not practiced safely and with caution, martial arts can be dangerous to you and to others. It is important to consult with a professional martial arts instructor before beginning training. It is also very important to consult with a physician prior to training due to the intense and strenuous nature of the techniques in this book.

Cover Design by Brian Rule

Printed in Hong Kong

A special thanks to Jake Bonacci and Ron Frazier. Without your help, this book would not have been possible.

CONTENTS

PART ONE: GENERAL PHYSICAL PREPARATION

SECTION ONE: METABOLIC CONDITIONING

FULL-BODY METABOLIC CONDITIONING

SECTION TWO: POSTERIOR CHAIN

DOUBLE EXTENSION

TRIPLE EXTENSION

SECTION THREE: UPPER BODY PUSH

HORIZONTAL PLANE

FRONTAL PLANE

OVERHEAD SUBTITUTES

SECTION FOUR: UPPER BODY PULL

HORIZONTAL PLANE

FRONTAL PLANE

SECTION FIVE: CORE

PART TWO: SPORT-SPECIFIC TRAINING

SECTION ONE: SPORT-SPECIFIC STANDING

SECTION TWO: SPORT-SPECIFIC GROUND

PART THREE: TRAINING ROUTINE

ALTERNATE WORKOUTS

INTRODUCTION

In the early days of mixed martial arts, it was possible for a fighter to attain victory based on technical ability alone. Those days are gone. In this age of shared information, most fighters will anticipate your plan of attack and present a suitable counter. While having superior technique will certainly help you achieve your goal of victory, to get the upper hand time and again, you must either move quicker than your opponent can counter or continuously counter his counters, dragging him deeper into the hole until you are finally able to get one step ahead and leave him defenseless.

Both of these qualities can be improved in every individual, but it must be done through superior strength-and-conditioning training. Having covered my preferred fighting techniques in my book, Wrestling for Fighting, I've dedicated this manual to helping you reach your athletic potential, which in turn will allow you to execute your game plan in the cage without fatiguing. I've outlined the complete physical training regimen that garnered me a reputation as a fighter with superior conditioning and stamina.

The first part of the book covers general physical preparation exercises, or GPP. These workouts are executed off the mat, most often in the weight room. Although the majority of them are very general in nature, they allow you to develop a base level of strength by progressively increasing resistance in each exercise. The second part of the book covers sport-specific training, which consists of the workouts that you do on the mat, using actual fighting technique to increase power and endurance in specific, individual movements. By utilizing sport-specific exercises and drills, you're able to increase your stamina while carrying out your actual game plan. This is an extremely practical way to train. Sport-specific training gives you a way to drill techniques you're familiar with, allows you to increase strength and stamina in the exact movements needed in a fight, and lets you get real face-to-face practice with your partners.

The combination of these training methods in the right manner and ratio will allow for vastly improved endurance in the cage. However, utilizing these methods improperly, or at an incorrect frequency, can actually harm performance. To ensure that you get the most out of the information presented in this book, I give sample workouts from my actual training camps at the end. This eliminates the guesswork of developing your own workout routine when first starting out in the sport. By following the template provided, you can mimic a proven routine and garner great strength and conditioning right out of the gate.

It is important to mention that this book is designed sequentially. The beginning of each chapter explains specific details necessary for understanding the pages that follow, and each section builds upon the previous section. As you read the book, you will discover not only what exercises I utilize in my fight preparation, but also why I utilize each individual exercise at various stages in my training regime. By the end of the book, you will be armed with the knowledge to either build your own training routine or to simply mimic my workouts correctly and efficiently.

PART ONE
GENERAL PHYSICAL PREPARATION

Many fighters make the assumption that working out in the cage or on the mats will supply all the strength and conditioning they need. Nothing could be further from the truth. Solely sparring and drilling MMA movements will increase your technical ability, but it will fail to develop your body to its maximum athletic potential. Sparring is hard on a fighter, and as intensity increases, so do injuries. It's impossible to spar or drill on a consistent basis with the intensity needed to develop strength and conditioning to peak levels. This is where general physical preparation comes into play. General physical preparation (GPP) is any non-sport-specific workout that develops a set of generalized athletic qualities. This increased athletic ability in turn helps an athlete more effectively train their sport-specific activities in other workouts.

While it may seem counterintuitive, general physical preparation exercises are often very dissimilar to your actual sport. The Principle of Specificity states that in order to become better at any activity, you must practice that activity in the exact way you want to perform it. This helps ingrain the motor pattern into your body and makes you stronger and more efficient at that exact movement. However, with GPP that is not our goal. Rather than improving specific movements, you develop general abilities that transfer over into a wide range of movements. This builds an athletic base and helps you learn specific sports movements in a more efficient manner. Since the movements are of a very general nature, the same GPP workout could be used for a fighter or an NFL running back with the same efficiency. The goal is to build a base of athleticism that will erect the foundation for the sport-specific training methods shown later in the book.

The general athletic qualities we seek to improve with GPP are broad, but they can be reasonably sorted into one of eight categories, the first of which is strength.

STRENGTH

Strength is the force that is applied to an object in order to make it move. In human beings this force is generated by muscular contractions that initiate movement in various joints of the body. Muscular strength is the base of all human movement, and the amount of strength that can be applied in any movement can only be increased in one of two ways.

The first way is by increasing the cross-sectional area of the muscle fibers used in the movement. Essentially, as a muscle gets bigger, it gets stronger. However, this method of increasing strength tends to plateau quickly. Due to the fact that a twofold gain in the cross-sectional area of an individual muscle is accompanied by a threefold increase in the mass, developing bigger muscles is not the most efficient way to increase strength. Increasing muscle size to improve strength rapidly leads to diminishing returns because at some point the weight of the increased muscle mass overcomes the strength gains it provides.

The other, more efficient, method of gaining strength is achieved by cultivating the central nervous system. The central nervous system (CNS), is the system of your body that controls and dictates conscious movement. As you consciously decide to initiate any action, your CNS breaks down the movement and sends signals to the necessary muscles telling them when to fire, in what order, and with how much force. The CNS not only acts as the controller of individual muscles, but also the safety switch. If allowed to contract unchecked, it would be possible for individual muscles to flex with enough force to damage bones and tendons. To prevent this from happening, your CNS commands the necessary muscles to contract with the minimum amount of force needed to complete the movement. Consistent strength training will disinhibit this process, allowing the CNS to signal individual muscle groups to contract with increased force. Developing the neural pathways can lead to extremely impressive strength gains, even while the cross-sectional area of the muscle fibers remains constant. More strength allows fighters to use less energy to execute their techniques, which leads not only to increased efficiency with these techniques, but also decreased energy output.

SPEED

The second general athletic quality we aim to improve with GPP workouts is the creation of speed. Speed is the rate at which any given muscle can contract, and thus the velocity of movement. The velocity of any given movement is determined in part by the muscle fibers initiating that movement. There are two types of muscle fibers: Type I, commonly referred to as "slow twitch," and Type II, called "fast twitch." The higher the percentage of Type II muscle fibers that make up a motor unit, the faster that muscle can contract. The ratio of Type I to Type II muscle fibers in any muscle group is mostly determined by genetics. There's no way to turn a Type I muscle fiber into a Type II or vice versa, but by training powerful movements it's possible to increase the size of the Type II muscle fibers, which changes the ratio of the Type I to Type II fibers. Simply put, the more Type II muscle fiber you possess, the greater your potential for speed. And for those looking to increase Type II muscle fiber, increasing muscular size is a good option.

Muscle fiber is not the only limiting factor on speed, however. An athlete who is genetically blessed with a large quantity of Type II muscle fiber could still be extremely slow. This is because his central nervous system is not allowing his muscles to contract with maximum velocity. It's another instance where CNS inhibits the speed of the muscle contraction as a safety device. However, this safety switch can be reset by consistently training in a quick manner. As your CNS relearns the maximum velocity at which your muscles can safely contract, it will allow your body to move in a much quicker manner. Similar to maximal effort strength training, utilizing short bursts of extremely quick movements is the best method to retrain the CNS to allow a higher capacity for speed. And as we all know, increased speed allows a fighter to execute his techniques more quickly than his opponent, which in turn allows him to catch his opponent off guard or advance position before his opponent has a chance to defend. Speed development is an absolutely essential part of training for an MMA athlete.

POWER

Power is the third athletic quality we seek to improve with GPP training. Strength and speed are generally thought of as opposite sides of the same coin. Increasing strength improves the amount of force you can apply to something, while increasing speed allows you to apply that force with more velocity. However, between these two sides lies power. Power is the rate at which work is performed. It is the force delivered to a specific object over a specific period of

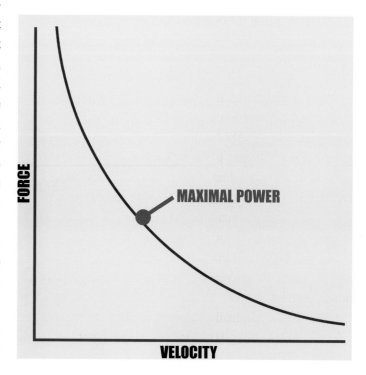

FORCE / VELOCITY CURVE

The relationship between strength and speed are inversely linked to one another. Because of the way human muscle fiber contracts, movements will always be limited to either high levels of force, or high levels of velocity, but never both at the same time. It's similar to a race between a semi truck and a Ferrari. The winner will always depend upon the load they're asked to carry. High-force movements will be executed at a slow velocity, while high-velocity movements will always exhibit low maximal force.

The Force/Velocity curve is the embodiment of this inverse relationship between strength and speed. On the far end of the curve is a high-velocity/low-force activity, such as a quick right cross, while on the other end of the spectrum is a high-force/low-velocity movement, such as a maximum-effort deadlift. In the middle, however, lies the balance between force and velocity. At this point, maximum power is attained. Movements in this range are things such as Olympic lifts, dynamic-effort squats, and powerfully executed double-leg takedowns. All these movements utilize power and speed in the best possible ratio to complete a powerful athletic movement. The middle of the curve is where maximum power is achieved, and also where the maximum amount of work is completed. By focusing your training on these moderate-force, moderate-velocity, high-power movements, you have the capacity to increase your fighting ability more than improving any other athletic quality.

time. As such, power is the middle ground between strength and speed. Since power is a function of speed and strength, as you develop those athletic qualities, your power production will amplify as well. Power is the most important athletic function we seek to improve with our GPP training. A fast, strong, and powerful fighter is a dangerous fighter.

SIZE

The fourth athletic quality we aim to develop with general physical preparation is size. Size refers to the mass of the athlete. Since MMA is a weight class–restricted sport, monitoring your mass is a very important part of the competition. There are three facets to weight gain and loss. Hydration is the most variable. The weight of the water in your body is a significant portion of your total body mass. Hydration is crucial for proper function of your muscles, brain, and organs. There is an optimal level of hydration, and permanently decreasing your mass through dehydration is unfeasible.

The second controllable factor in body mass is fat. Fat is the medium of long-term energy storage throughout your body. While fat is a survival mechanism for storing energy when food intake is high, for a performance athlete it has no function. Fat is released too slowly to serve as a fuel source in an MMA fight, so as long as there is a minimum level of body fat to maintain the function of the organs, it is useless to accumulate. Body fat should be kept as low as feasibly possible through proper diet during your training camp.

The method of size most affected by GPP training is muscular size. By altering the intensity and volume of your training cycles, you can increase or decrease the size of various muscle groups. This can have a profound effect on your total body weight. For optimal performance, you want to be as strong as possible in your given weight class. This means if you desire to move up in a weight class, you must increase the size of your muscles to provide the extra mass. Muscular hypertrophy, or increase in muscular size, can be accomplished through two means.

Sarcomeric hypertrophy is the act of increasing the size of the actual muscle fibers. This is accomplished mainly through heavy weight training. As the muscle becomes acclimated to increased tension, the muscle fibers increase in size to accommodate increasing loads. Sarcomeric hypertrophy is an important part of increased strength. As mentioned before, all things being equal, a bigger muscle is a stronger muscle. And by increasing the size of the muscle fibers through sarcomeric hypertrophy, you can expect increases in overall strength gain as well.

The other method of increasing muscular size is sarcoplasmic hypertrophy. The sarcoplasm is the fluid surrounding the muscle fibers. Sarcoplasm is the storage medium for glycogen, which directly powers the muscular contractions. As the stores of glycogen are depleted in the sarcoplasm through strenuous workouts, the body adapts by increasing the amount of sarcoplasm stored around the muscles. This is the source of the infamous workout "pumps" in localized muscle groups. Sarcoplasmic hypertrophy is best developed through higher repetition training. This adaptation is great for increasing endurance in local muscle groups. Sarcoplasmic hypertrophy essentially gives an individual muscle a bigger gas tank.

It should be noted that for an MMA fighter, both forms of hypertrophy are important. Sarcomeric hypertrophy will increase the maximum strength potential of the muscle group, while sarcoplasmic hypertrophy will increase the maximum endurance potential of the muscle group. Both operations have some overlap. Even high-repetition exercises will stress the muscle fibers and cause them to grow, and even low-rep lifts can cause depletion of glycogen. However, by combining both low- and high-rep workouts, you can reap the benefit of both methods of size increase. Fighters need to be powerful and well conditioned, and it's quite possible to increase both attributes while going either up or down in weight.

ENDURANCE

The fifth element to the athletic puzzle is endurance—the quality of being able to continue working for a long period of time. In modern MMA, all matches have set time limits. A UFC fight will be either fifteen minutes or twenty-five minutes maximum. So, for our purposes, endurance simply refers to the ability to maintain a high pace for the entire match. Fighters with poor endurance tend to start fast and slow down as the match progresses.

There are several mechanisms by which GPP increases the endurance of a fighter. The first is through increased efficiency of the cardiorespiratory system. The heart, lungs, and blood vessels play a crucial role in transporting oxygen to the muscles. By utilizing exercises that consistently elevate the heart and breathing rate, your body becomes accustomed to the high level of oxygen consumption of the muscles. This increases the maximum amount of oxygen your body can intake and utilize during strenuous activity, or VO2 max. The higher your VO2 max, the more work you're able to accomplish before your body resorts to anaerobic methods of producing power (i.e., without oxygen). As your VO2 max increases, your heart rate during intense exercise will drop. This gives you plenty of power in reserve when going into late rounds in a fight.

The second aspect of endurance is lactate threshold. As the intensity of exercise increases, the workload overcomes the body's ability to supply oxygen to power that work. At this point your body resorts to producing power through anaerobic means. As your body produces energy without using oxygen as a catalyst, it develops lactic acid as a by-product. Lactic acid is produced locally near whatever muscle group demands energy. Generally lactic acid can be cleared away into the blood stream, but as the intensity of an exercise increases, the lactate begins to accumulate in a local area. At the point when the lactate ceases to be cleared away and accumulates in the muscle tissues, it can cause pain and fatigue in that muscle. At the point of lactate threshold, the muscle in use becomes exhausted and unable to move effectively. This is common in many sports,

in which the athlete feels physically great, save for a small area of his or her body that is totally incapable of moving.

This nasty side effect can be delayed through proper training as well. By frequently inducing lactate development in individual areas of your body, the muscles can become tolerant to a certain level of lactic acid, allowing that muscle group to continue functioning even in a highly acidic environment.

COORDINATION, BALANCE, AND AGILITY

The five previous athletic qualities all deal with muscular contractions in some way. They all focus on increasing some quality of the muscle unit, whether size, force, or velocity potential. Although the muscles are the motors for the body, the brain needs feedback to ensure the muscles are contracting in the proper pattern. The following three athletic qualities deal with giving feedback to the athlete's brain and, in turn, making his or her motions more precise and accurate.

COORDINATION

The first feedback sense is called proprioception. Proprioception is an internal sense that tells a part of a body where it is in relation to other parts of the body. This is the physical sense that improves coordination. Proprioception allows a fighter to determine where each part of his body is without conscious effort. This sensory function is read by specialized nerves in the muscles and joints called "proprioceptors." These nerves are found all over the body, and they are constantly sending information about muscle tension, joint angle, pressure, and movement back to the brain. The pathways from the proprioceptors back to the brain can be developed like any other human function. By challenging the coordination of various areas of your body, the pathways between the proprioceptors and the brain are optimized, increasing the accuracy of the information relayed between the two points. This increases coordination, allowing a fighter to complete complex actions without having to think about them. Because of the complex motor patterns executed in MMA, a fighter needs to be extremely aware of where his limbs are in relation to his torso. An arm extended just an inch too far or a chin pushed forward just a bit too much can cause a premature end to the fight. By being aware of the location of all your body parts, you can avoid being caught out of position.

Coordination is improved through the sense of proprioception. While this helps your brain determine the proximity of certain body parts in relation to other body parts, another sense helps your body determine its relationship with the downward pull of gravity. This sense, called equilibrioception, monitors and adjusts balance. Human beings have a relatively narrow footprint and as such are inherently unstable. Without constant correction from the muscles, the body has a natural tendency to fall over. Equilibrioception uses input from the eyes and the inner ears, as well as the sense of proprioception to determine body position and to make minute adjustments to keep the body upright in relationship to gravity. By challenging your sense of balance, the inputs from the eyes, inner ears, and proprioceptors are refined, allowing the minute corrections coming back to the muscle to be even more precise. Using tools such as BOSU balls and wobble boards can challenge your balance, increasing the accuracy of the sense of equilibrioception, which in turns leads to increased overall balance for the athlete. Optimal balance is extremely important to any athlete fighting from the standing position. Your sense of balance is what enables you to keep a fight on the feet and deliver strikes or to disrupt your opponent's balance and force him off his feet and to the mat.

AGILITY

The internal senses of proprioception and equilibrioception increase coordination and balance respectively, but combining these two abilities together develops yet another athletic ability. Agility is the athletic sense concerned with improving the body's ability to change direction. An agile athlete is one who can halt his momentum in one direction and quickly send it in another. This is the last key to the athletic puzzle. By combining strength, speed, power, coordination, and balance—an athlete is able to recognize what position his body is in and in what direction it is moving, use powerful muscular contractions to stop his movement, maintain his balance as his weight shifts, and then explode in a new direction. This is a critical component of developing footwork and timing in the striking game, as well as an important function of dynamic grappling. Agility is the combination of increased balance and coordination with improved muscular contraction.

The eight athletic qualities must be trained and developed in every area of the body to become a better fighter. Having extremely powerful legs is of no use if your upper body is weak. Having quick hands will not help you if you have poor coordination and are unable to place punches with accuracy. Developing endurance in the legs is useless if you have poor balance and are unable to stay on your feet. However, this does not mean that each individual muscle group needs a different exercise to develop each of the eight qualities. This would take far too much time—time that would be better utilized increasing technique. When I'm doing general physical preparation workouts, I like exercises that give the most bang for the buck. Quality exercise selection can increase several athletic attributes as well as work many different muscle groups at the same time.

Rather than organize the exercises into muscle groups, which is common for body building routines, my workouts are broken down by movement. To a fighter, movements are much more important than muscles. Having strong hamstrings will never win you a fight. Using those hamstrings to turn on a cross and knock your opponent out will. With that in mind, this book categorizes exercises into various different movement patterns. These are broad movement patterns applied to various different activities in life and various activities in the sport of MMA. The goal with these movement patterns, again, is to be as general as possible. Increasing strength in a general plane of movement will carry over into all other similar movement patterns. This allows us to use nonspecific exercise selection and still increase strength in various other motions.

The first movement pattern covered in the book is lower-body pushing movement. This is the action of your legs pushing against the ground to move your body. It can include various different movements in various different planes. Forward, backward, and lateral movement are all initiated with the legs pushing against the ground. While pushing with the lower body uses the legs and hips to facilitate most movements, the entire back can become involved in many of the exercises shown in this section. The muscles of the back side of the body, or the posterior chain, are the strongest-linked muscle group. All powerful actions will depend upon the posterior chain in some degree to facilitate movement. This is why the lower-body push section focuses heavily on recruiting and involving the posterior chain in all of the exercises.

The next section is upper-body pushing. This is the action of your arms moving away from your body. This can involve either extending the arms and moving a weight away from your torso, or placing your hands on a fixed object and moving your torso away from that object. This is an important motion when striking, as well as grappling. To develop a powerful upper body you must increase your pushing strength in many different planes of motion.

Upper-body pulling is the next section of the book, and it is very closely tied with the previous section on upper-body pushing. Upper-body pulling is the motion of retracting the arms toward the body, either by pulling the body to a fixed surface or pulling a heavy load toward the torso. Because of the complexity of the shoulder joint, the upper body is capable of moving and exerting force in many different directions. To develop balanced upper-body strength, the amount of pulling and pushing movements must remain relatively equal. In this section I cover the various ways to increase pulling strength while keeping power output of the pushing and pulling motions equalized.

The final activity covered in this book can be more accurately described as inactivity. The last section covers the core function of stabilizing the torso. The muscles of the core are primarily charged with the task of keeping the spine safe, and to do this they must become extremely powerful at controlling and resisting movement. Although the core muscles control any twisting or bending at the spine, their main job is actually to prevent twisting and bending motions. Simply put, the core musculature is in charge of either preventing the spine from moving, or moving it in a safe, controlled manner. This is the final movement that must be addressed for a complete workout routine.

PROGRAM DESIGN

When working with my strength coach to develop a general physical preparation routine, we consider several things. The first question we ask is: What goals are we trying to accomplish? Which of the eight physical abilities are we trying to improve upon—strength, speed, power, size, endurance, coordination, balance, or agility? Or are we trying to build on all eight aspects at the same time? While it's often not practical for an experienced athlete like me to improve upon all aspects with the same workout, there are some great exercises that can improve upon many different athletic characteristics in one movement.

Different exercises improve different movement patterns, and different rep ranges and motions improve various athletic abilities. If looking to increase strength in the posterior chain, heavy squats may be the key to unlocking that strength. If looking to increase the endurance in the upper arms, high-repetition pushing and pulling motions may be the optimal exercise. When striving to boost agility, rapid directional changes with high repetitions are usually the best course of action.

Before any workout routine is started, one must ask the very important question first and foremost: "What goals am I looking to achieve?" After that question is asked, it's a simple route to find behaviors and exercises that will allow you to fulfill your goal. Without asking this question first, your workout routine will be disjointed and ultimately less successful than a directed exercise regimen.

The next part of developing an effective GPP program is ensuring that all applicable movement patterns are covered with the workout routine. For an MMA fighter it's important that every area of the body is covered with your

REP RANGES

When it comes to repetition ranges, each person seems to have their own ideas on the proper amount of reps for each given exercise. Some people feel that high reps are better suited for grapplers, while others feel that single-rep maximum lifts are the only way to build musculature strength. In reality there are many different repetition schemes that can be used for all exercises, and each range builds different musculature qualities. Depending upon what physical qualities you are seeking to improve, you can utilize low-, medium-, or high-repetition exercises to fulfill your goals. The chart below describes the physical qualities that can be improved upon via strength training, and what repetition range most strongly fulfills that goal. This is a general guideline, as all athletes' bodies are different. However when you're unsure whether to execute low or high reps to fulfill your goals, this chart will give you a solid starting point.

ATHLETIC QUALITY	NUMBER OF REPETITIONS						
	1	3	5	10	15	20	50
STRENGTH	■	■					
SPEED	■	■					
POWER		■	■				
SIZE - SARCOMERIC	■	■					
SIZE - SARCOPLASMIC				■	■		
VO2 MAX						■	
LACTATE THRESHOLD						■	

training routine. For an arm wrestler, leg strength may not be of critical importance. However, a fighter will rely on every part of his body at some point in his career, so each movement must be given equal attention. In general, for me, this means working my entire body with each workout.

In my workouts the goal is to spend time developing each of the four movements previously discussed, posterior chain, upper-body push, upper-body pull, and core stabilization. This is a great way to organize your workouts. Each movement can be adjusted with different speeds and intensities to target different athletic qualities, and assisting work can be added for extra volume to any given target muscle.

However, this isn't to say that you must work the full body in each training session. Sometimes when focusing on a specific goal of adding size or strength to a specific area, it can be beneficial to focus on a single movement or body part for an entire workout. But to cover the entire body with split workouts takes much more dedicated effort, sometimes as much as five or six sessions per week. When I'm deep into a training camp, I usually only have three, one-hour sessions per week to dedicate to GPP, so unless there's an injury preventing me from training a certain body part, I generally stick to full-body sessions.

While in a training camp I also focus on different athletic qualities at different periods of the training camp. Strength and size are the slowest physical attributes to develop. So if my goal is to develop these qualities, it must be done early in the training camp. Trying to gain twenty

pounds with only two weeks left before a fight would be futile. It varies for all fighters, but generally from twelve to eight weeks, my GPP sessions will focus primarily on gaining power, strength, and, if necessary, size. This allows me adequate time to develop these attributes, as well as affords me a solid base of strength to carry me throughout my training camp.

Early in my training camp, my strength workouts always follow the same format. The first movement is always a warm-up. This is generally a light, body-weight movement that induces blood flow to the various areas of the body that I'm preparing to train. After adequate warm-up I move on to core training. This extends the warm-up to the muscles protecting my spine, as well as ensures adequate volume to stress the abdominal muscles and other muscle groups surrounding the spine. Core training is generally followed by an Olympic lift variation. It can be any variation of an Olympic movement, usually rotated for different effects. This is the most important part of my strength- and power-training sessions. Olympic lifts are movements that must be executed with extreme power, which is a great way to develop full-body power, strength, and speed in a single exercise. Then I move on to various heavy exercises for different areas of the body. Sometimes I will do a lower-body exercise, sometimes an upper-body exercise, and sometimes I'll do both in the same session. Although the exercises vary, I'll perform those that can be loaded with heavy weight.

Finally, I move on to light assistance exercises, such as ones that are solely designed to strengthen the shoulder muscles or to strengthen the calves. These movements are generally done for higher reps and with lighter weight.

To conclude the workout, I'll do an adequate cool down, such as walking on the tread mill or body-weight squats. If there's time left at the end of the session, I'll do some stretching to increase flexibility.

As my training camp progresses and my work rate improves, my coach, Jake, begins to add in endurance workouts. These workouts are geared toward increasing my work capacity. Rather than schedule the workouts around a set amount of weight to be lifted, and slowly increasing the volume, endurance workouts are designed to give me a set amount of time to do an ever increasing amount of work. The two factors in determining the timing are total work time and work/rest intervals. If you are fighting for twenty-five total minutes, ideally you want an endurance session to last twenty-five total minutes. Anything less will result in inadequate preparation come fight time, and anything more

PROGRESSIVE OVERLOAD

While there are many different schools of thought and many different ideologies regarding strength-and-conditioning training, there is one universally accepted principle when it comes to increasing your athletic ability. Deliberately increasing stress in your training routine will yield steady results. This is called the Progressive Overload Principle. This principle is the key to increasing athletic ability in varying areas of development.

By targeting a goal, such as increased strength, speed, or endurance, and then measuring your progress on that goal, you can monitor the amount of progress made on each athletic ability. Regardless of whether you like to train with heavy weights for low reps, moderate weights for high reps, training to failure, or using high-speed plyometric work, unless you're progressively overloading your body, you will fail to see any adaptation and therefore fail to see gains in your athletic ability. Whether it's five more pounds, one more rep, or two seconds faster, each workout cycle should be better than the last. Only by measuring and then purposefully advancing with each workout will you become a better athlete.

will lead to a decrease in power production over the time span of the fight.

Work/rest intervals should also match the duration of the fight. In a twenty-five-minute UFC title fight, each round is five minutes long with a one-minute break between rounds. So come fight time, my endurance sessions should be aimed at five minutes of work time with a one-minute rest. These times are the ultimate goal, something to work up to. It would be impossible to go five five-minute rounds at the beginning of a training camp. The first session may be three three-minute rounds with a one-and-a-half minute break in between. As I become more and more conditioned, round times and the number of rounds will increase while rest times will decrease. Again, all fighters' training camps are unique, but I generally focus in on this type of training in the last four weeks of the camp. The middle of the training camp, from eight weeks to four weeks, can be a combination of strength and endurance sessions, perhaps alternating every other workout. This combination of strength training early in the camp with endurance training late in the camp allows me to walk into the fight with a good combination of strength and conditioning.

While general physical preparation can be an extremely complex and debated subject, there are some keys that are true for all athletes. First, you must train your entire body, and you must train it in movement patterns that are applicable to your sport. Then you must consider your goals, and select exercises, repetition ranges, and intensities that will help you fulfill those goals. When lifting or performing power exercises, train powerfully with maximum speed to gain the full benefit of those lifts. And finally, when seeking to increase endurance, select exercise intervals that mimic the intervals of your actual fight. If you follow these key points when creating an exercise regimen, you will give yourself the best chance to become a well-conditioned mixed martial artist.

PRILEPIN'S TABLE

Training volume is one of the hardest decisions to make when designing a routine. The amount of sets and reps utilized for any given exercise can have a huge impact on the efficiency of the workout. When first beginning a workout, it's often hard to determine how many total reps will be optimal for each given exercise. Too much volume will lead to premature fatigue and negatively affect future workouts, while too little volume will fail to elicit the desired training response. The solution to this is utilizing Prilepin's Table. This table was designed by Soviet scientist A. S. Prilepin in the 1960s. He determined optimal repetitions ranges and intensities for each individual set of workouts. By simply testing your one-repetition maximum on any given exercise, and then following the table, you can determine what weight to use for each individual repetition range and the optimal amount of repetitions to aim for in the entire set. Combining this knowledge with the Rep Ranges Chart shown will allow you to expertly select set and rep schemes. You must simply test your one-rep max, load the bar with the proper percentage of weight for your desired goals as shown in the Rep Ranges Chart, and then execute the optimal amount of reps provided by Prilepin's Table.

% OF 1 REP MAX	REPS PER SET	TOTAL REPS	OPTIMAL REPS
60 - 70%	3 - 6	18 - 30	24
70 - 79%	3 - 6	12 - 24	18
80 - 89%	2 - 4	10 - 20	15
90 - 100%	1 - 2	4 - 10	7

SECTION ONE
METABOLIC CONDITIONING

It's been said that fatigue makes a coward of all men—this is especially true in fighting. You could be the most technical martial artist on the planet, but if you get exhausted halfway through the first round, your technique will do little to help you win the fight. With no gas left in the tank, your strikes, takedowns, and submissions become sloppy and ineffective, forcing you to retreat.

To avoid such an outcome, you must become a well-conditioned athlete. Conditioning is somewhat of a broad term used to describe the rate at which you can work. If you have good conditioning, you can keep a constant medium/high pace throughout the fight and then initiate explosive bursts of energy when you need to execute a technique. By contrast, if you are a poorly conditioned fighter, then you will be unable to keep a high pace through the fight, and each time you explode with a particular movement, it will slow you significantly for the remainder of the fight. If you want to reach the top of the MMA mountain, you must be able to keep your techniques sharp into the later rounds, and this can only be achieved when strength and conditioning plays an integral part of your training.

AEROBIC CONDITIONING

For the purposes of this book, we will refer to conditioning as increasing the efficiency of the two metabolic pathways used to fuel your body. The aerobic pathway utilizes the oxygen that comes in through your lungs and is spread throughout your body via your heart and arteries. When the oxygen makes it way to your muscles, it combines with sugars and fats to form adenosine triphosphate (ATP), which is stored in the muscles. ATP is the most important molecule in an athlete's body because it is responsible for powering every movement. If your body were a high-performance sports car, ATP would be the gasoline. When one of your muscles needs to perform work, ATP is split and provides energy for that muscle to contract. If you have good aerobic conditioning, your body can produce ATP faster than it is consumed during aerobic exercise, which essentially means that you have an unlimited source of energy during low-intensity movements. However, there is a catch. Your body only uses the aerobic pathway for producing energy when your muscles receive an ample amount of oxygen. Through aerobic conditioning training it is possible to increase the efficiency of your lungs, heart, and circulatory system at supplying your muscles with oxygen while performing work, but there are limitations. When you perform a great amount of work in a very short period of time, your anaerobic pathway becomes the main producer of energy, which we will cover next.

While any physical activity will increase heart rate and breathing rate, in order to improve upon your aerobic conditioning, the increase must be maintained throughout your entire workout. This is why long-duration cardio exercises such as jogging and bike riding have been the training staple of fighters for more than a century. Moderate-intensity weight lifting exercise will also increase heart and lung capacity, but the key is to minimize rest times. Utilizing training circuits with a three-to-one or higher work-to-rest ratio ensures that your cardiorespiratory system is taxed through your entire training session. Whether it's a long jog or a fifteen-minute circuit training session in the gym, so long as your heart and lungs are being worked at a high rate for the entire session, your aerobic conditioning will increase.

Despite the low power output, the aerobic energy system is your base of conditioning. The more efficient your lungs are at taking in oxygen, and the more efficient your heart is at spreading that oxygen throughout your body, the less energy your anaerobic pathways need to provide during moderately intense activity. A good aerobic base ensures that you are able to keep a medium pace without fatiguing and still have plenty of energy left in reserve to execute a powerful, potentially fight-ending technique. If you are a beginner athlete, it is important that you focus on developing your aerobic conditioning first. When you neglect this aspect of your training, you will only be fresh in your MMA training for a few minutes, which causes you to lose focus and your technique to get sloppy as practice presses on. In order to become proficient in the sport, you must learn and practice a great number of techniques, which requires you to be focused and alert for long training sessions.

ANAEROBIC CONDITIONING

While the aerobic pathway is utilized during moderately intensive activity, the anaerobic pathway is utilized when your body requires a large amount of power, such as when you throw a powerful overhand or shoot in for a takedown. Unlike the aerobic pathway, which uses oxygen for the production of ATP, the anaerobic pathway has two different methods for creating energy, neither of which requires the muscles to receive oxygen. The first is called the ATP-PC system or the phosphate system, and it comes into play when you perform extremely powerful movements, such as a clean and jerk, sprint 100 meters, or pitch a baseball. The ATP-PC system relies upon an extremely small supply of creatine phosphate stored in the muscle cells that rapidly produce ATP molecules. The power produced from the creatine phosphate chemical reaction is available instantaneously, and it allows the muscles to contract powerfully. While this form of energy production allows you to do incredible things, it doesn't last long. The maximum output of this energy source only lasts a few seconds until the reserves of phosphates in the muscles are used up. And once phosphates are gone, it takes several minutes before it can re-accumulate in the muscles to significant levels.

The second anaerobic energy pathway is called the lactic acid system, which breaks down glucose, or blood sugar, into lactic acid. While the supply of phosphates in the muscles cells run out relatively quickly, the supply of glycogen in the body is much larger. This means that the energy from the lactic acid pathway can last anywhere from a few seconds to a several minutes. This comes in handy because when the ATP stored in the muscles ceases to provide the body with the power it needs to perform in-tensive activity, the lactic acid pathway steps in. However, because of the number of steps the body must go through before glucose can be converted to ATP via glycolysis, it is slightly less efficient and can't produce as much power as when the body uses the ATP stored in the muscles. There is another drawback to producing energy through the lactic acid pathway. The chemical reaction that enables your body to produce ATP without oxygen also releases lactic acid as a by-product. As a result of this by-product, your body becomes highly acidic in the regions where the lactic acid is being produced. This can cause great discomfort and fatigue in the muscle groups being exercised.

Training the anaerobic energy systems to make them more efficient is very similar to training the aerobic energy system. To develop the energy pathways, you must utilize and then overload that energy system in training. In other words, in order to make your body more efficient at producing power while in a state of oxygen deprivation, you must train in a state of oxygen deprivation. By increasing the intensity of your exercise, and then remaining at that elevated intensity for a relatively long duration of time, your body will adapt to the challenge and refine the anaerobic pathways, enabling more energy to be released from the chemical conversion of glucose into ATP. The other benefit of training with high intensity is that your body will develop resistance to the acidic effects of the lactic acid system. As the acid accumulates in your muscles groups, the pain can become overwhelming. This has a huge psychological impact on a fighter, as they know that every time they flex that muscle group, the pain will increase. By consistently training with adequate intensity to produce lactate in the muscle groups, the fighter can become acclimated to the increased acidity in his muscles and fight through the pain.

THE BIG PICTURE

All three of these metabolic pathways—aerobic, anaerobic-ATP, and anaerobic-glycolysis—must be developed and utilized to be a successful MMA fighter. Each energy system has both its positive and negative qualities. With the phosphate system, your body uses creatine stored in your muscle cells for instant bursts of power such as a big knockout punch, a powerful double-leg slam, and spinning from the mount into an armbar, but this energy system alone will not get you through a fifteen-minute fight. It only lasts a few seconds, and it takes minutes to recover. The lactic acid system is a useful bridge between explosive and low-intensity movements, as it can fuel powerful actions for a minute or more. When you engage in prolonged sessions of clinch fighting or struggle to keep your opponent pinned to the mat, you use your lactic acid system to its maximum potential. But this energy system also has its drawbacks. The process of converting glucose into ATP forces the accumulation of lactate in the muscle groups being used, which can cause localized fatigue. A perfect example is when you hold on to a guillotine choke for too long but fail to finish your opponent. With lactate built up in your arms, for several minutes they feel exhausted and are ineffective, making simple tasks such as keeping your hands up a very challenging task. Luckily you are equipped with the aerobic system, which is essentially an unlimited source of power. Granted, that power is of a low level and not conducive to dynamic movements, but it provides you with a base for all conditioning. With simple, nontaxing movements being powered solely by the aerobic process, you can still remain active while allowing your body to clear away lactate and rebuild the large supplies of energy needed for the other energy systems.

To increase your conditioning, you must train each of the energy systems. Jogging will not increase the maximum power capacity of the ATP energy pathway, just as doing heavy Olympic lifts will not increase the efficiency of your aerobic conditioning. However, this does not mean that you need an individual workout for each of the energy systems, as there is some overlap in all physical activity. A single workout could utilize both the phosphate energy system as well as the lactic acid energy system. Likewise, a single workout could increase not only aerobic conditioning, but anaerobic conditioning as well. The key is to make a conscious effort to develop all the energy systems. Utilizing the proper timing and intensity, workouts can be designed to give a multitude of benefits to your overall conditioning. To help you with this process, I have designed the following section to mimic the progression of my actual workouts, from the initial warm-up to high-intensity conditioning. The reason I didn't break it down into movements like the other chapters is because in metabolic training you do not target the muscles—you target the energy systems.

Before you dive into this section, it is important to realize that all of the movements demonstrated share similar qualities. The first quality is that each action is either a full-body movement or requires the use of many different muscle groups. This allows the greatest amount of work to be done, which in turn burns the most energy. The more energy you burn with each individual pathway, the more

efficient that pathway becomes. Choosing exercises that use only one or two muscle groups will lead to very rapid fatigue in those muscles, but very little energy burned overall. As a result, the exercise ends without training metabolic conditioning to the max.

The second aspect all the coming movements share is that you can ramp the intensity up or down, depending upon the stage of your training cycle. A poorly conditioned fighter coming off a long break of training will not be able to jump right into my fight camp and do the same exercises as me. Without that base level of aerobic conditioning, he will quickly fatigue and be unable to complete the routine. Therefore, all the exercises used in my conditioning routine are capable of being made easier or harder as the athlete requires, either by altering the amount of resistance used in the exercise or by altering the amount of work performed during a given time frame. A set amount of weight done ten times in a minute will elicit much less response than the same weight done fifty times in a minute. In the second scenario, the energy systems will work much harder to keep up with the demand, and it will become more efficient as a result.

Because these two elements are consistent in all of my conditioning exercises, they can easily be adapted into simple warm-up exercises as well. A warm-up is any movement performed at the beginning of a workout to prepare you for the more strenuous exercise ahead. The intention of a warm-up is to increase blood flow into the muscles and joints, and to excite the nervous system, allowing it to perform with maximum efficiency. Because of the full-body nature of my conditioning exercises, and their variable intensity, they fit perfectly into the definition of a warm-up. By lowering the intensity of the various exercises, either by volume or by level of resistance, I can perform any of these full-body movements at the beginning of my exercise to prevent injuries and prepare me for the workout ahead.

The first exercise shown in this section is my dynamic warm-up. The dynamic warm-up is a series of movements designed to get blood flowing into the muscles and loosen up the athlete for the harder training ahead. Next follows the dynamic foot-work drills. My strength-and-conditioning coach, Jake Bonacci, uses a few different implements, such as floor ladders and hurdles, to elicit different responses while training footwork. Again, just like the dynamic warm-up, these are large, full-body movements that get the hips moving in every direction and spread the energy expenditure across many different muscle groups. The chapter then progresses into individual conditioning movements such as jump rope and medicine ball slams. I've also included some of my favorite barbell complexes, as well as some unique exercises that are a favorite of my gym. Among these are the sledgehammer, the tire flip, and the ropes. These exercises require some special equipment, but because of the dynamic movements and immense boost they give to overall conditioning, they have become key exercises in my conditioning routine.

If you are unable to come across the equipment I have at my disposal, feel free to create your own metabolic conditioning exercises. There are thousands of different exercises that can be used to increase the efficiency of your metabolic pathways. As long as you use the proper intensity and time frame, as well as a large enough diversity of muscle groups, any exercise can be used to increase conditioning. Anything from dragging a sled to carrying heavy boxes can be employed to increase your work rate.

Metabolic training is a crucial element to develop to be a successful fighter. Without the ability to apply your techniques quickly and accurately into the late rounds, your MMA career will stall very quickly. Whether you adopt my favorite exercises or develop your own, you will be well on your way to becoming a complete fighter.

DYNAMIC WARM-UP

The dynamic warm-up is a series of functional, body-weight movements that I use at the beginning of all my strength and conditioning sessions to warm up my hips and core muscles. By moving my body on several planes of motion, including forward, backward, and laterally, I get a much more complete warm-up than I would by simply running on the treadmill. Like all warm-up movements, the goal is to elevate your heart rate and get blood flowing to your muscles, which helps prevent injury in your following workout. The nice part about this particular series of movements is that it warms up all muscle groups and forces blood into every joint. It also doesn't require any special equipment, which allows you to perform it at any time and location. And with it only taking about five minutes to complete, it is extremely time efficient. Most times, I like to do each warm-up movement down the length of the gym, and then move on to the next exercise in the series. After making these rounds, I'm ready to continue on with the more grueling and stressful movements in that day's workout routine without the fear of pulling a muscle or injuring a joint.

A-SKIP

The A-Skip is a forward-moving high-stepping walk that has alternating leg and arm motion. Jake begins this movement by raising his left leg high until his left thigh is parallel with the ground. At the same time, he raises his right arm and prepares to take a step forward.

As Jake steps his left foot forward, he drops his right arm. Next, he drives off his left foot, raises his right knee until it is parallel with the floor, and elevates his left arm.

Again Jake steps down onto his right foot and alternates the movement, concentrating on raising his knee high to properly warm up his hip flexors.

LATERAL SHUFFLE

The lateral shuffle is a simple lateral stepping motion designed to warm up the hip abductors and adductor muscles. Here Jake starts in a narrow stance with a slight bend in his knees.

Jake uses his hip abductor muscles to step his left foot toward the left side of his body. This effectively widens his stance.

Jake uses the adductor muscles of his right leg to pull his right foot close to his left foot and bring his stance into a narrow position again. Jake then moves down the length of the gym with this lateral motion. Once he reaches the far side of the gym, he will switch directions and come back. This ensures that the hip adductors and adductors of both legs are worked equally.

STRAIGHT-LEG SKIP

The straight-leg skip is a forward skipping motion where you raise your legs off the mat one at a time while keeping them straight. Here Jake demonstrates the straight-leg skip by first raising his left leg, and reaching to touch his toe with his right hand. This hand/toe touch ensures the leg is rising to the same height on each repetition.

As Jake plants his left foot on the mat, he raises his right leg and touches his toes with his left hand. This movement warms up the quads and the core muscles, as well as sends blood into the shoulder girdle.

Continuing to move forward with the straight-leg motion, Jake alternates sides once again. He will continue this motion down the length of the gym.

KARAOKE

RIGHT BEHIND LEFT — STRAIGHTEN — RIGHT IN FRONT OF LEFT — STRAIGHTEN — RIGHT BEHIND LEFT

1 **2** **3** **4** **5** **6**

1) Karaoke is a lateral movement used to warm up the hip adductors and abductors in a range of motion that often gets neglected. While all lateral warm-ups use the hips to some degree, with karaoke you cross your leg all the way across the midline of your body, both in the front and in the back. This makes the range of internal adduction much broader. Here Jake starts in a neutral position with his feet together. 2) Pivoting on his left foot, Jake transfers his weight onto his left leg, pivots on his left foot, and then uses his hip muscles to move his right leg behind his left leg. 3) As Jake's right foot makes contact with the ground, he transfers his weight onto his right leg and then moves his left foot toward his left side until he is once again in a neutral stance. 4) Shifting his weight onto his left foot, Jake moves his right leg in front of his left leg. 5) As Jake's right foot touches down, he transfers his weight onto his right leg and once again moves his left foot out to his left side, returning to a neutral stance. 6) Jake will continue this over/under motion rapidly down the length of the gym. To get an equal workout on both sides of his body, he will move back toward his right while facing the same direction. This will warm up the adductor and abductor muscles on both sides of his body.

BACKWARD DROP-STEP KICK

1 **2** **3** **4** **5**

1) The drop-step kick is a footwork exercise where you move backward, warming up your hip abductor and hamstring muscles. To perform this exercise, Jake starts with his feet together in a narrow stance. 2) To initiate the movement, Jake contracts his hip flexors and raises his right leg until he has a ninety-degree bend in his knee. 3) With his right knee pointing forward, Jake uses his right hip abductor muscles to pull his right knee toward the outside of his body. 4) Jake plants his right foot behind him. 5) Jake transfers his weight onto his right leg and then elevates his left knee until his thigh is parallel with the floor. He will continue this backward-moving exercise down the length of the gym.

LUNGE WALK

1) The lunge walk is a simple forward lunge, continued in a walking motion down the entirety of the workout space. The lunge mainly targets the quads, hamstrings, and glutes. To begin the exercise, Jake starts at the beginning of his lane with his feet together in a narrow stance and his arms at his side. 2) Jake steps his left foot forward. As his left heel hits the ground, he bends his knees and allows his hips to drop straight down. At the same time, he raises both his arms straight up overhead. Notice how he keeps his back perfectly erect, his arms straight up, and he lunges down until his back knee nearly touches the floor. 3) As Jake lowers his arms, he drives his body upward by extending his left leg and returns to an upright position. Once he is fully upright, he steps his right foot forward until it is once again even with his left foot. 4) This time Jake steps forward with his right leg. Again, he strives to keep his torso erect, his arms straight up, and a ninety-degree bend in his front knee. Jake will continue alternating this motion down the length of the gym.

LATERAL BOUNDS

1) This is a forward and lateral movement in one exercise. With the jump forward you warm up your calves, hamstrings, and glutes, and the side-to-side movement warms up your hip flexor muscles. To begin the exercise, Jake stands with both of his feet together. 2) For the first bound, Jake takes his right foot off the ground and uses the calves and hamstring muscles of his left leg to propel him forward. At the same time, he uses his hip abductor muscles to push him toward his right side. This has the net effect of moving him forward and to his right. 3) After Jake bounds in a diagonal motion, he lands on his right foot with his left foot off the ground. 4) Jake alternates the motion, using his right leg to propel him forward and toward his left side. It's important to note that he never comes to a resting position with both feet on the floor. As soon as his lead foot touches down, he immediately reverses direction and drives off it.

SWAN WALK

1) The swan walk is a forward movement drill that involves leaning forward after each step. The hamstrings, glutes, abdominals, and spinal erector muscles are all activated by this movement. This leads to ample blood flow to the hips and core and allows you to finish up your dynamic warm-up on a strong note. To start this exercise, Jake assumes a narrow stance and lets his arms hang at his sides. 2) Jake takes a small step forward with his right foot, shifts his weight onto his right leg, and then leans forward so that his torso is parallel with the floor. As the same time, he extends his left leg behind him to counter balance his torso and extends his arms out to either side of his body to increase his balance in this unstable position. It is important to note that he keeps his spine tense and perfectly straight. 3) Jake flexes his right hamstring and glute to pull his trunk back into the upright position. At the same time, he swings his left foot forward so that both feet are once again next to each other on the floor. In addition to being a great warm-up movement, this exercise also helps increase your stability due to the balancing aspect.

AGILITY LADDER

The agility ladder is an excellent tool for improving your speed, agility, and lower-body coordination. The various agility ladder drills begin with placing a cloth ladder lengthwise on the ground and then executing footwork movements down the length of the ladder, using the perpendicular lines for reference. There are many different movement patterns that can be utilized—forward, backward, lateral, or a combination of all three. Many of the footwork patterns are similar to or the same as the dynamic warm-up, but the emphasis of the movements is totally different. While the dynamic warm-up is movement based, the agility ladder is entirely based on speed. Instead of employing slow, controlled movement, the goal is to get your feet moving as fast as possible without touching the ladder. This not only increases your speed and lower-body agility, but it also does wonders to improve your coordination. By doing complicated footwork drills like this, you develop the pathway between the nerve bundles in your lower body and inner ear to give your brain a more accurate image of where your legs are in relation to the ladder on the ground. This increases proprioception and allows you to have more accurate footwork, which is extremely important in fighting.

SINGLE-LEG FORWARD HOP

1) This is a simple forward hop on a single leg. The idea is to keep one foot on the ground and hop into each box of the ladder successively. Here Jake begins the drill with his right foot on the ground in the first box of the hurdle and his left foot in the air. 2) Jake quickly hops out of the first box into the second box. As he moves down the length of the ladder, he uses his hands to help maintain his balance, which helps increase his coordination. 3) Jake jumps out of the second box into the third box. It should be noted that there is no pause between these jumps. Jake is not jumping, resting, and then jumping again. As soon as his foot lands, he recoils his leg, preparing to leap forward again. Once he reaches the end of the ladder, he will switch legs and come back in the other direction. This will ensure that he gets an even workout on both legs.

LATERAL SCISSORS

1) Jake begins the exercise with his left foot on the ground in the first box of the ladder and his right foot on the ground outside of the box. With each repetition, his staggered stance will alternate. 2) To initiate the lateral scissors drill, Jake quickly hops upward and scissors his legs in mid-air. As his left foot moves backward, his right leg moves forward. 3) Jake lands on the ground with his feet alternated. Now his right foot is in the first box and his left foot is outside of the first box. 4) Jake again takes a quick hop into the air, this time driving himself slightly to his left as he jumps. Again, he scissors his legs in mid-air so that his leg position alternates. 5) Due to his slight lateral hop and leg-scissoring motion, Jake now lands with his left foot in the second box of the ladder and his right foot to the outside of the second box. He will continue this motion down the span of the ladder, touching each foot into each segment of the ladder one at a time, then moving laterally onto the next segment. Just like the first drill in this series, he's not pausing in between jumps. Every time your feet land, you want to quickly explode into the next hop. The goal is to execute this drill as fast as possible while remaining accurate with your footwork.

SINGLE-LEG LATERAL HOP

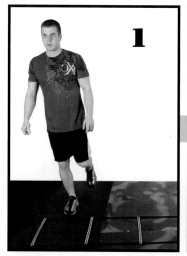   

1) This is a simple lateral hopping motion done on one foot that alternates into and out of the boxes. This gives the drill some forward and backward movement, as well as the primary lateral motion. Jake starts the drill standing on his right foot with his left foot in the air. His right foot is placed directly outside of the first box of the ladder. 2) Jake hops forward, landing with his right foot directly in the first box on the ladder. 3) Jake hops backward and to his left, landing on his right foot. The diagonal leap has placed his right foot directly outside of the second box on the ladder. 4) Jake hops forward and lands with his right foot in the second box on the ladder. Like all ladder drills, this hop is done as fast as possible. Building speed and accuracy is the main goal of the agility ladder, so speed should be your main focus while executing all of these drills. From here, Jake will rapidly continue this motion down the span of the ladder, and then switch legs and continue the motion in the other direction to ensure an equal workout with both legs.

SNAKE

Snake is a complex movement where you rotate around one planted foot, then alternate your pivot foot and continue to turn your body. You must use your hips in the exercise to quickly rotate, which helps you develop quick pivot steps. In the photo above, Jake begins with his left foot in the first box and his right foot on the ground just outside of the ladder.

Jake lifts his right foot off the ground and pivots in a counterclockwise direction for a quarter turn. This places his right foot to the right off the ladder, with his left foot still inside the first box.

Jake pivots and turns his hips another quarter turn in a counterclockwise direction. This places his right foot in the second box of the ladder.

Now Jake alternates his pivot foot. Keeping his right leg stationary, he moves his left leg in a clockwise direction. Notice how this places his left foot outside of the ladder.

Again, Jake pivots a quarter turn in a clockwise direction. This lands his left foot directly in the third box on the ladder.

Now that Jake's left foot is in the ladder, he again alternates his pivot foot and switches directions. He will continue this fast pivoting movement down the length of the ladder.

HOP IN / HOP OUT

1) This is a simple hopping drill where you abduct and adduct your legs while hopping forward. Just like all drills in this section, it not only improves foot speed and agility, but also body awareness. To begin the exercise, Jake stands with both feet in the first box of the ladder. 2) Jake takes a small hop forward. While in the air, he abducts his legs and moves them to the outside of his body. He lands with both feet directly outside of the second box. 3) Jake now takes a stationary hop, adducting his legs inward. He lands with both of his feet inside of the second box, one rung up from where he started. 4) Jake now duplicates the movement, hopping forward and abducting his legs, landing with his feet outside the third box. He will repeat this quick in-and-out motion down the length of the ladder.

KARAOKE

1) The movement in this sequence is identical to the movement of karaoke shown in the dynamic warm-up, except now you perform it on an agility ladder. Jake begins the exercise by standing with both feet together to the left of the ladder. 2) Jake lifts his left leg off the ground and moves it laterally behind his right leg, stepping his foot down to the inside of the first box. 3) Transferring his weight to his left foot, Jake moves his right leg laterally to the outside of the ladder. 4) Jake now adducts his left leg, moving it toward his body and slightly forward. 5) Jake transfers his weight onto his left foot and moves his right leg behind his left leg. This movement places his right foot in the second box of the ladder. 6) As Jake's right foot lands in the ladder, he transfers his weight onto his right leg and moves his left leg in front of his body, planting it on the ground on the left side of the ladder. He will continue this back-and-forth motion down the span of the ladder.

LATERAL TRIANGLE HOP-IN

This is a lateral hopping motion designed to keep your feet together throughout the entire movement. The drill moves forward, backward, and laterally, which helps you develop the ability to move quickly in any direction. To begin the exercise, Jake places both feet inside the first box on the ladder and faces to the side.

Jake takes a small hop forward and to his left, landing outside of the ladder. Notice how his feet are still together.

Jake quickly propels himself backward into the second box of the ladder.

Once again Jake hops laterally, only this time the lateral movement is paired with a backward hop. This diagonal movement places him just outside of the ladder, facing the third box.

Jake takes a small hop forward, landing in the third box of the ladder.

Jake repeats the original movement, hopping forward and to his left. He will repeat these diagonal hopping motions until he reaches the end of the ladder. At that point, he will change directions, moving to his right. This will challenge the muscles on both sides of his body equally.

SINGLE-LEG SLALOM

This is a single-leg diagonal movement exercise that helps increase balance as well as agility in your working leg. To begin the exercise, Jake places his left foot outside the first box, hangs his right foot in the air, and prepares to slalom his way down the length of the ladder.

Jake takes a small lateral hop to his left, landing with his left foot inside the first box on the ladder.

Jake takes a diagonal hop forward and to his left. This small leap places his left foot on the ground to the left of the ladder.

Jake now hops laterally once again, this time to his right, causing his left foot to land in the second box on the ladder.

Once again Jake makes a diagonal hop, this time forward and to his right. This places his left foot to the right of the ladder.

Jake will continue this slalom motion down the expanse of the ladder. When he reaches the end, he will switch legs and move back down the ladder to achieve an equal workout on both legs.

TWO-FOOT RUN-THROUGH

With the two-foot run-through, you move your body straight forward using a bilateral leg scissor. This develops agility from a split stance, which comes in extremely useful in fighting. To begin the exercise, Jake stands with both feet together at the beginning of the ladder.

Jake hops upward and moves his right foot slightly forward. This causes him to land with his right foot in the first box on the ladder.

Jake hops again, this time moving his left foot forward, causing him to land with both feet in the first box on the ladder.

Hopping upward again, Jake moves his right foot forward. He lands with his right foot in the second box on the ladder.

From the split-stance position, Jake hops forward and brings his feet back together, placing them both in the second box.

Jake repeats the movement once again, scissoring his legs and moving his right foot forward. He will continue this forward movement down the length of the ladder. When he reaches the end, he will reverse direction and alternate his foot position, moving his left leg forward on the return trip.

SINGLE-LEG LATERAL

This is a single-leg exercise that involves lateral movement. Much of your footwork in an MMA match involves pivoting on a single foot, and drills like this help develop balance in those types of motions. To begin the exercise, Jake stands on his right foot at the beginning of the ladder.

Jake hops laterally to his left. He keeps his left leg flexed to prevent it from touching the ground as he lands.

Jake lands on his right foot in the first box of the ladder.

With another lateral bound to his left, Jake moves through the air along the span of the ladder.

Jake will continue this single leg lateral motion until he reaches the end of the ladder, at which point he will switch legs to ensure both sides of his body get an equal workout.

HURDLES

While the agility ladder drills are a great tool for developing coordination and agility in your lower body, hurdle drills are exceptional for developing power and balance in your lower body. The goal with the various drills I have laid out on the coming pages is to explode into each jumping movement, reset your base upon landing, and then explode into your next jump with the same force as the first. Just as with the agility ladder, there are a multitude of different movement patterns you can utilize when doing hurdles. Backward, forward, and lateral movements should all be incorporated to build power in each direction. It can be a little time-consuming to do both the agility ladder and hurdles in the same workout, so by alternating them every other day, you get the best of both worlds. If you look at the sequence below, you'll notice that Jake is using plastic hurdles where the height can be altered to suit the strength level of the athlete. However, if you do not have these units, any obstacles will do so long as they are of uniform height.

TWO-FOOT FORWARD HOP

The two-foot forward hop is a simple bilateral hopping exercise that takes you over a series of hurdles. To begin, Jake stands in front of the first hurdle with his feet shoulder width apart.

Jake lowers his hips, preparing to leap over the first hurdle.

Jake contracts his hamstrings and calves and leaps over the first hurdle.

Jake lands on his feet, plants his heels, and resets his base. He immediately lowers his hips to once again to prepare for the following hop.

Jake leaps again, extending his hips, knees, and ankles in a powerful motion to carry him over the second hurdle.

Jake lands on the ground, plants his feet, and rebends his knees in anticipation of the next hurdle.

TWO-FOOT LATERAL HOP

This is another bilateral jumping motion. However, this time Jake will hop laterally over the hurdles. To begin, he stands to the right of the first hurdle with his feet shoulder width apart and his knees bent.

Jake extends his hips, knees, and ankles in order to leap into the air. At the same time, he pushes himself to his left using his legs.

Jake moves laterally over the first hurdle, landing on the ground. Rather than immediately rebound his legs and leap over the second hurdle, he plants his feet and resets his base before preparing for his second jump.

Jake bends his knees in order to build power for the second jump.

Jake contracts his posterior chain, extending his hips, knees, and ankles in order to leap over the second obstacle.

Jake lands between the second and third hurdle. He will continue this lateral hopping motion until he reaches the end of the hurdles, then come back in the opposite direction to ensure an even workout on both sides of his body.

SINGLE-LEG FORWARD HOP

The single-leg forward hop is a unilateral forward hopping motion, good for developing coordination as well as single-leg power. Jake begins the drill with his right foot flat on the ground and his left foot in the air, facing the first hurdle.

Contracting his right hamstring, glute, and calf muscle, Jake leaps forward over the first hurdle.

Jake lands on the ground, still balancing on his right leg.

Instead of immediately hopping over the second hurdle, Jake plants his right foot and regains his posture.

After planting his foot, Jake bends his right knee, preparing to hop over the second hurdle.

Jake powerfully extends his right leg, forcing him over the second hurdle. At the end of the course, he will switch legs and return down the length of the hurdle circuit.

SINGLE-LEG LATERAL HOP

This is a single-leg variation of the lateral hop shown earlier. Single-leg variations double the intensity of each action, while generally halving the volume. To begin the exercise, Jake stands on his left foot to the left of the first hurdle.

Jake bends his left knee in anticipation of the upcoming leap.

Jake contracts his left glute, hamstring, and calf to leap off the ground, and he abducts his leg to move him toward his right.

Jake lands on his left foot and takes a moment to regain his balance after the ballistic movement.

After planting his foot and resetting his base, Jake repeats the same hopping motion to his right.

Jake leaps over the second hurdle, landing on the ground on his left foot. He will repeat this motion until the end of the hurdle circuit, at which point he will switch legs to ensure an even workout.

BACKWARD HOP

The backward hop is a leaping variation drill that forces you to maintain your balance while executing an awkward motion. To begin the exercise, Jake spreads his feet at shoulder width and faces away from the first hurdle.

From his bent-knee position, Jake leans slightly back, extends his legs, and jumps backward over the first hurdle.

Jake lands on the ground, bending his knees to catch himself.

Jake plants his feet and settles his base rather than immediately rebending his knees and continuing the hopping motion.

Jake bends his knees, and then he leans slightly back and extends his legs, leaping over the second hurdle.

Jake lands with his feet flat on the ground. He will continue this backward hopping motion until he competes the circuit.

SINGLE-LEG BACKWARD HOP

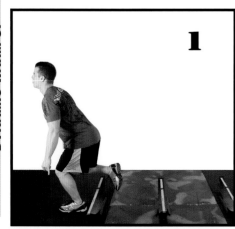

This is a unilateral variation of the previous hurdle drill. Here Jake is continuing with the backward hopping motion, except in this exercise he hops on a single leg. To begin the exercise, he stands on his left foot, elevates his right leg, bends his left knee, and faces away from the first hurdle.

Jake leans back and extends his left hip, knee, and ankle in order to leap backward over the first hurdle.

Jake lands on his left foot between the first and second hurdle.

Jake resets his base and regains his balance before moving on to the second leap.

Jake repeats the same motion, extending his leg and leaping backward over the second obstacle.

Jake lands on his left foot between the second and third hurdle. He will continue this backward hopping motion until the end of the circuit, then switch legs to ensure an even workout.

QUICK FEET

Quick feet is a simple drill that practices alternating diagonal footwork around the hurdles, rather than over top of them. To begin the exercise, Jake stands with his feet shoulder width apart in front of the first hurdle.

Jake abducts his right leg away from his body, stepping his right foot to the outside of the first hurdle. As he does this, he drags his left foot behind him to ensure his feet do not get spread too far apart.

Jake steps his left foot forward and toward his left side. Notice how this places his left foot between the first and second hurdle.

Jake slides his right foot toward his left foot to reestablish his original stance. Now both of his feet are between the first and second hurdle.

Jake steps his left foot forward and toward his left side. As his left foot moves to the outside of the second hurdle, he drags his right foot along to ensure his stance does not get spread too far apart.

Jake continues the diagonal stepping motion, alternating left and right and resetting his stance after every step. This is a great drill to train coordination in lateral stepping motions.

FIGHTING STANCE QUICK FEET

1) This exercise is similar to the previous one, except now you move laterally around the hurdles while in your fighting stance. This builds co-ordination and power while moving through actual sport-specific footwork patterns. To begin the exercise, Jake assumes his fighting stance in front of the first hurdle 2) Jake steps his left foot forward and toward his left side. 3) Shifting his weight onto his left leg, Jake pulls his right foot forward, moves it around the first hurdle, and then moves it back and reestablishes his fighting stance. 4) Jake steps his right foot farther behind him. 5) Jake shifts his weight onto his right leg, enabling him to pull his lead foot back under his body and reestablish his fighting stance. 6) Jake takes another step backward with his right foot. 7) Shifting his weight onto his rear foot, he pulls his left leg back under his body and reestablishes his fighting contance. 8) Now that Jake is outside of the obstacles, he is free to move laterally again. He steps his left foot forward and toward his left side, planting his foot between the second and third hurdle. 9) Shifting his weight onto his left leg, he pulls his right leg back under his body and reestablishes his fighting stance. From here, he will continue down the ladder, ingraining the footwork patterns into his muscle memory. At the end of the circuit, he will move back down the obstacle course to his right, ensuring an even workout.

ROPES

In this sequence Jake demonstrates the rope drill, which is exceptional for developing your stamina. If you look at the photos below, you'll notice that Jake is gripping the ends of two twenty-foot-long ropes, with the opposite ends attached to the wall. To perform the exercise, he comes up on his toes, drives his hips forward, and raises his arms, creating a wave motion down the length of the rope. With each repetition, he is forced to make a full-body, triple-extension movement, which is similar to the motion used in the power clean and jerk or any Olympic lift. In addition to being a great exercise to get beginner athletes familiar with triple-extension movements, it also lacks a true eccentric phase of motion. This means that throughout the exercise, some part of the rope is always moving upward, which keeps you from having to constantly overcome the force of gravity and leads to less injuries and muscle soreness at the end of the workout. In this particular sequence, Jake uses ropes that weight approximately forty to fifty pounds apiece. While this might seem like a light load, handling the ropes requires constant effort. There is no downtime when performing this exercise, which drives the work rate up very quickly. As a result, it is a great tool to develop your stamina and build full body power.

 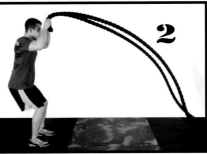 

1) With his knees bent and his feet spread at shoulder width, Jake begins the exercise by grabbing the ends of the ropes in his hands. 2) Dynamically flexing his shoulders, Jake raises his arms upward while at the same time driving his hips forward. This causes the portion of the ropes nearest to his body to rise. 3) As Jake drops his shoulders, elbows, and lower back slightly, the portion of the ropes nearest to his body descends, smacking the ground about four feet in front of him. This sends a wave down the length of ropes. As the exercise continues, Jake will continue this wave motion by flexing his knees, hips, and shoulders to elevate the ropes, and then extending his shoulders and back to smash the ropes back into the ground.

ALTERNATING ROPES

1) With his knees bent and his feet spread at shoulder width, Jake grabs the ends of the ropes in his hands. 2) Jake elevates his right arm slightly, causing the right rope to rise. Although this is the same motion as in the previous drill, because he is lifting his arms one at a time, his lower body becomes less involved and puts more of the load on his arms. It is important to note that with this first stroke, Jake only slightly lifts his right arm to get the wave motion started. 3) As Jake drives his right arm downward, he flexes his left shoulder and raises his left arm, causing the nearest portion of the left rope to rise off the ground. 4) Jake now extends his left shoulder, smashing the portion of the rope nearest his body into the ground. At the same time, he flexes his right side, raises his right arm, and elevates the right rope. 5) Jake now extends his right shoulder, smashing the portion of the rope nearest his body into the ground. He will continue this alternating motion for the desired amount of time.

TIRE HOP

The tire hop is a warm-up exercise that has been used in Muay Thai and boxing gyms for generations to build endurance and strength in the lower legs. When you hop on a tire as opposed to the ground, it produces a springy rebound effect that not only forces you to extend and contract your calves with each repetition, but also to use your calf muscles to maintain your balance. This generates a lactic acid buildup in your lower legs, which is similar to what you experience over the course of a long fight. The more you perform the tire-hop, the more immune you become to calf fatigue. In a fight, this allows you to stay on your toes and execute your footwork with maximum efficiency.

1) I place my feet on either side of the tractor tire, with my right foot slightly forward.

2) Contracting my calves, I make a slight vertical leap. As my feet come off the tire, I move my right foot back and my left foot forward.

3) I land on the tire with my left foot slightly forward. As the tire rebounds, I will flex my calves and leap into the air again, this time moving my right foot forward and my left foot back. I will continue leaping and alternating my feet in this fashion for at least several minutes.

JUMP ROPE

Just as with the tire hop, the jump rope is a staple exercise in most boxing and Muay Thai gyms around the world. By skipping your feet over the rope, you increase endurance in your lower legs, and by twirling the rope around and around, you receive a good shoulder and forearm workout. It is important to mention that the goal of this exercise is not to see how high you can jump, but rather to continuously lift your feet just high enough for the rope to pass underneath them. Unlike the tire hop, this requires good timing as well as conditioning.

When performing this exercise, it is important to use a rope that suits your purpose. The majority of boxing gyms use lighter ropes to focus on the development of the legs, while most Muay Thai gyms use heavy ropes to focus on the conditioning of the arms. In both cases, jumping rope is not something you want to do for a few seconds and then quit. To experience the benefits of this exercise, you should jump rope at a relatively quick pace for at least five minutes. The majority of professional trainers will have their fighters warm up with a twenty-minute rope-jumping session.

1) I grip a handle of the jump rope in each hand, extend my arms downward, and step my feet over the bottom of the rope.

2) I twirl my wrists in a counterclockwise direction, causing the rope to swing toward the top of my head. At the same time, I hop upward so that my feet elevate a few inches off the mat.

3) Continuing to twirl my wrists, the jump rope travels over my head, in front of my body, and underneath my elevated feet. As it moves to my backside, my feet touch down and I prepare to hop upward once again.

TIRE FLIP

When you flip over a tire such as the one shown below, the muscles of your legs, hips, back, and arms must all unite to get the job done. And due to the substantial weight of the tire, your lungs and heart must work extremely hard to send oxygenated blood to every corner of your body. The intense effort combined with the total-body nature of this movement makes it a killer cardio exercise. However, to experience its full benefits, it must be done for several repetitions. Flipping the tire over once and then backing away will have virtually no positive effect on your body.

1

To set up this exercise, I place a tractor tire flat on the floor, squat before it by bending my knees, dropping my hips downward, bending forward at the waist, and securing a narrow grip underneath the bottom edge.

2

To lift the edge of the tire upward, I straighten my legs, contract my back, and extend my hips forward. It is important to note that his is the most difficult part of the movement due to your lack of leverage.

3

Once I have the tire elevated, I step my right foot forward and push the tire into the upright position.

4

I step my right foot forward and continue to push on the tire, causing it to fall toward the floor.

5

As the tire lands on the floor, I bend down in front of it.

6

To return to the start position, I step forward until my feet are close to the tire, bend my knees, drop my hips, and bend forward at the waist. Next, I grab the bottom edge of the tire with both hands and prepare for another repetition. I will continue flipping the tire until I have reached the desired distance or time.

SLEDGEHAMMER ON TRACTOR TIRE

Although beating a tire with a sledgehammer might seem more like manual labor than a workout, it is an excellent exercise for strengthening your body. Unlike when you strike something solid with a hammer, the soft material of the tire absorbs the impact, allowing you to swing with maximum force and not damage your joints. If you look at the photos below, you'll notice that I stagger my feet while performing this exercise. To get the hammer moving from this position, I must twist my torso and drive my hips forward. Both movements have practical application to fighting. The twisting of your torso is similar to when you throw a punch or kick, and the hip drive is similar to the movements of a double-leg takedown. In addition to increasing sport-specific strength, the exercise taxes nearly every muscle in your body. Your forearms must powerfully contract to grip the handle of the hammer, and your legs and back must accelerate the end of the hammer downward into the tire. If your goal is to increase your overall strength and conditioning, this is a good exercise to include into your regimen. It might be old school, but it is highly effective.

1 To set up this exercise, I stand before a tractor tire with a sledgehammer gripped in both hands. Notice how my hand closest to the butt of the hammer is palm-in, while the hand closes to the head is palm-out. Next, I stagger my feet by placing my left foot in front of my right.

2 Contracting my calves and rising up onto my toes, I raise the hammer above my head. Coming up onto your toes is important, as it will allow you to drive the hammer down with more force.

3 I contract my abdominal muscles, thrust my hips back, and drop down onto my soles as I accelerate the hammer toward the tire with maximal force.

4 As the sledgehammer strikes the tire, it bounces back into the air, allowing me to easily reset my position and begin another repetition.

5 Instead of pulling the hammer back to my right side, I pull it back to my left side. Notice how this causes my torso to twist. From here, I will execute another repetition and then switch back to my right side.

OVERHEAD WEIGHT SWING ON ROPE

In this sequence I demonstrate the overhead weight swing, which is a very simple movement. All it entails is looping a rope through a small weight plate, holding both ends of the rope in your hands, and then swinging the weight overhead for a set amount of time. Despite its simplicity, it can be an extremely challenging exercise. Maintaining the constant swinging momentum is taxing to your shoulders, upper back, and arms. At the same time, your core and lower body must constantly strain against the shifting weight to keep your torso steady and your back straight. Just as with the majority of movements in this section, the overhead weight swing can be done with high intensity to challenge your upper-body endurance or at low intensity to warm up the muscles of your shoulder girdle and upper back.

1 To set up this exercise, I string a rope through the hole on a small weight plate and then grip the ends of the rope in both hands. Notice how both of my grips are facing inward.

2 I raise my arms overhead and then swing them circularly, causing the weight plate to begin rotating around my body

3 As I continue to swing the rope and weight, I isometrically contract my abdominal muscles, obliques, lower back, and legs to stabilize my torso and control the weight.

OVERHEAD PRESS AND REVERSE LUNGE COMPLEX

Weight lifting complexes are a method of exercise that forces you to grab a load, and then execute several different exercises without ever releasing the weight. By doing several repetitions of one exercise, maintaining your grip on the barbell, and then moving straight into a next exercise, you can challenge many parts of your body in a relatively short period of time. In this sequence I demonstrate a barbell complex that combines an overhead press with a reverse lunge. The combination of these two movements taxes most of the major muscle groups in the body. The overhead press covers the upper-body muscles and the reverse lunge covers the lower-body muscles. Like all complexes, it's a great tool for developing overall body conditioning and endurance. The nice part about this particular complex is its simplicity. Involving only two movements, it is a very easy exercise for beginners. And with a partner assisting you throughout the movement, you can focus more on form and less on stabilizing the load. Once you feel comfortable with this exercise, you can move on to the heavier-loaded, high-complexity barbell movements.

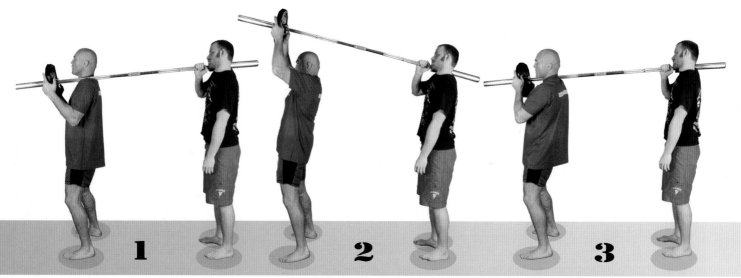

1 To set up this exercise, I load a weight onto one side of a barbell and heft it up onto my left shoulder. At the same time, my training partner hefts the opposite side onto his right shoulder. Notice how my back is straight and I'm gripping the weight to prevent it from sliding off the bar.

2 Flexing my shoulders and triceps, I extend my arms vertically and move the barbell over toward my right side.

3 Relaxing my shoulders and arms, I lower the barbell down to my right shoulder.

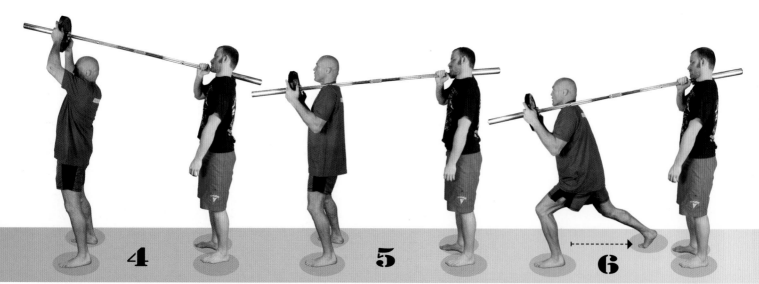

4 Flexing my triceps and shoulders, I extend the barbell vertically again and move it back toward my left side.

5 Relaxing my shoulders and arms, I lower the barbell back down to my left shoulder.

6 Immediately after lowering the barbell down to my left shoulder, I step my right foot backward.

7 I execute a reverse lunge by gently lowering my right knee down to the mat.

8 Contracting my left hamstring and glutes, I elevate my hips.

9 I return to the start position by stepping my right foot forward.

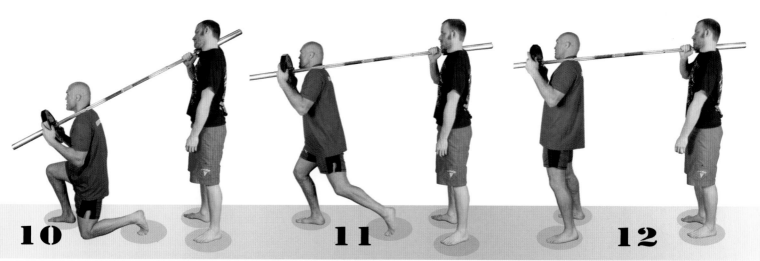

10 I now alternate sides by stepping my left leg backward, dropping my hips, and performing a reverse lunge.

11 I increase my elevation.

12 I return to the starting position by stepping my left foot forward. From here, I will complete a set number of repetitions.

GRAPPLER'S BARBELL COMPLEX

In the sequence below I demonstrate the grappler's barbell complex, which provides an intense workout. In a very short period of time, you perform nearly every movement and articulation of the human body, resulting in increased cardio and endurance with just one repetition of the complex. When first starting out, don't be afraid to go light. Even with just a few pounds loaded onto the barbell, this exercise can be a killer.

BENT-OVER BARBELL ROW

1 To begin this exercise, I grip a barbell at slightly wider than shoulder width, bend forward at the waist, and let the barbell hang down by my knees.

2 Contracting my latissimus dorsi, trapezius, and biceps muscles, I pull the barbell to my chest.

3 Relaxing my arms and upper back, I lower the barbell back down to knee level.

UPRIGHT BARBELL ROW

4 I straighten my posture and slide my hands inward along the bar.

5 Contracting my trapezius muscles, I pull the bar straight up to my chin.

6 Relaxing my arms, I lower the barbell back down to waist level.

BARBELL MILITARY PRESS

7 I slide my hands outward along the barbell until my grips are at shoulder width. Next, I clean the barbell upward so that it is resting on the front of my shoulders. Notice how I have angled my elbows forward to keep the bar locked in place.

8 I extend the barbell vertically by straightening my arms.

9 Relaxing my arms, I lower the barbell back down onto the front of my shoulders. Once again, I angle my elbows forward to hold the barbell in place.

BARBELL GOOD-MORNING EXERCISE

10 I extend the barbell overhead once again, and then lower it down onto the back of my shoulders.

11 Slightly bending my knees, I push my hips back and bend forward at the waist, lowering my torso toward the ground.

12 Contracting my glutes and hamstrings, I push my hips forward and straighten my posture.

SPLIT SQUAT WITH BARBELL

13
Holding the barbell across my upper back and shoulders, I take a big step backward with my right foot.

14
I perform a split squat by dropping my hips. Notice how my back is perfectly straight, my left thigh is parallel with the ground, and my right knee is hovering just above the floor.

15
Pushing off of the floor using my left foot, I increase the elevation of my hips and straighten my legs. From here, I will alternate the positioning of my legs and perform another split squat, this time with my right leg forward.

SQUAT AND PUSH PRESS

16
After completing a split squat on both sides, I bring my feet back together. Notice how they are roughly shoulder width apart.

17
I perform a squat by bending at the knees and moving my hips backward.

18
Flexing my quadriceps and hamstrings, I increase my elevation and straighten my legs.

19

Once I have reached the standing position, I extend my arms vertically. It is important to mention that I use my legs to generate momentum for this lift.

20

I lower the barbell back down behind my head and place it across the back of my shoulders.

21

At the end of my last push-press repetition, I immediately drive the barbell overhead.

ROMANIAN DEADLIFT

22

I lower the bar down in front of my body and let it hang from my arms.

23

Slightly bending my knees, I thrust my hips back and bend forward at the waist. Notice how the barbell is hanging directly below my abdomen. If it is positioned underneath your chest, you most likely need to move your hips farther back.

24

Contracting my glutes and hamstrings, I elevate my torso and return to the standing position. From here, I will begin the complex once again until I have completed a set number of repetitions.

DB SNATCH

With the Olympic lifts taxing your entire body and being explosive in nature, they can be a great conditioning workout on their own. However, standard Olympic lifts require the use of a barbell, which are quite heavy, and it can be difficult to maintain proper form when executing the higher repetitions needed for increasing stamina. This can be alleviated by using a single dumbbell. Dumbbells are easier to handle than barbells, and you can drop the weight as low as you need to achieve your desired number of repetitions. In addition to this, dumbbells also require no setup, which cuts down on the lag time between exercises. All you have to do is grab the dumbbells off the rack, lift it to waist height, and begin executing repetitions.

In this series, I demonstrate how to execute the dumbbell snatch. It is similar to the hang snatch performed with a barbell in that you use your hips to drive the dumbbell upward and overhead in one clean motion. The primary difference is that because you perform the exercise with one arm at a time, you must switch arms after a set number of repetitions in order to attain equal benefits on both sides of your body. In addition to taxing the muscles of your posterior chain, the dumbbell snatch also has a tendency to work out the muscles in your lower arm.

1) With my feet shoulder width apart, I grip a dumbbell in my left hand and let it hang at waist level. 2) I bend slightly at the knees and move my hips back. This bend gives me the space I need to drive my hips upward and generate the momentum needed to heft the dumbbell overhead. 3) From the knee-bend position, I drive my hips forward, extend my legs straight, and move my torso explosively upward. At the same time, I pull my left elbow toward the ceiling. The combination of these actions moves the dumbbell upward rapidly. 4) With the dumbbell moving upward at a high velocity, I now need to lower myself under the weight in order to catch it correctly. To do this, I rebend at the knees, lower my hips slightly, and pull my elbow down. This allows me to bring my arm completely under the weight, which I then straighten to support the dumbbell overhead. From here, I will simply extend my legs fully and rise into the standing position.

MEDICINE BALL SLAM

In this sequence I demonstrate the medicine ball slam, a very simple exercise geared toward increasing endurance and stamina. Just as with many of the exercises in this section, it is very easy to perform. All you do is position a medicine ball over your head, and then use the muscles of your abdomen, arms, and hips to slam it down to the ground. Once accomplished, you snatch the ball back up on the rebound and repeat the process. Due to it being a large-amplitude, high-intensity movement, the medicine ball slam is a good tool for developing overall body conditioning.

1   **2**   **3**

Standing with my feet spread slightly less than shoulder width apart, I grip the sides of a medicine ball in my hands and straighten my arms over my head.

Contracting my abdominal muscles, I drive my hips back and force the medicine ball toward the floor using my hands.

I slam the medicine ball into the floor. As it rebounds, I will catch it with my hands, raise it back overhead, and perform another repetition.

MEDICINE BALL CHEST PASS TO SPRAWL

In this sequence I demonstrate the medicine ball chest pass to sprawl, which requires you to have both a training partner and a medicine ball. If you look at the photos below, you'll notice that this drill involves elements of both a horizontal press and a push-up. You perform the chest press part of the drill as you toss the ball to your partner, and then you perform the push-up part of the drill as you sprawl out on the canvas. While neither the push-up nor the chest press are challenging pressing movements considering the light weight of the medicine ball, when combined over the course of several minutes, the drill can become exhausting. It builds great endurance in the pressing muscles, which is critical in the course of a long fight. Personally, I like to do this drill as a warm-up or as part of a circuit training routine.

I begin the exercise on my knees with a medicine ball held in my hands. I'm facing a partner, and he's in the same kneeling position.

I explosively extend my triceps, pushing the ball away from my body. As the ball is in the air, I allow my momentum to carry me forward, forcing me to fall toward the mat.

I sprawl my hips back and catch myself with my hands, allowing my arms to absorb the impact of the landing. At the same time, my partner catches the medicine ball.

I explode upward out of the push-up position, forcing myself back to a kneeling position.

My partner extends his arms, passing the medicine ball back to me. I raise my hands in front of my body in preparation to catch the ball as it moves towards me.

I catch the ball in my hands, absorbing the impact of the ball with my arms. At the same time, my partner drops into a push-up position. With this drill it's good to develop a rhythm with your partner and work together to time your passes and catches.

POSTERIOR CHAIN

For athletes, the posterior chain is the most important, and often most neglected, muscle group. It's made up of several muscles that must work together in order to generate maximum power. Among the muscle groups of the posterior chain are the calves, hamstrings, gluteal muscles, and the erector spinae. When these muscle groups fire in unison, they allow you to exert a "pushing" force off the ground, which is responsible for the majority of the dynamic and explosive movements that you make as an athlete. For example, the core movements of sprinting, Olympic lifting, and ice-skating are all directly powered by the posterior chain.

In the sport of MMA, nearly every movement initiated from the standing position, as well as many grappling movements, directly benefit by increasing the strength of your posterior chain. To throw a proper punch, kick, knee, or elbow from the standing position, you must plant one or both of your feet firmly on the mat and pivot at the waist. These actions allow your legs, hips, and lower back to propel your strike forward. If you try to execute these strikes without generating momentum from your hips, they will lack any real power. No matter how strong your upper body, without powerful hips and legs, you will never become a devastating striker. The same thing applies to takedowns. All wrestling shots and takedowns begin from the ground and work their way up. Without the ability to lower your hips and drive through your opponent, your chances of completing a successful takedown diminish greatly. Even when you are grappling on the mat, the muscles of your posterior chain

come heavily into play. Every time you bridge while on your back, you use your glues to drive your hips into your opponent, allowing you to elevate his hips and escape out from underneath him. When you perform a shrimping maneuver, you must use your hip flexors to adduct and abduct your legs to and from your body.

With such a vast number of movements in which your posterior chain comes into play while competing in MMA, training these muscle groups, and especially training them in different ways to prepare them for your variety of techniques, is very important. In this section I cover the methods that my strength-and-conditioning coach, Jake Bonacci, developed to increase the strength, explosiveness, and endurance of my posterior chain. The first section involves knee- and hip-dominant exercises. As you will see, these exercises primarily involve bending at the knee and hip joint. Everything from heavy power movements such as the traditional back squat and deadlift, as well as assistance movements such as the hip thrust and band pull-throughs, are detailed. While all of these movements can be done with an emphasis on either speed or max effort, the barbell movements are easier to load heavy, which allows you to focus on max effort, while the body-weight movements are simpler and more efficient to set up and knock off multiple repetitions quickly.

Since it is important to train each of the muscle groups that make up the posterior chain from different angles, I demonstrate both bilateral and unilateral hip-knee- and hip-dominant exercises. Bilateral posterior chain exercises, or any movement where the athlete is standing on both feet, are important as they allow for maximum loading. When both feet are together and working equally to move the load in any given exercise, it effectively doubles the volume of work compared to a single-leg movement. This not only saves time, but it also initiates a stronger training effect, leading to greater results. However, unilateral leg exercises must not be overlooked. When exercising the posterior chain, there are many joint angles and movement patterns that can only be duplicated when using a single leg. As you know, when fighting you often ask your legs to perform separate tasks, such as when you throw a front kick, pivot on your rear leg to throw a cross, or use your legs to control your opponent form the half guard. In order to maximize your posterior chain muscles for fighting, you must perform both single- and double-leg exercises.

In the next section, I cover triple-extension exercises. While the first section focused strictly on knee and hip extension, this section adds in ankle extension as well. When the ankle, knee, and hip joints flex simultaneously, it can produce more force than any other human movement. Having the ability to produce large amounts of force is critical in the sport of MMA. If you want to execute a technique with maximum power, whether it is a straight right cross while boxing, a powerful double-leg takedown from the standing position, or a wrestler's switch from your knees, you need to explosively flex your ankle, knee, and hip joints. To help you train your triple-extension movements, I cover two different types of exercises. The first is a series of jump variations. Jumping is the simplest triple-extension movement in any athlete's athletic base. With jumping being such a simple movement, any athlete can immediately begin training triple-extension movements regardless of his current level of strength or conditioning. This makes standing jump training a good starting point for athletes who have built a foundational level of strength from performing double-extension movements shown earlier in this section but who are also unfamiliar with the more advanced triple-extension movements show at the end.

At the end of the jumping section, I demonstrate plyometric jumps, which are among the most challenging and physically taxing lower-body exercises. Due to the specific way in which these exercises cause the muscles to relax and then contract over a short period of time, they have the ability to increase your power production more than almost any other exercise. While the benefits of plyometric jumping exercises are first rate, you must be prepared to handle the stress of the movements. Before you begin to perform

them, you must develop a solid base of physical strength, as well as a good capacity to recover from stress.

Finally, I cover the Olympic lifts and their variations, which is perhaps the most important section in this book. There are only two lifts performed competitively in the Olympic Games, the snatch and the clean and jerk, but there are many different variations of these lifts. With both the snatch and the clean and jerk, the goal is to lift a loaded barbell off the ground and move it to an overhead position where your arms are fully extended. With the snatch, this movement is performed in one fluid motion, and with the clean and jerk, it is performed in two steps. Both exercises move your body through different ranges of motion, and thus build power in different ways. Therefore, it is imperative to include variations of both into your training program to cover all the necessary joint angles. As you will see, some variations require you to heft the barbell off the ground, while others begin from the standing position with the barbell hanging at an arm's length. Additionally, the clean and jerk can be separated into two movements, with the clean being practiced separately from the jerk. Performing these variations allows you to get the benefits of full-power triple extension in every workout. By constantly switching up your Olympic lifts, you can keep your body from plateauing, yet still tax your central nervous system in every workout. As we have already covered, this is key to increasing your ability to produce speed and power in every part of your body.

A final note on Olympic lifts: they are very difficult to learn correctly. To get the full benefit of these amazing lifts, it may be necessary to find yourself a good coach and have him teach you the fundamentals and critique your form. Trust me when I tell you that it's worth the effort. Olympic lifts have been a critical component of my strength-and-conditioning development.

Within this chapter I cover all the necessary tools any person—fighter or regular Joe—will ever need to develop his posterior chain. Starting with simple body-weight knee and hip exercises, and progressing down to the most difficult and beneficial triple-extension Olympic movement, this section covers it all. The posterior chain is the foundation of your athletic abilities. Taking the time to support and strengthen the muscles of your legs and lower back will translate more directly to your ability to perform your sport than any other exercise you can do in the weight room. So take your time, start from the beginning of the chapter, and work your way through each section until you're capable of performing plyometrics and Olympic lifts efficiently and safely.

DOUBLE EXTENSION

BACK SQUAT

The back squat has been called the "king of all exercises," and for good reason. Very few exercises can match the benefits of an intense squat session due to the heavy loads you can utilize and the broad range of motion. When you perform a squat, you tax the muscles on both the front and backside of your body. On your anterior chain, your quadriceps and abdominals receive an excellent workout. And on your posterior chain, your calves are taxed as you walk the bar out of the rack and your upper back is challenged as you squeeze the barbell tight to your trapezius muscles. It is important to mention that a small segment of athletes feel that squats are dangerous due to the possibility of injuring your spine. Personally, I disagree. The squat is a natural human motion, and as long as you perform it correctly (with your hips moving back, your chest up, and driving the weight up through your heels), you will experience positive results. As with all exercises, utilizing proper form is much more important than seeing how much load you can lift.

1   **2**   **3**

Standing with my feet shoulder width apart and my toes facing slightly outward, I hold the barbell on my shoulders and trapezius muscles using my hands.

I slowly lower my elevation by moving my hips backward and bending at the knees. This causes the barbell to move straight downward, driving its weight through my heels and into the floor. To ensure that the barbell travels vertically, I keep my back straight and look forward. When I reach the bottom of my movement, which in this case is roughly a seventy-degree bend in my legs, I halt my downward momentum and prepare to increase my elevation. Note, it is very important to keep your weight on your heels throughout this exercise. If you lean forward, the bar will move in front of your body, causing your back to round.

To increase my elevation from the bottom of my movement, I force my hips upward by flexing my glutes, hamstrings, and quadriceps. Just as during my descent, I keep the weight of the bar on my heels. Once my body is fully erect, I prepare to execute another repetition.

PARTNER SQUATS

The partner squat is nearly identical to the back squat shown in the previous sequence. The primary difference lies in the form of resistance. While the typical back squat utilizes a barbell and weight plates for resistance, the partner squat employs the body weight of another person. The same muscles are taxed—the hamstring and glutes are the prime movers, and the spinal erectors, quads, abdominals, calves, arms, and upper back all play a role in stabilizing the movement. Although the execution of both squats is the same, the initiation of the partner squat differs from the traditional back squat in that you must pick your opponent off his feet at the start of the exercise and then return him to the standing position at the end. With both exercises being so similar, deciding which one to utilize should be based on availability. If I'm working out in the weight room, I'll use the barbell and perform traditional back squats. If I'm on the wrestling mats and want to work on developing my posterior chain strength before or after my workout, I'll perform partner squats. Having this technique in my arsenal is key because it allows me to perform my squat sessions when I am on the road or training at a foreign gym lacking a weight room.

1) Both partners face each other. Since Lance will perform the first squat, he grabs Jake's right wrist with his left hand. This will help him control Jake's body throughout the movement. 2) Lance lowers his level and hooks his right arm to the inside of Jake's right leg. As he lowers his level, he drives his head underneath of Jake's right armpit, essentially dropping himself into a Fireman's Carry position. 3) Lance now plants his feet under his shoulders and pulls Jake's weight onto his back. As he pulls Jake over his shoulders, he extends his back and comes into the fully upright standing position. When in this position, it is important to balance your partner evenly on your shoulders or it will make the exercise much more dangerous for both parties. 4) Lance bends his knees and hips, relaxes the muscles of his posterior chain, and lowers Jake toward the ground. 5) At the bottom of the squat, Lance contracts his hamstrings and glutes, drives his hips forward, and elevates his torso. It is important to note that like standard barbell squatting, Lance drives his weight through his heels as he ascends. 6) After the desired number of reps, Lance lowers Jake down by relaxing his glutes and hamstrings. However, at the bottom of this repetition, he allows Jake to slide off his shoulders and land on his feet. 7) Lance slides Jake off his back and releases his leg. From here, Lance will move back into the standing position.

FRONT SQUAT

Although the back squat is considered by many to be the king of all exercises, it's not ideal for everyone. When you squat with heavy weight loaded onto the back of your shoulders, it can push your shoulders down at a faster rate than your lower back, which forces the lumbar spine into hyperflexion and can result in injury. In addition to this, back squats require good flexibility to lower the weight in the proper fashion. If you have poor hip and ankle mobility, you will be incapable of achieving the needed depth with your squats or fall over backward as you descend. To eliminate these potential dangers, a lot of athletes perform front squats instead. By placing the barbell in front of your neck instead of behind it, the leverage on the lumbar spine decreases, which reduces the potential for lower-back injury. Placing the barbell in the front position also has the added advantage of providing counterweight as you move your hips backward, which eliminates much of the flexibility needed when performing the traditional back squat. Despite the alternate positioning of the barbell, the front squat maintains the advantages that make the back squat such an amazing exercise. It's possible to move very heavy loads, and a broad range of muscles is employed to perform the movement. However, due to the change in leverage, the front squat tends to shift the emphasis away from the hamstrings toward the quadriceps. While the front squat is an excellent exercise to help unseasoned lifters learn the squatting motion without needing to focus as heavily on lumbar stability and hip and ankle mobility, by no means is it a novice lift. It is the choice exercise of many Olympic lifters, who are some of the strongest athletes in the world, because it carries over more completely to their sport.

1

Jake begins the front squat standing with his feet about shoulder width apart. The barbell is resting on the front of his deltoid muscles and his clavicle bones, running across the front plane of his body. To secure the barbell, Jake crosses his arms so his hands are resting on the opposite shoulder muscle. This traps the barbell in between his shoulders and his hands.

2

Jake descends in the front squat position by flexing his knee joints and forcing his hips to move back. It is important to note that he is keeping his back as vertical as possible and his weight on his heels.

Jake begins the ascent by contracting his glutes, hamstrings, and quadriceps muscles. As his hips move forward and his knees and hips extend, his torso elevates.

Jake completes the front squat by locking out his knees and resting in the fully upright position. From here he can either rebend his knees and descend for another repetition or rack the weight and move on to another exercise.

ALTERNATE FRONT SQUAT GRIP

In this photo Jake demonstrates an alternate front squat grip. The barbell is still resting on the front of his shoulders, but rather than fold his arms over top of the bar, he bends his elbows straight back and uses his fingers to push the bar into his deltoids. This prevents the barbell from rolling forward. While it may appear as if the weight is being held up by just a few of Jake's fingers, the majority of the weight is still resting on his shoulders and clavicle. This is the preferred grip for the front squat utilized by Olympic lifters, as the hand position is identical to the hand position in the clean and jerk. However, when attempting the front squat, either grip will work. Neither method significantly affects the mechanics of the squat, so try them both and discover which one works best for you.

OVERHEAD SQUAT

While the back squat is a great exercise that utilizes nearly every muscle in the body, it's not a movement that fighters should perform daily. Like any exercise that is performed too often, your body will quickly adapt and eventually fatigue the nervous system. To combat this, you can incorporate simple variations of the back squat to keep your body guessing. One such variation is the overhead squat, which is utilized by many Olympic weight lifters and MMA fighters. Olympic weight lifters use this variation because it closely resembles the squatting motion they perform in order catch the barbell after executing a snatch. MMA fighters and other athletes use the overhead squat because it forces them to isometrically contract their shoulders and upper back to stabilize the bar, which leads to increased strength and injury prevention in those muscle groups. The prime movers in the overhead squat are identical to the back squat—the glutes and hamstrings provide the majority of the force to elevate the bar, but due to the unstable overhead position of the barbell, the core faces a much greater challenge than with the regular back squat in keeping the spine stable. However, due to the dynamics of this exercise, the overhead squat is performed with lighter weight than a traditional back squat. When first attempting this exercise, it is not uncommon for an athlete to begin with one-third or even one-fourth of the weight they use when performing back squats. As your core becomes more adept at stabilizing the bar at this awkward angle, overall strength and power will increase dramatically. When used as an intermittent variation, the overhead squat's ability to increase core and upper-back stability more than make up for the reduced load.

To begin the overhead squat, Jake moves the bar into the overhead position. This is generally done by unracking a loaded barbell at the chest, and then using a push press motion to elevate it overhead. Once he has the barbell overhead and his arms extended, Jake establishes a shoulder-width stance and prepares for the squatting motion.

Jake begins the squatting motion by flexing his knees and moving his hips backward. As he descends, he keeps his lower back arched and his upper back shrugged upward. This stabilizes his entire posterior chain and helps keep the barbell in place. Note that although his back is leaning forward, the barbell is still centered over his heels. He accomplishes this by pulling his shoulder blades back until his arms are behind his neck. If he failed to do this, the barbell would not remain in the proper position.

Jake ascends from the bottom of the squat position by flexing his glutes and hamstrings and driving his hips forward. As his torso elevates, he straightens his posture. It is important to mention that throughout the entire movement you must keep the barbell centered over your heels to maintain control of the weight. Additionally, you must isometrically contract your upper back and core muscles to keep your spine neutral.

LOWERING THE BARBELL

Overhead exercises provide a multitude of benefits, but they present a unique challenge as well. Anytime the barbell is moved over your head, it must be lowered again in a safe manner. With lighter weights, this is a minor concern. If the weight of the bar is trivial, the strength of the arms alone can set the barbell down without much effort. However, when executing the Olympic Lifts shown in this section, the mass of the barbell will rise drastically as you become more skilled at the movements. By definition, Olympic lifts use the strength of the entire body to boost the weight overhead, so the strength of the arms alone is insufficient to lower the barbell. Olympic lifters have developed a special technique, as well as a special set of tools, to lower the barbell safely and efficiently from the overhead position. Instead of trying to slowly lower the barbell with their arms alone, Olympic lifters actually aim to drop it from overhead. It's much safer to allow gravity to lower the weight while the lifter simply controls the barbell as it descends. Below Jake demonstrates the proper method to lower a barbell from overhead. The goal with this motion is to safely move out from underneath the barbell as it drops to the ground, using the arms to control it as it falls. The motion is important, but some specialty lifting equipment can make dropping the barbell safer and less damaging to the floor. A proper lifting platform, with a wooden base and rubber strips on the edges, provides a stable place for Jake's feet and a layer of cushion underneath the weight plates. The plates themselves are also specialty products. Rather than using standard metal plates, Olympic lifting is commonly done with rubber bumper plates. These absorb the impact of the landing, causing less noise and collateral damage if they happen to get loose. Although it won't make you a stronger or more powerful athlete, learning to lower the barbell properly from the overhead position will allow you to safely utilize the Olympic lifting techniques shown in this section without injury to yourself or innocent bystanders at your gym.

Jake stands on the lifting platform and positions a barbell loaded with rubber plates overhead. With arms extended and his feet less than a shoulder width, his entire body supports the weight, making it a relatively stable position.

To lower the barbell, Jake rotates his shoulders forward slightly. This moves the barbell out in front of his body, giving it an unobstructed path to the floor. As the weight begins to fall, Jake relaxes his arms and allows gravity to pull the bar straight down. Notice his hands stay on the barbell until it passes his hips. This control prevents the barbell from moving too far forward and getting loose.

After the barbell passes Jake's hips, he completely releases his grips and allows it to hit the lifting platform. Notice how he positioned the weights so that they land on the rubber strips of the platform. With the weight plates also being constructed of rubber, the impact is absorbed nicely and creates minimal noise and damage. Now that the weight is safely back on the floor, Jake can continue with another Olympic lift.

HIP THRUST ON STABILITY BALL

Although you rarely see the body weight hip thrusts performed, it's an excellent exercise for building strength in your hamstrings and glutes. As a matter of fact, it stresses your glutes to such a degree that I've seen many well-conditioned athletes quickly burn out while performing them. Personally, I feel hip thrust exercises such as the one demonstrated in this sequence are very beneficial for mixed martial artists because the motion is similar to the bridging motion you perform while executing sweeps and other grappling techniques. By including hip thrusts into your regimen, you will undoubtedly develop a more powerful bridge. In addition to this, you will also reduce the potential for hip, knee, and lower-back injury in every athletic movement.

In this sequence I perform the hip thrust on a physiotherapy ball to decrease stability and make the exercise more difficult, but it is important to mention that there are other variations. You can place your feet on a stable object such as a bench or box to make the exercise easier. You can eliminate back support by placing your shoulders on one bench and your feet on another. And if you want to make things really challenging, you can perform single-leg hip thrusts or place a barbell over your hips to increase the load. With a variation available for everyone from beginning to advanced practitioners, there is no reason to avoid this valuable exercise.

Lying flat on my back, I place my heels on the top of the stability ball and spread my arms out to my sides. It is important to notice that my hips are currently positioned on the floor.

Using my glutes and hamstring muscles, I thrust my hips upward off the floor.

Once my hips are elevated, I continue with my hip flexion by rolling my feet across the top of the stability ball and extending my legs until my body is flat.

Once I have straightened my body, I keep my hips elevated and move my feet toward my body by rolling them across the top of the stability ball.

Without letting my hips drop, I once again move my feet away from my body by rolling them across the top of the ball. Once my body has straightened, I will bring my feet back toward my body to complete another repetition. It is important to note that the only time your hips touch the floor is at the start and end of the exercise.

BAND RESISTED PULL-THROUGH

The pull-through is another underutilized exercise that targets your glutes and hamstring muscles. If you look at the first photo in the sequence below, you'll notice that both of my hands are gripping a flex band that is tied to a dumbbell behind me. To perform the exercise, I straighten my legs and posture, just like I do when executing a squat. However, with the resistance coming from between my legs, my body wants to fall backward. To prevent this from happening, I shift my weight onto my heels, drive my hips forward, and focus on activating my posterior chain muscles. Personally, I feel this is a great supplement to squatting. A lot of people take very wide stances and perform shallow movements while squatting. This does wonders for developing their quadriceps, but not so much their hamstrings and glutes. By performing the pull-through in conjunction with squats, you guarantee a well-rounded lower-body workout. The other nice part about this technique is that it trains you to be on your heels, which is ideal when executing squats. By ingraining this foot positioning into your subconscious, you automatically drive your heels into the ground while squatting, leading to a far safer and more productive squat session.

With my feet spread roughly at shoulder width, I bend at the hip and knees and grab one end of a flex band between my legs using both hands. It is important to notice that the opposite end of the flex band is tied to a dumbbell, and the dumbbell is secured in place. It is also important to notice that my back is perfectly straight and I am looking forward.

I flex my glutes and hamstrings to extend my hips forward and straighten my body. This movement increases tension on the flex band, which in turn pulls my body backward. To maintain my posture, I force my weight down through my heels.

Keeping my weight on my heels, I slowly bend my hips and knees to return to the starting position. It is very important to notice that I have kept my back straight throughout the entire movement. If you allow your back to curve forward, it increases your risk of injury.

HEAVY BAG ZERCHER SQUAT

The Zercher squat taxes your glutes and hamstring muscles, but instead of loading the weight across your upper back like in the back squat or across your shoulders like in the front squat, you hold the weight in your arms. Personally, I feel this is a more practical application for a fighter. For example, when you are in your opponent's guard and get caught in a submission such as a triangle choke, having the strength to pick his body up off the mat and then slam him back down can save you from having to tap. This particular exercise mimics the awkward weight distribution of such a lift better than either the back or front squat. If you look at the photos below, you'll notice that I execute the exercise using a heavy bag rather than the more common barbell, and the reason is threefold: it more closely resembles a human body, it is less painful to hold, and it is harder to hang on to, which provides your arms with a workout.

1   **2**   **3**

Standing with my feet roughly shoulder width apart, I secure a heavy bag to my chest using my arms. It is important to notice that despite holding a rather unwieldy object, my back is perfectly straight.

Keeping my back straight, I lower my butt toward the ground by bending at the hips and knees.

I increase my elevation by flexing my hamstrings and glutes and straightening my body. Once my body is fully erect, I prepare for the next repetition.

GOOD-MORNING

The good-morning is a great supplemental exercise for developing all the muscles in your posterior chain. Although the glutes are the primary muscles being taxed, the muscles of your hamstrings and lower back play a big role in stabilizing your body as you execute the movement. One of the nice advantages about incorporating good-mornings into your regimen is that by their very design you are forced to work the muscles in your posterior chain. There is no way to shift your weight so that your quadriceps do all the work, which is a common problem inexperienced athletes often face when doing squats. If you feel that your glutes and hamstrings could use more development, you can't go wrong with this exercise.

1 Standing with my feet spread at slightly less than shoulder width, I place the barbell across my upper back and hold it in place using my hands.

2 With a slight bend in my knees, I bend forward at the waist and lower my torso to a forty-five-degree angle in relation to the ground. If you go lower with the movement, it is important to keep a good grip on the barbell to prevent it from rolling forward and up your neck.

3 Flexing my glutes and hamstrings, I elevate my torso. Now that I have returned to the upright position, I will immediately execute my next repetition.

DOUBLE EXTENSION

GOOD-MORNING WITH PARTNER

The movement in this exercise is similar to that of the standard good-morning, except here you use a human body for resistance. There are a few adjustments you must make. Instead of holding your training partner across your upper back, which would cause too much pressure on your spine as you lean forward, you hold him in front of your body using your arms. In addition to taxing your glutes and hamstrings, it also provides your arms with an excellent workout. Personally, I like to utilize this exercise when I don't have any weights on hand or when I am performing a workout with a training partner. It should be noted that performing good-mornings with a body can be extremely difficult due to the added weight, and you should adjust your repetitions accordingly.

1 With my feet spread roughly at shoulder width, I scoop my training partner off the mat and hold him in my outstretched arms. It is important to notice that my knees are slightly bent and my head is up. In addition to challenging my posterior chain, my arms are getting a good isometric workout from holding my partner.

2 I elevate my torso until my body is perfectly vertical. At the same time, I use my arms to curl my training partner up and into my chest.

3 As I bend forward at the hips, I lower my training partner toward the mat.

4 Flexing my glutes and hamstrings, I reverse my movement and straighten my posture. At the same time, I curl my training partner back into my chest using my arms. From here, I will continue the exercise for a set number of repetitions.

ROMANIAN DEADLIFT

The Romanian deadlift is a very similar movement to the good-morning. Both are performed with a slight bend in the knees and hip flexion, and both primarily tax the glutes and hamstrings. The only difference is how you carry the weight load. Instead of placing the barbell across your upper back as you do in a good-morning, you hold the bar in your hands as you do when performing the traditional deadlift. With both exercises being supplemental to the bigger compound exercises such as squats and deadlifts, they are generally done later in the workout with lighter weights. Oftentimes, deciding which one to perform boils down to efficiency. They both tax the same muscle groups in a similar way, so I will choose the one that requires the least amount of moving around between sets. For example, if I am doing a squat workout, I'll usually follow up with good-mornings because the barbell is already positioned up on the rack. If I am doing a deadlifting workout, I'll follow up with Romanian deadlifts because the bar is already positioned on the ground.

1 Standing with my feet roughly shoulder width apart, I grip the barbell at shoulder width and let it hang at an arm's length.

2 As I slightly bend my knees and flex my hips, I tilt my torso forward until my upper body is nearly parallel with the floor. Notice how I have kept my back perfectly straight.

3 Flexing my glutes and hamstrings, I elevate my torso until my body is completely erect. From here, I will continue the exercise for a set number of repetitions.

DEADLIFT

When an athlete hits a plateau in his strength training routine, oftentimes the best solution is to put more weight on the bar, and very few exercises can be loaded heavier than the deadlift. The deadlift is one of the simplest movements in my workout routine. The extent of the workout involves reaching down, grabbing a barbell, and then standing back up. But the simplicity of the movement accounts for it's great efficiency. Due to the relatively short range of motion and simple movement patterns, it's possible to progress very rapidly on the deadlift. As an athlete becomes stronger and stronger at this motion, he can load the bar heavier and heavier. That makes the deadlift a great max effort movement. As a test to see one's own strength development, or as a periodic workout to challenge the body in a profound way, the deadlift is a great developmental tool.

Much like the squat, the deadlift is primarily a posterior chain exercise. However, unlike the squat, the range of motion in the hips tends to be shallow. This shallow hip angle steers the focus of the exercise away from the hamstrings and more toward the spinal erector muscles. In both exercises the glutes are a prime mover in pushing the hips forward. Although there are many variations of the deadlift involving different starting heights of the bar, this is the most basic set up. The barbell is loaded with plates, and the plates are set on the ground. This basic deadlift is a great starting point to develop your lower back.

1

After loading a barbell on the lifting platform, Jake spreads his feet at shoulder width and grabs the barbell with both hands. Notice that his grips are also roughly shoulder width apart and that his shins are as close to the bar as possible without his shoulders moving over the top of the bar.

2

Jake contracts his spinal erector muscles and glutes. This drives his hips forward and pulls his shoulders back. The combined action of these two motions causes his torso and the bar to slowly elevate. While pulling the barbell upward, Jake drives his weight through his heels. If he begins to lean forward or lets the bar drift away from his body, it will amplify the effort needed to hoist the load. It is important to notice that his back has remained flat.

As Jake nears the top of the movement, he shrugs his trapezius muscles up and pulls his shoulder blades together. This locks out the deadlift in a safe position and allows him to rest for a moment before reversing the motion.

To lower the barbell, Jake reverses the previous actions. He extends his spinal erector muscles and moves his hips backward. This allows the barbell to drop back down in a straight line. While lowering the barbell, he maintains his arched back, never allowing his shoulders to come forward. This could compromise his spinal safety and cause him injury. Although it's possible to simply drop a barbell from the top of a deadlift, without the proper equipment, it can cause serious damage to the floor due to the heavy weights involved.

BACK HYPEREXTENSION

When training your posterior chain, it is easy to get into the habit of focusing exclusively on your glutes and hamstring muscles. However, the muscles of your lower back play a very important role in all athletic movements. Anytime your hips tilt forward or backward, your spinal erector muscles contract to keep your shoulders up, your lower back arched, and your spine stable. The more you develop the muscles in your lower back, the more you reduce the risk of injuring your spine while working out and training. Although there are many ways to strengthen the muscles of your lower back, I like the back hyperextension exercise due to its simplicity. If you look at the photos in the sequences below, you'll notice that in both variations of this exercise I fix my legs to the bench press prior to arching my back. This reduces the role of my hamstrings and glutes and forces my spinal erector muscles to move my torso up and down. While it is possible to increase resistance by using bands, dumbbells, or a barbell, performing the exercise using body weight alone is usually enough to give even a well-conditioned athlete a strenuous workout. If you do decide to add weight to the movement, it is very important to pay special attention to your form. You want to keep your shoulders back, your lower back arched, and your spine in a straight line. If you allow your lower back to relax and your shoulders to slump, you risk injuring your spine. Most find back hyperextensions to be most effective when using body weight alone for medium to high repetitions.

1

On a decline bench, I wrap my hamstrings around the backstop and rest my quadriceps against the front cushion. Notice how I am using my right arm to keep my body upright.

2

With my legs secured to the bench, I remove my right hand from the bench and keep my body upright using the muscles in my posterior chain. Next, I place both hands behind my head to ensure strict movement. It is important to notice that even though I am leaning forward, my back is completely straight.

3

Keeping my back straight, I bend at the hips and lower my torso until it is parallel with the decline bench press. In this position, my glutes and hamstrings are working hard to stabilize my body. It is important to notice that instead of dropping my torso all the way down to the bench, I keep it suspended a few inches above.

4

I flex the spinal erector muscles in my back and elevate my torso back to the starting position. From here, I will continue with the exercise for a set number of repetitions.

OPTION 2

1

I lay flat on a bench so that my hips are at one end and my feet are at the other. As my partner grips my ankles to hold my lower body in place, I place my hands behind my head.

2

With Jake keeping my legs secured to the bench, I flex the spinal erector muscles in my back and elevate my torso until it is positioned slightly above my lower body. Notice how my back is perfectly straight.

3

I lower my torso back toward the floor.

4

I perform a second repetition. From here, I will continue with the exercise for a set number of repetitions or a set amount of time.

LATERAL BARBELL LUNGE

When performing a lower-body workout, athletes often focus so intently on exercises that involve front-to-back movement that they neglect to perform exercises that involve side-to-side movement. In fighting, lateral movement is often more important than moving forward or backward, especially when it comes to evading strikes, acquiring a dominant angle of attack, or executing takedowns from the clinch. Performing the lateral barbell lunge is an excellent way to round out your lower-body training and prepare you for lateral movement in a fight. Although the exercise primarily stresses the hip flexors by abducting and adducting the legs from the body, it also taxes the glutes and hamstrings as your hips lower and your knees flex.

Standing with my feet close together, I rest the barbell across the back of my shoulders and trapezius muscles and hold it in place using my hands.

1

I employ my hips' abductor muscles and take a long step toward my right side using my right foot.

2

I bend my right knee and squat toward the floor. With my upper body having shifted toward my right, my right leg is forced to do the majority of the work.

3

Flexing my hamstrings and glutes, I increase my elevation and straighten my posture. Next, I step my right foot back toward my left foot.

4

I step my left foot toward my left side. From here, I will execute another lunge.

5

STEP-UP

The step-up is a great single-leg training exercise. Although its execution is simple, the benefits are broad. It can correct muscular imbalances, increase stability and coordination, and provide an excellent workout for both your glutes and quadriceps muscles. If you look at the photos below, you'll notice that the movement is very similar to walking or running, just with the added load of a barbell. With the step-up being such a common movement, its carryover is great for all sports, not just fighting. However, unlike many other types of single-leg training, the step-up does require extra equipment, most importantly something to step up onto. Here I use a bench, but anything with a broad base and an elevated platform will work just as well. It is important to note that when you increase your load using a barbell as I do in this sequence, you should take extra caution. With both of your hands tied up, you won't be able to brace yourself should you slip. If you feel shaky when starting out, replace the barbell with dumbbells. Although they are harder to hold because they are grip dependent, they are easily dropped, which allows you to catch yourself with your hands.

1 To prepare for this exercise, I stand in front of a bench with my feet close together and a barbell perched on my shoulders and trapezius muscles.

2 Keeping my back straight, I step my left foot up onto the bench.

3 Transferring my weight onto my left foot, I flex my glutes and left quadriceps to straighten my left leg and begin pulling my body upward. It is important to mention that as I do this, I drive my weight downward through my left heel.

DUMBBELL VARIATION

4

As my left leg straightens, I place my right foot next to my left foot. If you look closely, you'll notice that I am driving my weight down through my heels.

5

I reverse my previous actions and step my right foot back down to the floor.

6

To return to the starting position, I step my left foot off the bench and position it next to my right foot on the ground. From here, I will alternate sides by stepping my right foot onto the bench first. I will go back and forth like this for a set number of repetitions.

FORWARD BARBELL LUNGE

The forward barbell lunge is another beneficial single-leg exercise, especially for the MMA athlete. Although it's not as natural a movement as the step-up, it's almost identical to the movement involved when you change levels and shoot in for a takedown. As a result, performing the forward barbell lunge on a regular basis will increase the speed and power of your single- and double-leg takedowns. However, it should be noted that it can be a relatively difficult exercise for beginner athletes to perform correctly. If you've never done lunges before, it's best to start with just your body weight and pay special attention to your form. To perform the lunge correctly, make sure your back is vertical and that your lead knee does not travel too far forward as your hips drop. At the bottom of your lunge, you want your lead leg to be bent at a ninety-degree angle in relation to the ground. If you have a difficult time finding your balance or keeping your spine straight during the exercise, it's probably best to start with the split squat variations shown in the next sequence.

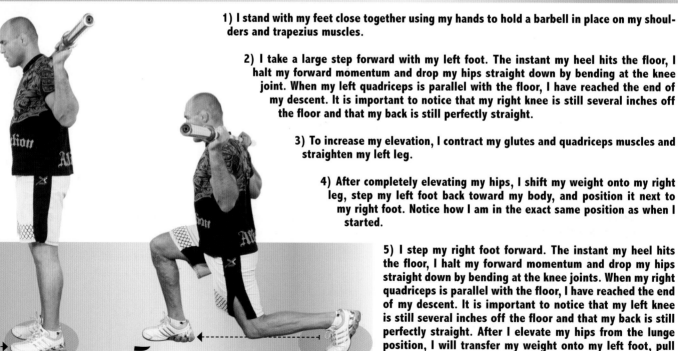

1) I stand with my feet close together using my hands to hold a barbell in place on my shoulders and trapezius muscles.

2) I take a large step forward with my left foot. The instant my heel hits the floor, I halt my forward momentum and drop my hips straight down by bending at the knee joint. When my left quadriceps is parallel with the floor, I have reached the end of my descent. It is important to notice that my right knee is still several inches off the floor and that my back is still perfectly straight.

3) To increase my elevation, I contract my glutes and quadriceps muscles and straighten my left leg.

4) After completely elevating my hips, I shift my weight onto my right leg, step my left foot back toward my body, and position it next to my right foot. Notice how I am in the exact same position as when I started.

5) I step my right foot forward. The instant my heel hits the floor, I halt my forward momentum and drop my hips straight down by bending at the knee joints. When my right quadriceps is parallel with the floor, I have reached the end of my descent. It is important to notice that my left knee is still several inches off the floor and that my back is still perfectly straight. After I elevate my hips from the lunge position, I will transfer my weight onto my left foot, pull my right foot back, and prepare to execute another repetition.

OVERHEAD BARBELL LUNGE

In this sequence I demonstrate a variation of the barbell lunge. The movement of my lower body is identical to the previous exercise, but in this version I'm holding a barbell in a fixed position over my head rather than across my upper back. While this may seem like a minor change, it significantly increases the difficulty of the exercise. The lunge is a hard exercise to stabilize even with the bar held close to the body. When it is held overhead, the challenge of stabilizing your body during the movement increases dramatically. It is important to mention that the overhead barbell lunge can be done with moderately heavy weight for a challenging workout or with light weight as a warm-up. Personally, I like to perform it as a warm-up to increase blood flow to the upper and lower body.

1) **Standing with my feet close together, I grip a barbell at slightly wider than shoulder width, extend it straight overhead, and lock out my arms.**

2) **I take a large step forward with my left foot. The instant my heel touches down, I stop my forward momentum and drop my hips straight down by bending at the knees. When my left quadriceps is parallel with the ground, I have reached the bottom of my descent. Notice how my right knee is positioned several inches off the floor.**

3) **I elevate myself out of the lunge position by flexing my quadriceps and glutes and straightening my left knee. Once my body is erect, I transfer my weight onto my right foot and step my left foot back, returning to the starting position.**

4) **I switch sides by stepping my right foot forward. The instant my foot touches the floor, I stop my forward momentum and drop my hips straight down by bending at the knees. When my right quad is parallel with the floor, I have reached the bottom of my descent. Notice how my left knee is positioned several inches off the floor.**

5) **I elevate myself out of the lunge position by flexing my quadriceps and glutes and strengthening my left knee. Once my body is erect, I transfer my weight onto my left foot and step my right foot back, returning to the starting position. From here, I will continue to repeat the exercise for a set number of repetitions.**

SPLIT SQUAT

The difference between the split squat and the lunge is the positioning of your feet. With the lunge, you start with your feet together and then step forward into your lunge. With the split squat, you start with your feet already staggered and simply drop and raise your hips to complete a repetition. By eliminating the step forward, it becomes much easier to maintain your stability. The only time you have to deal with a shift in your body weight is when you step forward to begin the exercise and when you step back after finishing all of your repetitions. As noted earlier, this is a great option for beginner athletes. It taxes all the same muscles as the standard lunge, but doesn't challenge your coordination so heavily. Once you're able to perform the split squat efficiently, you can move on to the lunge previously shown or try the Bulgarian split squat, which is demonstrated in the next sequence.

1   **2**   **3**

Keeping my feet spread roughly at shoulder width, I position my left foot in front of me, and my right foot behind me. I rest a barbell across my shoulders and trapezius muscles and hold it in place using my hands.

Bending my left knee, I drop my hips straight down toward the mat. When my left quadriceps is parallel with the ground, I have reached the bottom of my descent. Notice how my right knee is positioned a few inches off the floor.

I elevate my hips by contracting my glutes and quad muscles and straightening my legs. Once I have returned to the starting position, I do not step my left foot back as I did when performing the lunge. Instead, I keep my left foot forward and prepare to once again lower my hips. After completing a set number of repetitions, I will alternate sides by positioning my right leg in front of me, and my left leg behind me.

BULGARIAN SPLIT SQUAT

The Bulgarian split squat is a variation of the standard split squat demonstrated on the previous page. The difference is that instead of having both feet on the ground, you elevate your rear leg by placing your toes on a bench. Unlike the lunge or the other split squat variations, this exercise forces nearly all of your weight onto your lead leg. The goal of doing single-leg exercises is to work each leg independently as much as possible, and this exercise works great in that regard. As you lower and raise your body, your lead leg does all the work. All your rear leg does is stabilize your body. However, it is important to mention that stabilizing your body is no easy task, making this exercise relatively advanced. To reduce your risk of injury, I strongly recommend becoming comfortable with the standard split squat first.

1   **2**   **3**

With a bench positioned behind me, I place my left foot flat on the floor, rest the top of my right foot on the bench, and hold a dumbbell in each arm for resistance.

Keeping my back perfectly straight, I bend my left knee and drop my hips toward the mat. Once my left quad is parallel with the floor, I have reached the bottom of my descent. Notice how my right knee is elevated several inches off the floor.

I elevate my hips by contracting my glutes and quad muscles and return to the standing position. From here, I will complete a set number of repetitions and then switch the positioning of my legs.

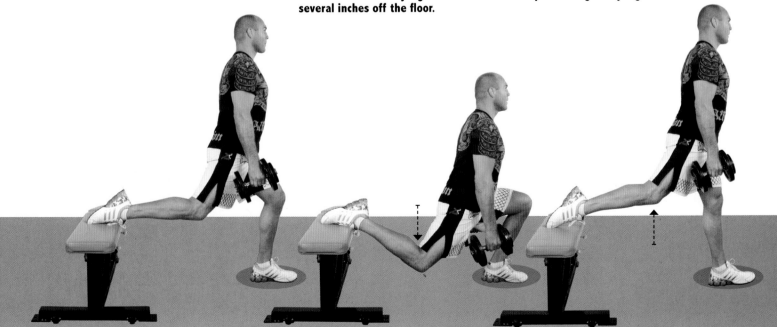

ROCKER

Instead of the knee flexion involved in many of the other single-leg exercises demonstrated in this section, the rocker concentrates on flexion at the hip. If you look at the photos below, you'll notice that my grounded leg remains relatively straight throughout the exercise. This forces my hamstrings and glutes to work together to extend my hips, and guarantees that my quadriceps will not take charge of the movement. When performing this exercise, it is important to keep your lower back extremely tight to prevent the spine from rounding, which could potentially put your spine in an unsafe position. As long as you perform it correctly, this is a great exercise for building or rebuilding size and strength in your posterior chain.

1 Standing with my feet close together, I grip a weight plate in my hands and let it hang at waist level.

2 I transfer my weight onto my left leg, bend forward at the waist, allow the weight plate to dip toward the mat, and extend my right leg behind me to maintain my balance. It is important to notice that I only have a slight bend in my left leg. When my back is parallel with the floor, I have reached the bottom of my descent.

3 I flex my left glute and hamstring to elevate my torso, pull my right leg back toward my left leg, and return to the starting position. I will complete a set number of repetitions before switching to my right leg.

SQUAT WITH BOSU BALL

In this sequence I demonstrate how to perform a body weight squat on a BOSU ball. The challenge of this exercise is not the squat, but rather stabilizing your body as you perform the squat. It's akin to running on ice—even though you can't move very fast, maintaining your balance is extremely challenging and taxing. Although your maximum power reduces dramatically when squatting on an unstable surface, the exercise should not be written off as inconsequential. As you drop your hips, your ankles are forced to adjust and rebalance your body, which is a very important trait in fighting. While all athletes can benefit by incorporating this exercise into their regimen, it is particularly useful for people who have lost balance and coordination due to injury, such as a broken ankle. In the sequence below, I have included three variations of this exercise. In option 1, you perform the squat with just your body weight. I recommend this for all beginners or if you are rehabbing an injury. In version 2, you perform the squat with a barbell in the back squat position. This enables you to easily add resistance to the movement, which will allow your muscles to adapt to the off-balance position more rapidly. In the final variation, option 3, I demonstrate the squat utilizing a weight plate in front of the body. This is another option to add resistance, but by placing the weight in the front of the body it allows those with inflexible ankles to more readily achieve the full squat position. This enables you to obtain the full the benefits of the squat even with inadequate flexibility.

SQUAT WITH BOSU BALL (OPTION 1)

1

2

3

4

With a BOSU ball positioned in front of me, I step my left foot on the far edge to force it to the floor.

Transferring my weight onto my left foot, I step my right foot onto the opposite side of the BOSU ball. Once accomplished, I shift my weight so that all edges of the BOSU ball are off the floor.

Once I have found my balance, I bend my knees and drop my hips straight down until my quadriceps are parallel with the floor. It is important to note that the primary challenge in this movement is not the squat, but rather stabilizing yourself at the ankle and knee joints. It is also important to notice that I use my hands to help balance myself during my descent.

Still maintaining my balance, I flex my quadriceps, glutes, and hamstrings to elevate my hips back to the starting position.

DOUBLE EXTENSION

SQUAT WITH BOSU (OPTION 2)

1   **2**   **3**

Holding a barbell across my upper back using my hands, I step carefully onto a BOSU ball. Notice how I place my feet on the outer edges.

I lower my elevation by bending at the knees and moving my hips back. Because my hands are unable to shift to maintain my balance, during my descent I retain my balance using the muscles in my ankles and knees.

I contract my glutes and hamstrings, raising my hips and moving back into the standing position. As I drive my heels into the BOSU ball to ascend, the ball constantly shifts, causing me to maintain focus and adjust my balance.

SQUAT WITH BOSU (OPTION 3)

1   **2**   **3**

I begin the front squat standing on a BOSU ball. My feet are placed on the outer edges of the ball and I'm holding a weight plate in both hands in front of my body. Notice how the plate is close to my chest in the upright position.

I lower my elevation by bending at the knees and moving my hips back. As I descend, I extend my arms in front of my body, which moves the weight plate away from me. This provides a counterbalance to my hips and compensates for inflexibility in my lower legs.

I contract my glutes and hamstrings, raise my hips, and return to the standing position. As my hips elevate I retract my arms, pulling the weight plate in close to my body.

JUMPING SQUAT

As you now know, there are many different variations of the squat. Each variation offers different benefits, which allows you to achieve various goals. Some variations focus more on building strength and muscle mass, while others focus on increasing stability. The jumping squat is an excellent exercise for developing power and stamina. Rather than simply rising from the bottom and returning to the standing position, the jumping squat requires you to finish each repetition by leaping off the ground, which develops explosive power and ensures that maximal force is used on each repetition. There is no way to cheat in this movement—if you fail to utilize maximum power, your feet will not leave the floor. However, due to the ballistic nature of jumping squats, I tend to use much lighter loads than I do with other squat variations. Oftentimes, I just use a medicine ball as demonstrated below. While this does not provide much resistance, should I lose control of the load during the exercise, the soft nature of the medicine ball poses very little risk. To make up for the lack of resistance, I will increase my repetitions, which does wonders for improving stamina. When I become too exhausted to execute the jumping squat with maximum effort, I realize it immediately due to the diminished height in my jumps and can terminate the set.

1) Standing with his feet shoulder width apart, Jake holds a medicine ball in front of his body with both hands. 2) Jake bends at the knees and descends into the bottom of the squat position, still holding the medicine ball in front of his chest. 3) Jake contracts his glutes and hamstrings powerfully to extend his hips and knees. As his body elevates, he flexes his calves and extends his ankles. At the same time, he flexes his shoulders and raises his arms into the air to assist in generating momentum for the leap. The combination of these movements catapults him into the air. 4) As Jake lands with his feet spread at shoulder width, he bends his knees and transfers his weight through his heels.

PLYOMETRIC DEPTH JUMP CIRCUIT

In this sequence I demonstrate a simple plyometric obstacle course that challenges your jumping ability and leg stamina. If you look at the photos below, you'll notice that I have spread four low, plyometric boxes roughly a foot and a half apart. The goal is to keep both feet together as you jump on top of a box and down to the opposite side. Due to the low height of the boxes, developing maximum power is not your goal. While any plyometric drill will increase strength—especially drop jumps due to the stretch/shortening cycle of the muscles—the main goal is to build stamina in the lower legs. This is extremely important in mixed martial arts, especially when fighting in the stand-up position. If you lack stamina in your legs, you will be more inclined to rest your heels on the mat as the fight goes on, which dramatically hinders your movement. Personally, I like to include this exercise as a part of a full-body circuit. I'll perform plyometric depth jumps for a set amount of time, and then move on to the next exercise.

I lay out a plyometric obstacle course by spreading four boxes approximately a foot and a half apart in a straight line. Next, I stand in front of the first box with my feet close together, bend my knees, and tilt my torso forward by bending at the waist.

Extending my ankles and knees, I jump up onto the first box. I land with my feet close together, my knees bent, and my torso bent forward.

I flex my calves and take a very small jump forward, which positions me between the first and second box. As I absorb the force of the landing, I prepare to immediately rebound straight into my next jump.

I flex my calves, hamstrings, and hip flexors and immediately jump forward onto the next box. From here, I will continue to jump all the way to the end of the boxes and then back again, completing one repetition.

PLYOMETRIC HURDLE CIRCUIT

In this sequence I have once again placed four plyometric boxes in a row, spaced approximately a foot and a half apart. However, instead of jumping on top of each box as I did in the previous exercise, I jump over each one. By eliminating one step, each jump you make must be twice as powerful. In addition to having to jump high enough to clear the edge of the box, you now also have to jump far enough to clear the box entirely. To get a true plyometric workout from this circuit, it is important not to rest between jumps. The instant your feet touch down, contract the muscles in your legs and jump again. While it is clear that this is a more challenging variation of the previous drill, both essentially accomplish the same thing—lower-leg endurance. Personally, I like to use the previous circuit as a warm-up for this one.

I lay out a plyometric obstacle course by spreading four boxes approximately a foot and a half apart in a straight line. Next, I stand in front of the first box with my feet close together, bend my knees, and tilt my torso forward by bending at the waist.

Powerfully flexing my calves, hamstrings, quadriceps, and hip flexors, I jump forward and over the top of the first box.

As I land between the first and second box, I immediately prepare to contract my muscles and jump again.

I jump over the second box.

I land between the second and third box. From here, I will continue down the line and then return, completing one repetition in a set number of repetitions.

PLYOMETRIC LATERAL DEPTH JUMP CIRCUIT

In this sequence I demonstrate how to use the same plyometric box course to perform lateral jumps. Instead of facing the boxes and jumping straight toward them, as you did in the previous two circuits, you stand with the boxes at your side and jump laterally on top of them. Similar to the first box circuit shown, you jump into the air, land on top of each box, and then jump down into the gap between the boxes. Just like the plyometric depth jump and the plyometric hurdle, this exercise works your ankles, hips, and knees. However, due to the lateral movement involved, it challenges the abductor muscles as well. To equally stress both hip abductors, make sure to reverse the direction of the jump after completing a set number of repetitions.

I lay out a plyometric obstacle course by spreading four boxes approximately a foot and a half apart in a straight line. Next, I stand with my right side facing the first box and spread my feet roughly at shoulder width.

I jump sideways and land on top of the first box. The upward jump required me to employ my calves, hamstrings, quadriceps, and hip flexors, and moving my body laterally required me to employ my left hip abductor muscles.

I jump sideways again and land between the first and second box. As I absorb the impact of the landing with my legs, I prepare to immediately drive upward and onto the second box.

Driving off the ground, I jump laterally onto the second box. From here, I will continue down the line and then back again, completing one repetition in a predetermined set of repetitions.

PLYOMETRIC LATERAL HURDLE CIRCUIT

In this sequence I demonstrate a more advanced variation of the previous circuit. You still jump laterally toward the plyo boxes, but instead of hopping on top of each box, you jump over them. As I mentioned earlier in this section, jumping over the boxes requires a higher degree of intensity and permits shorter rest times. While the calves are the primary movers in the forward box jump exercises, the hip abductor and adductor muscles are heavily involved in the lateral jumps. If you plan on fighting, these muscles play a very important roll. In a stand-up battle, no fighter moves exclusively forward or backward. To avoid a strike or create a dominant angle of attack, you must step laterally. By performing lateral jumping drills such as this one, you build stamina in your hips and calves, which allow you to keep your foot movement sharp late in the fight.

I lay out a plyometric obstacle course by spreading four boxes approximately a foot and a half apart in a straight line. Next, I stand with my right side facing the first box and my feet roughly shoulder width apart.

I leap over the first box. This requires me to employ my calves, hamstrings, and hip abductor muscles.

I land between the first and second box. As I flex my legs to absorb the impact of the landing, I prepare to immediately jump over the second box.

I leap powerfully into the air yet again, propelling myself over the second box.

I land in between the second and third boxes. Again, I bend my knees to absorb the impact of the landing and prepare to immediately jump over the next box. I will continue down the line and then come back again, completing one repetition in a predetermined set of repetitions.

PLYOMETRIC LATERAL COMBINATION CIRCUIT

In this sequence I demonstrate how to combine the lateral jumping variations previously shown to create a grueling plyometric circuit. It combines the plyometric lateral depth jump as well as the plyometric lateral hurdle. To perform this circuit correctly, start by jumping laterally on top of the first box and then down to the opposite side. Instead of continuing on to the next box, reverse your direction by jumping back on top of the first box and then down to the starting position. Next, hurdle over the first box. Once these three steps are completed, you move on to the next box and do the exact same thing. Like the previous lateral jumping circuits, this exercise increases stamina in your legs, as well as the accuracy and efficiency of your footwork. But due to the constant changing of directions, it does so to a much higher degree.

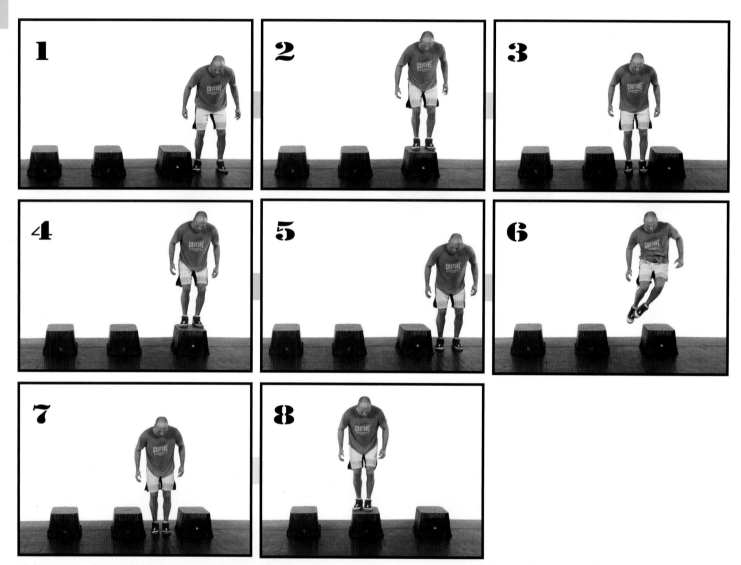

1) I lay out a plyometric obstacle course by spreading four boxes approximately a foot and a half apart in a straight line. Next, I stand with my right side facing the first box and my feet roughly shoulder width apart. 2) I jump laterally and land on top of the first box. The upward motion of this jump employs my calves, hamstrings, quadriceps, and hip flexors, while the lateral motion employs my left hip abductor muscles. 3) I leap off the first box and land on the ground between the first and second boxes. 4) Immediately after my feet touch down, I rebend my legs and leap back on top of the first box. This change in direction employees my right hip abductor muscles. 5) I return to the starting position by jumping off the first box. As I land, I bend at the knees. Not only does this allow me to absorb the impact of the landing, but it also allows me to immediately initiate another jump. 6) Instead of jumping back on top of the first box, I leap over it. 7) As I land, I bend my knees to absorb the impact and immediately prepare to jump to my right. 8) I jump laterally and land on top of the second box. From here, I will continue the drill down the line and then back again, completing one repetition in a set number of repetitions.

ADDUCTION PLYOMETRIC DROP JUMP

This is a simple stationary box jump. Rather than jumping over a series of obstacles, it's quite possible to get an efficient plyometric workout with one box. In this series, I simply straddle a box, jump on top of it, and then reverse my movements to drop back down. The exercise works many of the same muscles as the lateral box jumps, just in different patterns. My calves and hamstrings are the primary movers driving me off the ground, and my hip muscles are active to abduct and adduct my legs while in mid-air. The movement should be performed in the same way as all plyometric box jump exercises—either for a set amount of repetitions or a set amount of time. The big difference why I might choose this rather than utilizing several boxes for a plyometric circuit is practicality. If space is tight, I might not have room to lie out a big obstacle course. Similarly, if there are twelve people working out with me, waiting for each person to complete backward and forward reps on a long obstacle course may cause too much down time. By giving each person their own box to utilize for plyometric jumps, it's possible that everyone on the team can get a good workout at the same time.

1 **2** **3** **4**

1) I start by straddling the box with my feet slightly greater than shoulder width apart on either side of the box.

2) I jump straight up. While in mid-air, I use my hip adductor muscles to pull my feet together, allowing me to land on top of the box.

3) I take a small leap upward to gain elevation off the box, then quickly use my hip abductor muscles to move my feet outward, allowing me to drop back to the ground. I absorb the impact of the landing by bending my knees and immediately prepare to jump again.

4) Immediately after I absorb the impact of the landing, I jump straight into the air again, flex my hip adductor to pull my legs inward, and land on top of the box.

TRIPLE EXTENSION

STANDING LONG JUMP

The standing long jump is an excellent tool for developing explosive power in your legs, which is extremely important in MMA competition. Having the ability to drive powerfully forward benefits all aspects of your game, from throwing strikes to executing single- and double-leg takedowns. The standing long jump is also a handy tool for measuring the progression of your lower-body strength on a weekly or monthly basis. The more strength you develop in your legs, the farther you will be able to jump. As far as the execution of this exercise, it's fairly straightforward—simply bend at the knees and leap forward as far as you possibly can. If you look at the photos below, you'll notice that I provide two versions of this exercise. The first one requires you to jump with your feet parallel to one another, and the second one requires you to stagger your feet prior to jumping. The former variation is more of a general strength and speed development movement. By jumping with your feet together, each limb must produce the same amount of work. The second variation allows you to increase strength and speed in your actual fighting stance. With your legs split apart, each limb moves in a slightly different pattern and carries a different percentage of your body weight. As long as you perform the jump from the stance you employ in an MMA match, the power gained will carry over more directly to your fighting techniques.

I stand with my feet spread roughly at shoulder width.

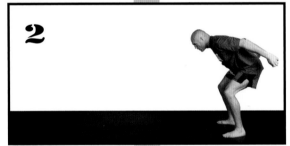

In one fluid motion, I move my hips backward, bend at the knees, and swing my arms behind me to prepare for my jump. It is from this position that I can generate the maximum amount of jumping power.

Explosively flexing my hips, quadriceps, and hip flexor muscles, I leap forward as far as possible. As I move through the air, I swing my arms forward to help maintain my momentum. It is important to notice that I keep my legs bent to prepare myself for the landing.

I land with my feet spread roughly at shoulder width. To absorb the impact, I keep my knees bent.

STANDING LONG JUMP (OPTION 2)

In this version of the long jump, I begin with my feet staggered. This is a more sport-specific version because in a fight the majority of the time you have one foot positioned in front of the other. By performing this jump on a regular basis, you will develop more explosive and powerful strikes and takedowns.

In one fluid motion, I move my hips backward, bend at the knees, and swing my arms behind me to prepare for my jump. It is from this position that I can generate the maximum amount of jumping power.

Explosively flexing my hips, quadriceps, and hip flexor muscles, I leap forward as far as possible. Due to my split stance, my rear leg leaves the ground sooner than my lead leg. This transfers a greater percentage of the workload onto my lead leg, as opposed to an equal workload distribution with the previous long jump variation.

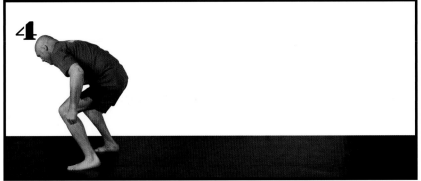

I land with my feet roughly shoulder width apart. To absorb the impact, I keep my knees bent.

STANDING LONG JUMP WITH FLEX BAND

While the standing long jump is an excellent exercise to develop power in your legs, at some point the muscles of your posterior chain will become so developed that your body weight alone will no longer provide enough resistance to continue building strength. When you reach a point in your training where the standing body weight long jump with no resistance stops yielding results, meaning you're jumping the same distance every workout, switching to the band-resisted long jump is a wise option. To perform the exercise, tie one end of the flex band around your waist, have your training partner hold the opposite end while in a firm stance behind you, and then jump forward just as you did when performing the standing long jump. The band provides resistance, but unlike adding weight to your body, it doesn't increase the risk of injuring your joints and muscles by adding to the impact of your landing. It is important to mention that the resistance in this exercise can be adjusted with the positioning of your training partner. For less resistance, have him stand close behind you so there is some slack in the flex band at the beginning of your jump. For more resistance, have him stand farther away so that there is tension in the band.

I secure a flex band around my waist and then hand the opposite end to my training partner, who takes position behind me. Next, I stand with my feet roughly shoulder width apart and my hands at my side.

In one fluid motion, I move my hips backward, bend at the knees, and swing my arms behind me to prepare for my jump. It is from this position that I can generate the maximum amount of jumping power. Notice how there is currently no slack in the flex band. Due to this added resistance, I must perform a lot more work to propel my body forward.

Explosively flexing my hips, quadriceps, and hip flexor muscles, I leap forward as far as possible. As I move through the air, I swing my arms forward to help maintain my momentum. It is important to notice that I keep my legs bent to prepare myself for the landing.

I land on the ground with my feet spread at shoulder width and absorb the impact with my legs. Note that my partner still has a tight grip on the flex band. There is now much more tension on the device, and he must hold fast to keep it from snapping me in the back. From here, my training partner will walk forward slightly and I will perform another jump.

VERTICAL JUMP WITH FLEX BAND

In this sequence I demonstrate how to perform a vertical jump using a flex band. Just as with horizontal jumps, the calves, hamstrings, and glutes are heavily taxed. The nice part about executing the vertical jump with the flex band is that the resistance is far less at the bottom of the jump than it is at the top. While in the squatting position there is slack in the back, which allows you to generate maximum speed right out of the gate. As your legs begin to straighten, the band tightens and resistance increases. This forces you to fight through the resistance using the muscles in your legs. The combination does wonders to increase your explosive power. As you probably already know, having this type of strength in your legs transfers extremely well to finishing takedowns. When you pick an opponent up into the air to finalize a double-leg takedown, your body goes through a motion very similar to doing a vertical jump. From the squatting position, you must extend your ankles, knees, and hips, and drive straight up until your opponent's feet come off the mat. The more you practice vertical jumps, the more success you will have with completing your takedowns and dumping your opponent to the mat.

1	2	3	4
I slide my body inside a flex band so that it wraps around the front of my shoulders and the back of my neck. As I stand with my feet shoulder width apart, my training partner steps on the opposite side of the flex band to provide resistance.	In one fluid motion, I move my hips backward, bend at the knees, and swing my arms behind me to prepare for my jump. It is from this position that I can generate the maximum amount of jumping power. Notice how there is currently no slack in the flex band. Due to this added resistance, I must perform a lot more work to propel my body upward.	I flex my calves, hamstrings, and quadriceps to explode straight up into the air. As I gain elevation, the resistance of the flex band increases, slowing my ascent.	As I land on the floor, I keep my knees bent to absorb the impact.

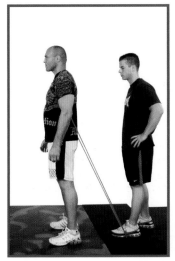   

PARTNER-RESISTED SPRINT

In this sequence I demonstrate how to do partner-resisted sprints. While sprinting is a very different motion from jumping, both movements essentially flex at the same three joints—the ankles, knees, and hips. They both also utilize the hamstrings and glutes as the primary workhorses. To set up this exercise, I attach a flex band to my back using a chest harness and have my training partner stand behind me and hold the other end of the band. As I begin my sprint, my partner uses his body weight to provide resistance, which challenges the muscles in my legs more than if I were doing a regular sprint. However, getting down the proper resistance can be tricky. It is important that your partner resist your sprint rather than run along behind you, but it is also necessary for him to move forward to prevent the band from breaking and causing injury to you. Personally, I recommend working with a strength-and-conditioning coach or an athlete who is already familiar with this exercise. It is also very important to utilize proper equipment. A flex band is ideal because it makes the towing process smooth and consistent. If you use a rope instead, your sprint will be uneven and jerky, which carries a high risk of injury. While this exercise can be performed for a set amount of time or distance, it's best to keep it short and explosive to maximize your power output.

I slip into a chest harness to secure the flex band to my back and then hand the opposite side to my training partner. Next, I walk forward to eliminate any slack in the band. It is important to mention that it is much more difficult for your partner to hold the flex band in this exercise because both of your feet remain on the floor, which provides you with traction to drive forward. As a result, we are using a flex band with handles to ensure that he does not lose his grip.

Once I have removed all slack from the flex band, I assume the three-point position by placing my left foot in front of my right, bending my knees, bending forward at the waist, and touching the fingers of my right hand on the mat. This position will allow me to initiate the sprint with a powerful forward drive.

Driving off my left foot, I explode my right leg forward. Notice how I swing my right arm back and my left arm forward to help generate momentum.

As I sprint, I drag my training partner along behind me. He maintains the same distance through the exercise to ensure constant resistance. From here, I will continue running for a set distance or a set amount of time.

VERTICAL BOX JUMP

This is another vertical jump variation that's used to develop your primary jumping muscles, which are the calves, hamstrings, glutes, and quadriceps. It's a very simple drill to execute. Starting from a standing position on the ground, you jump as high as you possibly can in an attempt to land on top of the box. Unlike in other jump variations shown, you do not want to add any additional resistance, either in the form of a plyometric stretch/shortening cycle or in the form of added resistance from a weight or a flex band. The challenge in this movement is simply to leap as high as possible. Unlike the Plyometric circuits I demonstrated earlier in the chapter designed to increase stamina, this is a maximum-effort, one-repetition exercise. With a box of adequate height, simply reaching the top of the box will require full exertion of the jumping muscles. After completing one rep, you want to drop off the box and rest for two to three minutes before performing another repetition. This exercise is designed solely to increase maximum vertical jumping ability.

When performing box jumps, it's important to use something that will adequately support your weight. In the sequence below I use a purpose made plyometric box, which has a wide base, rubber surface for grip, and square edges. Often you see people jumping onto stacks of wooden pallets or other makeshift platforms. While some are all right to jump on, those with warped bases, jagged edges, and uneven landing surfaces present too many obstacles to complete a safe workout.

1) I stand in front of a medium-height plyometric box with my feet shoulder width apart.

2) I move my hips backward, flex at the knees slightly, and move my arms backward to prepare for my jump.

3) I flex my calves, hamstrings, and quadriceps to explode into the air. I jump slightly forward, clearing the lip of the plyometric box.

4) I land on the box, bending my knees to absorb the impact of the landing.

5) I stand straight up.

DEPTH JUMP HOP-UP

Not only do jumping drills challenge nearly every muscle group in the lower body, but they also call upon the muscles of the upper body for balance and support. And with all jumping movements being dynamic in nature, they force the athlete to incorporate a high degree of power into each and every repetition. However, certain jumping exercises stand out above others in their ability to develop maximum power in the posterior chain. Plyometric exercises are a specific method of working out that involves a rapid stretch/shortening cycle in the muscles, which does wonders for making incredible gains in power and strength. If you look at the sequence below, you'll notice that Jake steps onto a platform and then drops off. As his feet make contact with the ground, his legs are forced to absorb the weight of his body. As his glutes, hamstrings, and calves decelerate the momentum of his fall, they rapidly stretch. After stopping his downward momentum in this fashion, there is a brief amortization phase in which his muscles cease to extend and begin contracting, at which point he executes a high amplitude upward leap. It is important to note that by dropping off the box prior to executing the leap, he builds up stored energy, allowing him to apply that energy to the upward leap. This allows him to produce more power than he would have been able to without the rapid stretch of the muscles prior to the shortening phase, which in turn allows him to teach his body to accept a new level of power output in his muscles and increase his overall strength. In other words, by dropping off the box he added more power to his jump, which in turn made him stronger than if he had simply jumped upward off the ground. For this reason, there are few exercises that can match the depth jump hop-up for increasing power in your lower body, but it comes at a cost. Plyometric exercises are inherently tough on the body due to the increasing tension in both the concentric and eccentric phases of the movement. However, by limiting the number of plyometric sessions to once or twice a week, as well as using very low volume on these movements, the depth jump hop-up will give you tremendous gains.

1

Jake begins the exercise standing in front of two drop boxes, one spaced a few feet behind the other. Like all vertical drop jumps, it's best to err on the side of caution with the height of the box. The higher the drop box, the greater the acceleration, but it also places greater stress on your joints. Even elite athletes generally stick to twenty-four to thirty inches as max heights for their drop box.

2

Jake lifts his left leg, places his foot on the first drop box, and begins to step up on the platform.

As Jake moves onto the top of the box, he positions his right foot on the far edge.

As Jake drops off the box, he accelerates. The instant his heels touch down, he begins to powerfully contract his glutes, hamstrings, and calves in order to slow his acceleration. This stretches those muscles, causing them to store energy.

After Jake's legs absorb the impact of the landing, he reverses his direction and leaps toward the top of the second box. It is important to mention that the period between the up and down motions, the amortization phase, should be as short as possible. The longer you pause in between phases, the weaker the jump will be.

Jake leaps vertically, landing on top of the second box. When performing this exercise, you can use the height of the second box to gauge the progression of your leaping ability. As you become stronger, you can increase the height of the second box.

DEPTH JUMP-HOP OVER

There are many different variations of the plyometric jump, and each one has a different emphasis. The plyometric leap shown previously is a great tool for adding inches to your vertical leap, but jumping upward is a movement rarely seen in the sport of MMA. More often, a fighter will use his legs to drive forward into his opponent, making the depth jump-hop over demonstrated in this sequence an excellent tool for increasing your ability to drive forward for a takedown or move quickly into the pocket to release a series of punches. If you look at the photos below, you'll notice that the hop over variation is very similar to the hop up plyometric jump is very similar to the depth jump hop-up. Even the boxes used are the same. However, the trajectory of the jump-hop over requires you to jump over the second platform rather than on it, making the trajectory more horizontal. Instead of focusing on jumping as high as possible, you want to jump just high enough to hurdle the obstacle. The main emphasis should be on distance. As you develop your strength with this movement, you want to maintain the same height of boxes but increase the distance you cover on the far side of the box, allowing you to measure your gains. Much like the depth jump hop-up, the jump-hop over can lead to amazing gains in your power development, but it also comes at a cost. The jump-hop over can be even more taxing on your body than the depth jump hop-up, which means you should limit it to once or twice a week. It is also important to perform depth drop jumps on the proper surface. There is a fine line between too hard and too soft of a landing surface. A floor made of concrete or hardwood would transfer too much of the shock into your joints and make recovery a long process. Conversely, a surface made of soft foam could provide instability upon landing, leading to injury to your joints. Simple rubber tiles are an ideal flooring for plyometric jumping, as is outdoor grass.

1

Jake begins the exercise standing in front of two drop boxes, one spaced a few feet behind the other. Like all depth jumps, it's best to err on the side of caution with the height of the drop box. Even elite athletes generally stick to twenty-four to thirty inches max in height for their drop box.

2

Jake lifts his left leg, places it on the drop box, and begins to step up onto the platform.

As Jake moves onto the top of the box, he steps his right foot off the far edge.

Jake drops off the first box and lands on both feet. As his heels touch down, he powerfully contracts his glutes, hamstrings, and calves in order to slow his acceleration. This stretches the muscles being utilized, causing them to store energy.

Jake's legs absorb the impact of the landing, and his muscles eventually stop his downward momentum. Immediately he reverses his motion. (The period in between the up and down motions, the amortization phase, should be as short as possible. The longer you pause in between phases, the weaker the jump will be.) After a brief amortization phase, Jake contracts and shortens his muscles, allowing him to leap forward. Instead of aiming to hop vertically, he leaps in a horizontal arc over the second box.

After Jake clears the hurdle, his heels land flat on the ground well beyond the second box. It is important to mention that in this exercise the second box is just an obstacle to clear. His goal is to get over the top of it and jump as deep as possible.

POWER CLEAN

The power clean is one of the core barbell movements used to increase explosive strength. While there have been entire books dedicated to the instruction of this one lift, the movement is rather easy to explain. You pick the barbell up off the floor, pull it high, and rest it on your shoulders. If you look at the photos below, you'll notice that this essentially involves performing a vertical jump and an upright row at the same time. What makes this exercise so difficult are the small details. In order to perform it correctly, the instant the barbell begins to slow, you must rebend your knees, pull your body underneath the barbell, and then turn your elbows upward to catch the bar between your palms and clavicle, all in a fraction of a second. While it can take years to master the form needed to compete in lifting competitions, it's still a great exercise for novice athletes. You might not be able to clean a massive amount of weight, but that is not important. By simply performing this exercise to the best of your ability, you will increase the strength of your posterior chain muscles, as well as increase your overall ability to generate power. These types of results will benefit you greatly in fighting. Having the ability to generate power improves all aspects of your game, from striking to bridging to executing takedowns and throws. Simply put, if you are looking to become faster and more powerful, the power clean should be a part of your training regimen.

1) I stand in front of a barbell with my feet roughly shoulder width apart. Next, I bend at the knees and waist and grip the bar with my palms facing toward me—the standard grip when doing Olympic lifts. Notice how my grip is only slightly wider than my stance and that there is no curvature in my back.

2) I drive my body upward by flexing my glutes and hamstring muscles and straightening my legs. It is important to mention that at this halfway point, the goal is to move the bar upward as quickly as your muscles will allow. However, it is very important not to jeopardize your form in an attempt to generate more speed. Notice how I am not leaning forward and my back is still perfectly straight.

3) As my posture straightens and the bar reaches hip level, the speed at which the bar is traveling begins to slow. This is due to the fact that I have fully contracted the primary movement muscles, which are the hamstrings and glutes. To help the bar continue along it's upward path, I execute a powerful shrug by elevating my shoulders using the muscles of my upper back.

4) To continue to help the bar along its upward journey, I flex my calves and come up onto my toes, completing the triple extension (hips, knees, and ankles). At this point, I have moved the bar as high as my muscles will allow me to.

5) To catch the barbell, I need to move my body underneath it. I accomplish this by driving my heels back down into the floor, rebending my knees, and dropping my hips. Notice how I rotate my elbows underneath the bar and fix them in a forward position. This allows me to catch the barbell in my hands and prevent it from falling back to the floor. It is important to mention that this rebend is not only a very explosive movement, but also one of the hardest movements to learn in weight lifting.

6) As the barbell drops toward the floor, I catch it in my palms and pin it against my shoulders. Notice how my elbows are forward, keeping the barbell locked tight to my clavicle. To complete the movement, I straighten my legs so that my posture is erect. With the barbell off the ground, it's now necessary to lower it back down safely to the floor. This is demonstrated on page 65.

OLYMPIC SPLIT JERK

In this sequence I demonstrate how to perform the Olympic split jerk, which begins where the previous exercise left off—with the barbell racked on the front of your shoulders, your elbows pointing forward, and your palms curved backward to press the bar into your body. From this starting position, the goal is to move the bar overhead. Instead of using your arms to accomplish this task, you want to employ your entire body. If you look at the photos below, you'll notice that I use my legs to drive the bar upward. Once I have removed the barbell from my shoulders in this fashion, I drop my torso below the bar by splitting or staggering my feet. While it is possible to simply drop your hips down and squat below the bar, this tends to tilt your body forward. When lifting heavy objects overhead, it is best to keep your spine as vertical as possible for maximum safety, and split jerk is the most effective way to accomplish this.

It is important to mention that this is a very athletic movement that requires a lot of preparation, good balance, and proper equipment. Without all of these things, the split jerk can be a very high risk lift. It is also important to mention that you will make very little muscular gain with this exercise. It's primary function is to make your central nervous system more efficient at performing this particular movement. Unfortunately, these central nervous system gains will not transfer over to your fighting game as well as the benefits made through many of the Olympic lifts demonstrated in this book. As a result, the spit jerk should usually be phased out of your training as you draw closer to your fight.

1) Standing with my feet shoulder width apart, I catch the barbell between my hands and shoulders. Notice how my elbows are locked in a forward position to prevent the barbell from dropping to the floor.

2) I slightly bend my knees and drop my hips back. This position will allow me to generate the momentum needed to drive the barbell over my head.

3) I explode my hips upward to get the barbell moving vertically. As I do this, my feet momentarily lift off the ground. Before they touch back down, I split them apart by moving my left foot forward and my right foot backward. This allows me drop my body underneath the bar and still maintain a powerful position with a vertical spine. As the bar travels upward, I extend my arms underneath it. However, it is important to mention that I am not forcing the barbell upward using my arms—that task was already completed with the previous explosion of my hips. I am simply extending my arms to match the ascent of the barbell. Once it is extended overhead, the lift is nearly complete.

4) With the barbell extended over my head, I bring my feet back together by stepping my right foot forward and my left foot backward. Once accomplished, I keep the barbell locked overhead as I stabilize my position. With the barbell off the ground, it's now necessary to lower it back down safely to the floor. This is demonstrated on page 65.

1

2

3

4

DEAD CLEAN

The dead clean is nearly identical to the power clean—the only difference is that instead of starting in a squat position with the barbell on the floor, you start in the standing position with the barbell clutched in your hands at hip level. Just as with the power clean, you perform an explosive jump to initiate the pull, and then rebend your knees with an explosive downward movement to position yourself underneath the bar and catch it on your shoulders. While this might seem like a less strenuous exercise to perform than the power clean, it's not. To heft the barbell up onto your shoulders from waist level, you must get the barbell moving at the same speed as you did when hefting it up from the floor. However, with there being less distance between your waist and your shoulders, that speed must be generated over a shorter period of time, which requires a much greater output of power. As a result, you will most likely have to reduce the load to get the same number of repetitions.

Partial Olympic lifts such as the dead clean are great for novice athletes. They usually offer all of the benefits as the complete Olympic lifts, but there are fewer steps involved, which makes the learning curve shorter. The dead clean also allows you to focus on the most important part of the lift, which is the explosive triple extension. After all, this is what helps develop the power needed in fights. In addition to these benefits, the dead clean is also an easier exercise to do in repetitions. When performing power cleans, you must lower the barbell all the way down to the floor, which causes the weights to bounce and often displaces your grips. With the dead clean there is no bounce, which eliminates the need to regrip the bar. In turn, this allows you to perform one repetition after another without any breaks. For these reasons, the dead clean is probably my favorite of all the Olympic lift variations.

1) Standing with my feet roughly shoulder width apart, I grip a barbell in my hands and let it hang slightly below my waist.

2) I explode my hips upward and shrug my shoulders to generate vertical momentum with the bar. Just as with the power clean, the goal is to move the bar upward. To accomplish this, I must generate the same amount of speed as I did when hefting the bar off the floor. However, with less distance for the bar to travel, I must generate this same speed in a much shorter period of time, making this a more powerful movement.

3) To help the bar along its vertical path, I flex my calves and come up onto my toes, completing the triple extension (hips, knees, and ankles). At this point, I've moved the bar as high as my muscles will allow.

4) To catch the barbell, I need to move my body underneath of it. I accomplish this by driving my heels back down into the floor, rebending my knees, and dropping my hips. Notice how I rotate my elbows underneath the bar and fix them in a forward position. This allows me to catch the barbell in my hands and prevent it from falling back to the floor. It is important to mention that this rebend is not only a very explosive movement, but also one of the hardest movements to learn in weight lifting.

5) As the barbell drops toward the floor, I catch it in my palms and pin it against my shoulders. Notice how my elbows are forward, keeping the barbell locked tight to my clavicle. To complete the movement, I straighten my legs so that my posture is erect.

6) To return to the start position, I move my elbows backward and allow the barbell to drop down. Instead of letting it fall all the way to the floor, I catch it slightly below waist level using my arms.

TRIPLE EXTENSION

PUSH PRESS

If you look at the photos in the sequence below, you'll notice that the initial movements of the push press are very similar to the power clean in execution. You start with the barbell on the floor, and then pull it up onto the front of your shoulders. However, once the barbell is loaded, you drive it overhead much like you did when performing the Olympic split jerk, but instead of splitting your legs apart and moving the weight overhead using the muscles of your lower body, you keep your feet together and heft the weight overhead using the muscles of your arms and shoulders. To perform the exercise properly, you want to flex your legs just enough to get the weight moving upward. Once it is off your shoulders, you complete the pressing movement using the muscles of your upper body. This helps spread the load more evenly across the lower and upper body, enabling a more complete workout. Additionally, with your feet remaining together, it is much easier to reset the movement and complete higher repetitions.

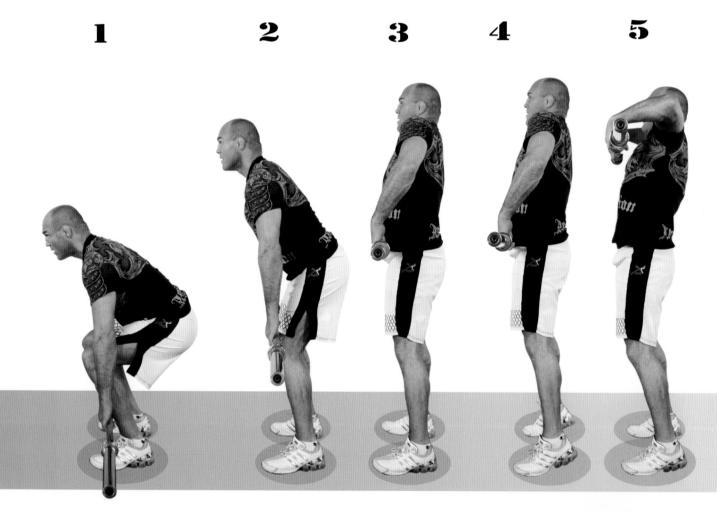

1) I start with the barbell at roughly mid-shin height. My feet are spread at shoulder width, and my toes are tucked slightly underneath the bar. Although my knees are bent to allow me to reach the bar, my chest is up to enable me to execute a powerful pull. My hands are extended down, gripping the barbell just to the outside of my legs. 2) I contract my hamstrings and glutes, forcing my hips to rise explosively upward. 3) As my hips fully extend, I contract my trapezius muscles in order to continue to aid the upward momentum of the barbell. 4) I flex my calves to extend the height of my pull, adding velocity to the barbell as it continues to move up. 5) With the barbell at it's peak, I now flex my wrists and point my elbows back.

6) As I bend my knees and move my body underneath the barbell, I continue rotating my shoulders until my elbows are pointing forward. This enables me to catch the barbell on the front of my shoulders. 7) I fully extend my legs, allowing me to move in the fully upright position. 8) I slightly bend my knees to add momentum to the overhead pressing movement of the barbell. 9) As I extend my legs I simultaneously extend my arms, flexing my shoulders and triceps muscles to force the bar overhead. 10) I straighten my legs, ending with the barbell in the overhead position. With the barbell off the ground, it's now necessary to lower it back down safely to the floor. This is demonstrated on page 65.

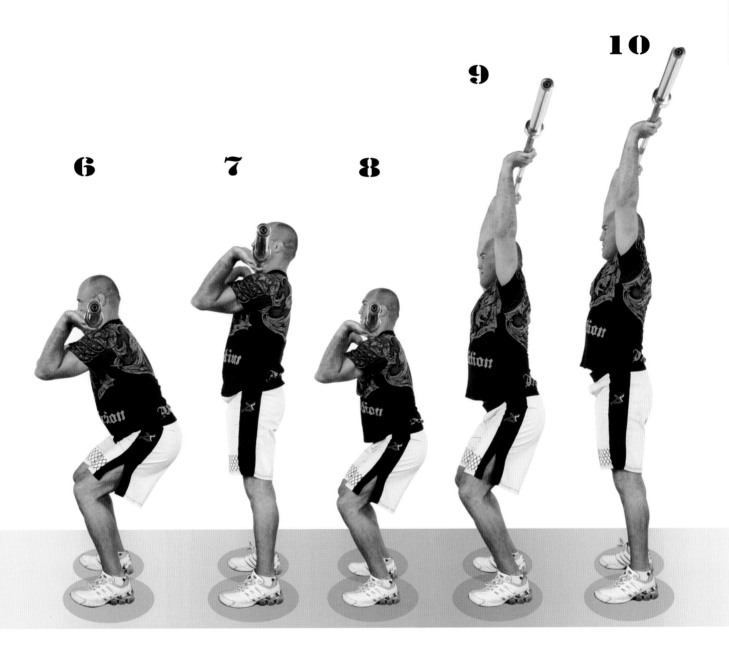

SNATCH

Just like the clean and jerk, the snatch is a great way to build full-body power in one simple movement. The exercise involves lifting a barbell resting on the floor to the overhead position in one continuous movement. Your legs and hips are employed to power the bar upward, and your shoulders and core are utilized to support the bar as it makes its journey. As a training tool, the main advantage of the snatch over the clean and jerk is that it involves a much larger amplitude of motion. In order to perform it properly, you must generate a lot of speed off the ground. If you fail to do this, you will be unable to move your body underneath the bar and catch the bar overhead by locking out your arms. The disadvantage of the snatch is that because more work is being done in a single motion, you generally use a much lighter load. Both lifts are excellent tools for building speed and power, but the clean tends to lean a bit more toward the power side of the spectrum, while the snatch builds a bit more speed. Personally, I recommend adding them both into your routine, as they will make you a better athlete and a more powerful fighter.

To begin the exercise, Jake positions his feet underneath the barbell, assumes a shoulder-width stance, and grabs the bar with a pronated grip. Notice how his shoulders are slightly ahead of the bar. This allows him to keep his knees and hips bent, as well as keep his back tight.

Jake begins the first pull by driving his heels down into the floor and extending his legs. This pulls the barbell off the floor. In this position, Jake keeps the bar very close to his legs and his back very tight.

In the second pull, Jake powerfully extends his hips, knees, and ankles. This gives him the momentum needed to elevate the bar past the sticking point into the overhead position. In this position Jake has his chest forward, allowing him to keep his back tight as the bar moves overhead.

As the barbell moves upward due to the momentum Jake generated with his second pull, he dynamically pulls himself downward by contracting his hamstrings and moving his torso underneath of the bar. The combination of these actions allows him to keep his arm straight and catch the barbell in the overhead position. It is important to note that in this position, you use your core muscles to help stabilize the bar.

Jake extends his hips and knees and rises into the upright position with the barbell overhead. From here, he will lower the barbell back to the floor using the technique demonstrated on page 65.

HANG SNATCH

In this sequence I demonstrate how to perform the hang snatch, which is a variation of the regular snatch. The primary difference between the two is that instead of beginning in a squat position with the barbell on the floor, you start with it clutched in your hands at waist level. Similar to the power clean previously demonstrated, you want to perform an explosive jump to initiate the pull, and then rebend your knees to position your body underneath the bar. However, instead of catching the bar on your shoulders as you do in the power clean, you catch the bar over your head by straightening your arms. Although this exercise taxes all the muscles of your posterior chain like the power clean, catching the bar overhead requires a much higher degree of balance. If your goal is to increase your power, stability, and coordination, which should be the goal of all fighters, I highly recommend incorporating this exercise into your regimen. Personally, I like the hang snatch over the regular snatch for the same reasons I like the dead clean over the power clean—it requires you to generate the same amount of speed over a shorter distance, which demands more power. It is also an easier exercise to do in repetitions because you only have to lower the weight down to waist level, which eliminates the bouncing of weights and the need to regrip the bar.

1 Standing with my feet roughly shoulder width apart, I slightly bend my knees, establish a wide grip on the barbell, and let it hang at waist level.

2 I explosively flex my ankles, knees, and hips to get the barbell moving vertically. Once accomplished, I drive my heels into the floor, rebend my knees, drop my hips, and move my body underneath the barbell to catch it. Notice how I extend my arms to match the ascent of the barbell.

3 As the barbell reaches the peak of its ascent, I lock my arms to prevent it from falling back toward the floor. At the same time, I straighten my knees until my posture is completely erect.

SECTION THREE
UPPER-BODY PUSH

When it comes to working out, pushing and pulling are intimately tied together. Anytime you execute a pulling motion with your upper body, a muscle responsible for pushing must dynamically stabilize the joint as it moves. Without equal power in both the target muscle group and the dynamically stabilizing muscle group, your total power output will be handicapped. The only way to exhibit maximum strength and minimize the potential for injury is to develop a balanced physique with an equal capacity to both push and pull. And the only way to ensure equalized power output in both pushing and pulling movements is to train both actions with the same amount of volume and intensity.

In this chapter, I demonstrate all of the pushing movements that I've incorporated into my routine. The target muscle groups for all pushing exercises are primarily the deltoid, pectoralis, and triceps muscle groups. However, depending on the movement patterns, the latissimus and teres major/minor, serratus, and even the rhomboid muscle groups can become heavily involved. These pushing motions are designed to be the opposite of those of the next section of the book, which focuses on upper-body pulling exercises. Pushing exercises are defined as any action where the hands move away from the body in a concentric manner. So, a simple motion like opening the hood of a car would fit the definition of a "pushing" movement, as you must begin with the hands near the body and contract the triceps in order to move the hands away from the body and push the hood upward.

In the sport of MMA, pushing motions play an important role. For example, a jab is primarily a pushing motion of the lead arm that involves glenohumeral flexion and elbow extension. In fact, all punches have some pushing element to them. Although the energy for a strong punch is generated in the posterior chain, it's finalized with a quick pushing motion of the arm. If you lack the stamina or power needed in your shoulders and upper arms to extend your fist into your opponent, you will fail to connect, despite the strength of your posterior chain. Much like a whip, the power is generated at the base of your body, but the tip of the whip is the portion that inflicts the damage. If you can't move your hands quickly, your punches will often miss their mark.

While not as technical a motion as a well-executed punch, there are also situations in the clinch that require you to put both hands on your opponent's chest and push him away. When fighting a superior clinch tactician, oftentimes the best-case scenario is to keep your hands close to your body to prevent him from obtaining control of your head and then use the muscles of your back and arms to shove your opponent away and create space. In both the punching and clinch scenarios, the ability to forcefully thrust your arms away from your body will help you dictate the pace and domain of the fight.

In this section, I demonstrate all of the exercises needed to boost the strength and endurance of the muscles used in pushing movements. The first portion of the chapter demonstrates a multitude of horizontal pushing exercises. It begins with the bench press, which is a great tool for building pressing strength, and then moves on to its many variations. I demonstrate how to use barbells, dumbbells, and stretch bands, as well as discuss how using these various implements allows you to tailor the traditional bench press to fit specific needs in your workout. I even show how to perform pressing exercises on a stability ball to incite additional motor recruitment. Many of the exercises in this section are shown both bilaterally and unilaterally, with some interesting hybrids of single-arm and double-arm movements that can be executed using a stretch band. And at the end of the section, I also demonstrate how to properly utilize upright horizontal pressing exercises to more closely simulate pushing in an MMA fight, as well as several other pressing techniques that allow you to stress your body at various joint angles and muscle lengths.

In addition to the standard bench press and dumbbell press variations, I also cover a variety of push-ups designed to tax your upper body in contrasting ways. While a simple bench press and a push-up both activate the same muscles and move the arms along the same trajectory, the bases of the movements are very different. The bench press is what trainers call an "open-chain" exercise, while the push-up is referred to as a "closed-chain" exercise. In this case, the difference between them is the base that the hand is connected to. If your hand is anchored to an immovable object when doing a pushing exercise, your body moves away from your hands as you extend your elbow joints. An example of this would be a push-up. Conversely, an "open-chain" movement is one where the concentric extension of your arms forces the object in your hands to move away from your body, such as in a bench press. While the differences may seem trivial, the final effect can be very significant. Closed kinetic chain exercises have been found to be more effective for rehabbing injuries and tend to spread the stress across the entire body, rather than focusing the burden exclusively on the targeted joint. In addition, with your body weight unsupported in a closed-chain exercise, you must activate many different muscle groups to bear the weight of your frame throughout the movement. Many trainers say this makes closed-chain exercises more functional, as controlling your own body weight is a necessary ele-

ment of being a good athlete. However, open-chain exercises have a very specific advantage. Because the effort is focused directly on the targeted joint in open-chain movements, the muscle is taxed much more strongly. This is useful for maximum muscle growth, as well as maximum strength potential. Because of this key difference, I show many different push-ups to compliment the various open-chain movements shown earlier in the section. While the open-chain pressing movements are great at stressing the muscles and causing growth, any athletes with joint injuries would be well served to take a look at the push-up variations as well.

It is important to mention that vertical pressing movements should supplement the horizontal pressing movements covered in this section. While there aren't a lot of situations in MMA that require a fighter to extend his arms vertically, vertical pressing is an important element of shoulder anatomy. If you exclude these exercises from your routine entirely, you will eventually develop musculature imbalances that will increase the risk of injury. To prevent this from happening, I demonstrate many different variations of vertical pressing exercises in this section, from handstand push-ups to overhead dumbbell pressing designed to stress the deltoids, triceps, and trapezius muscles. These exercises will help tax the shoulder joint in all its articulations of movement. However, not all people have an adequate range of motion and enough shoulder stability to safely execute overhead pressing movements. For athletes who suffer from minor shoulder injuries, performing vertical pressing exercises can lead to pain or even increase the severity of their injuries. Since this book is designed for the sport of MMA, where bad shoulders are all too common, I show some great rehab pressing exercises that can be used in place of overhead pressing. These are excellent tools that can build the shoulder joint in a manner similar to vertical pressing but without the high risk for injury or aggravation of the shoulder joint.

In summary, this chapter includes all of the tools needed to increase your capacity to execute pressing movements. When combined with the pulling movements covered in the next chapter, you'll have your blueprint for increasing the power, strength, and endurance of your upper body, as well as for injury prevention in your arms, upper back, and shoulders. If you equalize the volume, intensity, and movement patterns with both pushing and pulling motions, you'll be guaranteed to increase your athletic ability and your performance in and out of the cage.

HORIZONTAL PLANE

FLAT BENCH PRESS WITH MEDIUM GRIP

At any gym around the world, the second question you'll most likely be asked after your name is "How much do you bench?" This exercise has developed such a stellar reputation because it is one of the most efficient ways to build strength in your upper body. When you perform the standard bench press demonstrated below, your grip is slightly wider than shoulder width, which places the majority of the workload on your pectoral muscles. However, due to the nature of the movement, your triceps, biceps, shoulders, and abdominal muscles receive a difficult workout as well. The bench press is a staple of nearly every workout routine.

1 Lying flat on a bench, I place my feet on the floor, grip a barbell at slightly wider than shoulder width, and extend my arms so that the barbell is positioned directly over my chest.

2 Keeping my chest pushed out, I bend my elbows and lower the barbell until it touches my lower chest. It is important not to bounce the weight off of your chest. While this is popular in gyms everywhere, it's dangerous and masks weaknesses in your musculature. If you can't move the bar off your chest in a controlled manner, you should be pressing lighter weight.

3 Contracting my pectoralis major and triceps muscles, I force the bar vertically until my arms are once again fully extended. From here, I can lock out my elbows and finish my set or bend my elbows and begin another repetition.

FLAT BENCH PRESS WITH CLOSE GRIP

In this sequence I demonstrate how to perform a close grip bench press. Although the range of motion is the same as the standard bench press, the close grip shifts the emphasis of workload off the chest and onto the triceps. While it is good to include both variations into your routine, the close-grip bench press is often more beneficial to fighters because they keep their arms close to their body when in the ring. This is true while fighting standing up and on the ground. The chest is a powerful muscle group, but when both of your arms are tucked to your sides, your triceps are more important for delivering punches or shoving your opponent away while on the mat. Unless you throw all looping punches and grapple with your arms far to your sides, neither of which are recommended, I suggest adding this exercise into your regimen. It will help you develop pushing power with your arms tight to your sides, which is extremely beneficial when fighting in MMA competition.

1 Lying flat on a bench, I place my feet on the floor, grip a barbell at slightly narrower than shoulder width, and extend the barbell vertically so it is positioned above my chest.

2 Keeping my chest pushed out, I bend my elbows and lower the barbell until it touches my lower chest. It is important to notice that instead of angling my elbows toward the outside of my body as I did when my grip was wide, I keep my elbows tucked tightly to my sides. This allows me to further isolate my triceps muscles.

3 Keeping my elbows tight to my sides, I contract my triceps muscles and drive the bar upward until my arms are fully extended. Once accomplished, I can lock out my elbows and finish my set or bend my elbows and begin another repetition.

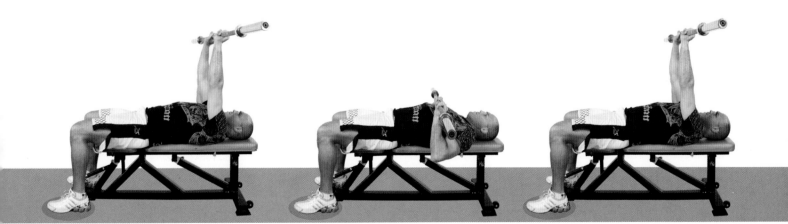

FLAT BENCH PRESS WITH FLEX BAND

In this sequence I demonstrate how to perform a bench press using the added resistance of a flex band. To set up the exercise, I wrap the flex band around one side of a barbell, loop it underneath the bench, and then wrap it around the other side of the bar. Although the movement is the same as with the standard bench press, the flex band increases the resistance as the bar travels upward. For a lot of athletes, the most difficult part about the bench press is lifting the weight off of their chest. To solve this dilemma, they decrease the load they are pushing, but then there is not enough resistance at the top of the press to get an adequate workout through the full range of motion. This exercise is an excellent alternative because it provides less resistance at the bottom of the lift, which allows you to move the weight off your chest, and then the resistance increases at the top of the lift, allowing you to apply an overload to the muscles at the top of the movement. Just as with the standard bench press, the chest and triceps are the primary movers, with the triceps gaining dominance as your grip gets narrower.

1

To set up this exercise, I loop the flex band around one end of the barbell, string it underneath the bench, and then loop it around the opposite side of the barbell. Once accomplished, I lie flat on the bench, grip the bar at slightly wider than shoulder width, and press it vertically so it is positioned over my chest.

2

Keeping my chest pushed forward, I bend my elbows and lower the barbell to my torso. The instant it touches my lower chest, I begin to reverse the movement and press the bar back up. It is important to mention that in this position the band provides very little tension, which makes it easier for me to press the weight off of my chest.

3

Contracting my pectoralis major and triceps muscles, I press the bar vertically so it is once again positioned directly above my chest. It is important to mention that the band gets progressively tighter as you increase the elevation of the bar. Once my arms are extended, I can lock out my elbows and finish my set or complete another repetition.

DUMBBELL BENCH PRESS

The dumbbell bench press is similar to the barbell bench press as far as the muscles challenged, but because you are now holding two separate weights, each arm has to work independently. With a lot of athletes, one side of their body is stronger than the other. When they perform the barbell bench press, the strong side of their body will often lift more of the load than the weak side. This is not possible with the dumbbell bench press, making it a good exercise to correct any imbalances. If you look at the second photo in the sequence below, you'll notice that my hands angle inward at the bottom of the press, which removes stress from my wrist, elbow, and shoulder joints. In addition to this, as I press the weight upward and lower it back down, I can follow a more natural arc by bringing the weights slightly closer together and farther apart. Due to these benefits, the dumbbell bench press is superior to the barbell bench press when nursing an upper body injury.

Lying flat on a bench, I place my feet on the floor, grip a dumbbell in each hand, and straighten my arms vertically above my chest. Notice how my palms are facing my legs.

I bend my elbows and lower the dumbbells toward my armpits. As the dumbbells dip below my chest, the natural arc of my arms causes them to tilt slightly toward one another.

Contracting my pectoralis major and triceps muscles, I press the dumbbells vertically. Once my arms are fully extended, I can lock out my elbows and finish the set or perform another repetition.

SINGLE-ARM DUMBBELL PRESS

As I previously mentioned, the benefit of using dumbbells for pressing movements is that each arm works independently. This is very important in fighting because seldom are both of your arms performing the same movement at the same time. This is true when striking and executing submissions. In this sequence, I demonstrate how to further isolate your arms by performing the pressing movement one arm at a time. By incorporating this type of press into your regimen, you become more familiar with pressing movements utilized in a fight. Personally, I don't feel that single arm presses should replace your more powerful two-handed presses, but they are a great supplemental tool. As you can see below, I demonstrate two variations of the single-arm dumbbell press. In the first one, you do continuous repetitions with one arm before switching to the opposite side, which allows you to really isolate each arm. In the second one, you hold a dumbbell in each hand and alternate between arms. I recommend trying them both to see which one fits your needs best.

SINGLE DUMBBELL PRESS

1 Lying flat on a bench, I place my feet on the floor, grip a dumbbell in my left hand, and position it slightly above my left armpit. To keep my balance, I place my right hand on my right hip.

2 I flex my left triceps and pectoral muscle and press the dumbbell vertically.

3 I relax my left arm and slowly lower the dumbbell down toward my left armpit.

ALTERNATE DUMBBELL PRESS

1 Lying flat on a bench, I place my feet on the floor and grip a dumbbell in each hand. To assume the start position, I elevate the right dumbbell vertically and position the left dumbbell down by my left armpit.

2 I lower the right dumbbell down to my chest.

3 Flexing my left triceps and pectoral muscle, I push the left dumbbell vertically. By alternating pressing arms, I can train both of my arms in the same set without having to switch the weight from one hand to the other.

DUMBBELL PRESS WITH FLEX BAND

In this sequence I demonstrate how to use flex bands to increase the resistance at the top of your dumbbell press. However, instead of looping the flex band underneath the bench press as you did with the barbell, you loop the band around your back prior to picking up the dumbbells. The reason for this is practicality. When performing the barbell press, the bar is generally sitting on a stationary rack, which makes looping the band over the bar and under the bench easy to accomplish. When you perform the dumbbell press, you need to pick up the weights and then move into position. For obvious reasons, this makes it difficult to secure the band under the bench.

FLEX BAND POSITIONING

1) I grip the flex band in my hands, turn my palms toward the outside of my body, and then stretch the band by pulling my arms out to my sides. 2) Keeping the flex band tight, I pass it over my head and wrap it across my upper back. 3) With the flex band gripped in each palm and wrapped around my upper back, I pick up the dumbbells and prepare for my exercise.

DUMBBELL PRESS WITH BANDS

1 **2** **3**

With the flex band in place, I lie flat on the bench, place my feet on the floor, and position the inner plates of the dumbbells in my armpits at chest level.

Flexing my triceps and pectoral muscles, I extend my arms vertically.

Relaxing my arms, I lower the dumbbells back down toward my chest. Once I have reached the start position, I can continue doing more reps or use my legs to swing my body back into the upright position and finish the movement.

SINGLE-ARM DUMBBELL PRESS WITH FLEX BAND

In this sequence I demonstrate how to perform the single-arm dumbbell press with a flex band. It is set up the same as the previous technique, and it works the same muscles—the only difference is that you're pressing with one arm instead of two, which can prove useful for building supplemental strength or rehab. However, this exercise is different from the standard single-arm dumbbell press because your free arm comes into play. Instead of resting it on your torso, you extend it upright with flex band in hand to provide tension for your working arm. Keeping your free arm stable while your working arm tugs at the flex band is not all that easy, and as a result your free arm gets a great isometric workout.

1 After looping the flex band around my upper back, I grip a dumbbell in my right hand, lay flat on the bench, and extend my left arm upward to draw the band tight.

2 Keeping my left arm extended, I flex my right triceps and pectoral muscles and press the dumbbell in my right hand vertically. At the top of the movement, my left hand must work very hard to stabilize the band, which is at full tension.

3 Relaxing my right arm, I lower the dumbbell back down to chest height. From here, I can continue with more repetitions or finish the set by lowering my left arm to release tension in the band.

DUMBBELL PRESS SERIES WITH STABILITY BALL

In this series I demonstrate how to perform various dumbbell presses with your back positioned on the top of a stability ball. As you drive the dumbbells upward, your weight shifts, causing the ball to roll beneath you. To prevent from rolling off of the ball, you must flex your abdominals, back, quadriceps, glutes, and hamstrings muscles throughout the entire movement. This provides an excellent workout to your core. It's not possible to lift as much weight on a stability ball as you can on a bench, but the goal of this exercises is not to isolate your pressing muscles, but rather challenge your core while training your pressing muscles. In fighting, this is a very important attribute. Unless you are lying flat on your back or are pressed up against the cage, you will be forced to employ your pressing muscles without a solid and stable backdrop.

DUMBBELL PRESS ON SWISS BALL

1) I lay my upper back on the surface of a stability ball, place my feet on the ground, and hold a dumbbell in each hand at chest level. 2) Flexing my pectoral and triceps muscles, I press the dumbbells vertically. At the same time, I flex my abdominals, back, quadriceps, glutes, and hamstrings to stabilize my body and prevent me from rolling off the top of the ball. 3) Relaxing my arms, I lower the dumbbells back to my chest. To prevent from rolling off the ball, I keep my core muscles flexed.

ALTERNATING DUMBBELL PRESS ON SWISS BALL

1) I lay my upper back on the surface of a stability ball, place my feet on the ground, and grip a dumbbell in each hand. To reach the starting position for this exercise, I keep the right dumbbell positioned by my chest as I drive the left dumbbell upward using my pectoral and triceps muscles. Just as with the last exercise, I use my core muscles to stabilize my position. 2) I relax my right arm and lower the dumbbell back down to chest level. 3) Alternating sides, I now drive the left dumbbell upward while keeping the right dumbbell at chest level.

SINGLE-ARM DUMBBELL PRESS ON SWISS BALL

1) I lay my upper back on the surface of a stability ball, place my feet on the floor, and hold a dumbbell in my left hand at chest level. 2) Contracting my left triceps and pectoral muscles, I extend my left arm vertically. At the same time, I contract my core muscles to stabilize my body on the ball. 3) Relaxing my left arm, I lower the dumbbell back down to chest level.

DUMBBELL PRESS WITH FLEX BAND ON SWISS BALL

1) After securing a flex band around my upper back, I lie on the surface of a Swiss ball, place my feet on the floor, and hold a dumbbell in each hand at chest level. 2) Flexing my triceps and pectoral muscles, I extend my arms vertically. At the same time, I contract my core muscles to keep my body stable. 3) Relaxing my arms, I lower the dumbbells back down to chest level.

ALTERNATING DUMBBELL PRESS WITH FLEX BAND ON SWISS BALL

1) After securing a flex band around my upper back, I lie on the surface of a Swiss ball, place my feet on the floor, and grip a dumbbell in each hand. To reach the starting position, I keep the left dumbbell at chest level and extend my right arm vertically. 2) Relaxing my right arm, I lower the dumbbell back down to chest level. At the same time, I contract my core muscles to stabilize my body on the ball. 3) Alternating to the other side, I extend my left arm vertically by flexing my left triceps and pectoral muscles. As the dumbbell rises, the tension on the band increases, making the press more difficult at the top of the movement.

SINGLE-ARM DUMBBELL PRESS WITH FLEX BAND ON SWISS BALL

1) After securing a flex band around my upper back, I lie on the surface of a Swiss ball, place my feet on the floor, and grip a dumbbell in my left hand. To assume the start position, I extend my right arm vertically to increase tension in the flex band. 2) Keeping my right arm raised, I extend my left arm vertically by contracting my pectoralis major and triceps muscles. At the same time, I contract my core muscles to keep my body stabilized on the ball. 3) Relaxing my left arm, I lower the dumbbell back down to chest level. As my arm drops, the tension in the band decreases.

DUMBBELL PRESS SERIES ON FLOOR

In this series I demonstrate how to do a number of dumbbell presses while lying flat on the floor, which limits the range of motion of the movement. This means that your chest muscles are never allowed to move into a stretch position, causing your triceps to play a larger roll. The chest muscles are still responsible for a large portion of the power generated in this movement, just not as much as they would when lying on a traditional bench. As I already mentioned, triceps strength comes in very handy when grappling, especially when you are lying flat on your back and need to push your opponent away from you. It is important to mention that all of the dumbbell presses previously shown can be performed on the floor. If you want to tax your triceps muscles yet still provide your chest with a substantial workout, dumbbell floor presses are a great option.

DUMBBELL FLOOR PRESS

Lying flat on the floor, I grip a dumbbell in each hand and point my elbows toward the outside of my body.

Contracting my triceps and pectoral muscles, I extend both arms vertically.

Relaxing my arms, I lower the dumbbells until my triceps are once again resting on the floor. From here, I can either complete another repetition or finish the set by sitting up.

ALTERNATING DUMBBELL FLOOR PRESS

Lying flat on the floor, I grip a dumbbell in each hand. To assume the start position, I keep my left elbow on the ground and extend my right arm vertically.

Relaxing my right arm, I lower the dumbbell back down until my triceps is resting on the floor.

Alternating sides, I keep my right triceps pinned to the floor and extend my left arm vertically. From here, I can continue with alternating repetitions or finish the set by sitting up.

DUMBBELL FLOOR PRESS WITH FLEX BAND

After securing a flex band around my upper back, I grip a dumbbell in each hand and lie back flat on the floor. Notice how both of my triceps are currently resting on the ground.

Contracting my triceps and pectoral muscles, I extend my arms vertically. As the dumbbells rise, the tension in the band increases.

Relaxing my arms, I lower the dumbbells back down until my triceps are once again resting on the floor. From here, I can complete more repetitions or finish the set by sitting up.

ALTERNATING DUMBBELL FLOOR PRESS WITH FLEX BAND

After securing the flex band around my upper back, I grip a dumbbell in each hand and lie back flat on the floor. To reach the start position, I keep my left triceps resting on the ground and extend my right arm vertically.

Relaxing my right arm, I lower the dumbbell until my triceps is once again resting on the floor.

Keeping my right triceps on the floor, I extend my left arm vertically. From here, I can continue with more repetitions or finish the set by sitting up.

CHEST PRESS WITH FLEX BAND

When strength training, it is important to perform exercises that mimic the movements involved in your sport to ensure the best possible transference. A perfect example is the chest press with flex band exercise demonstrated in the sequence below. If you look at the first photo, you'll notice that I'm standing in my fighting stance with one side of the flex band held in each hand. Although this is not the exact positioning I assume while fighting, it is pretty close. Using my legs and core to keep my body balanced, I execute a horizontal press. This exercise works the same muscles as the other pressing techniques already demonstrated, but it trains my body to unleash that strength from the standing position, which in turn increases my punching power and speed. If you plan on fighting, this is a great supplement movement to add into your pressing routine.

After wrapping a flex band around the vertical post of a power rack, I turn my back to the rack, grip the handles of the flex band in my hands, step my left foot in front of my right foot to increase tension in the band, and then lean slightly forward. Notice how I have positioned my hands at chest level.

Flexing my pectoral and triceps muscles, I extend my arms away from my chest, which increases tension in the band.

Relaxing my arms, I allow the flex band to slowly pull my arms back to the start position. Once I have completed a set number or repetitions, I will alternate my positioning by stepping my right foot forward.

LUNGE CHEST PRESS WITH FLEX BAND

The lunge chest press with flex band is another horizontal press that translates well to the sport of mixed martial arts. Instead of doing the press from your fighting stance, you lunge forward, press, and then return to the starting position. As you know, executing takedowns such as the double-leg often requires you to lunge forward, and this exercise will help increase your pressing power while in the lunge position. Just as with the previous technique, it is a good supplement workout to include into your pressing routine.

After wrapping a flex band around the vertical post of a power rack, I turn my back to the rack, grip the handles of the flex band in my hands, and then assume the lunge position by stepping my left foot dramatically forward. Notice how my left thigh is nearly parallel with the ground and my right knee hovers just a few inches off the floor.

Flexing my pectoral and triceps muscles from the lunge position, I extend my arms horizontally.

Relaxing my arms, I allow the flex band to pull my hands back to the start position.

I step my left foot back to my right foot and straighten my posture. Notice how there is currently no tension on the band.

I assume the lunge position on the opposite side by dropping my hips and stepping my right foot dramatically forward. Notice how my right thigh is almost parallel with the ground and my left knee hovers just a few inches off the floor.

Flexing my pectoral and triceps muscles, I extend my arms horizontally. From here, I will retract my arms, return to the standing position, and then continue to alternate lunges until I have completed a set number of repetitions.

PUSH-UP WITH ELEVATED TORSO

The push-up is one of the most fundamental movements in strength training. It's utilized everywhere, from kindergarten PE class to army boot camp. Its universal popularity is due to the fact that it builds strength in a very useful way—it teaches you to move your body away from something rather than moving something away from you. This not only develops the primary movement muscles such as the pectoralis major and triceps, but it also forces many other muscle groups to help stabilize your body as it moves, including the abdominals, biceps, shoulders, and even the quadriceps. Mastering moving your body weight should be a prerequisite before tackling heavier-loaded movements. However, the push-up does have some downsides. While it is a great pushing exercise, your body quickly adapts to the amount of resistance. Unable to easily increase your body weight, you become so strong after a short time of training push-ups that you are forced to perform them in higher repetitions. To solve this dilemma, later in this section I demonstrate how to execute push-ups in a way that makes them more challenging and suitable for strength development. But as I already mentioned, it is very important to master the basics first. In this sequence, I demonstrate one of the easiest ways to execute a push-up. If you look at the photos below, you'll notice that I perform the movement with my torso elevated. This shifts my weight toward my feet, causing less stress and weight to be placed upon my upper body. If you are new to working out or are trying to rebuild a base level of strength, this push-up variation is a great place to start.

1

I fix a barbell several feet off the floor in a squat rack. Next, I grab the bar at slightly wider than shoulder width, place my toes on the floor behind me, and straighten my body.

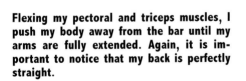

2

Relaxing my arms, I lower my upper body down to the barbell. Notice how my back is straight and my shoulder blades are pulled tight together.

Flexing my pectoral and triceps muscles, I push my body away from the bar until my arms are fully extended. Again, it is important to notice that my back is perfectly straight.

3

ONE-ARM PUSH-UP WITH ELEVATED TORSO

In this sequence I demonstrate a more challenging variation of the previous push-up exercise. Instead of positioning your feet close together and placing both of your hands on the bar, you spread your feet apart and place just one hand on the bar. Lowering your torso from this position is no easy task. With just three points of base, your body naturally wants to twist during your descent. To prevent that twist and keep your spine stable, you must employ your abdominals and other core muscles. Your arm positioning is also different. Unlike the two-arm push-up, which allows you to angle your elbows outward and focus on developing your pectoral muscles, you must keep your working arm tucked tight to your side to maintain your balance over the bar. This removes much of the workload from your pectoralis major and places it on your triceps. Although this technique isn't for everyone, it's a great exercise for athletes looking to accomplish a true one-arm push-up off the ground. Starting with your torso elevated allows you to build the necessary muscles and learn how to stabilize your body. As it becomes easier and easier, you can progressively lower the bar until your body is horizontal with the floor.

I fix a barbell several feet off the floor in a squat rack. Next, I grab the bar using my right hand, place my toes on the floor behind me, and straighten my back. With this version, it is important to notice that my right grip is lined up with my right shoulder and I have spread my feet apart to help stabilize my body as I perform the push-up.

Keeping my right elbow tucked to my side, I slowly lower my chest down to the barbell. I keep my back as flat as possible and flex my oblique muscles to prevent my shoulders from twisting.

Contracting my right triceps and pectoral muscles, I push my body away from the barbell until my right elbow is in the locked position.

I alternate slides by gripping the barbell with my left hand and releasing my right grip. Again, notice how my left grip is lined up with my left shoulder and my feet are spread apart. From here, I will execute a one-arm push-up with my left arm.

ELEVATED LEG PUSH-UP ON DUMBBELLS

In this sequence I demonstrate an even more challenging push-up variation. If you look at the photos below, you'll notice that I rest my feet on a bench press positioned behind me and grip two dumbbells instead of placing my hands on the floor. By elevating my legs, it transfers the majority of my body weight onto my arms, which is the opposite effect of the previous technique and increases the difficulty of the movement. And by gripping circular dumbbells, my upper body must fight to keep my base stable as I perform the push-up. It is important to mention that I position the dumbbells differently in the two sequences below. In the first series, I position them so that my palms are facing my feet, which causes my shoulders to become the prime stabilization muscles. In the second series, I position the dumbbells so my palms are facing each other. This forces my chest to stabilize the dumbbells. Personally, I like to switch back and forth between the two positions to alter the muscles being challenged.

1) To set up this exercise, I grip two dumbbells and place them on the floor shoulder width apart. In the sequence above, I position the dumbbells so my palms are facing my feet. In the sequence on the left, I position the dumbbells so that my palms are facing one another. I recommend trying them both because they require different muscles to stabilize your body. In both cases, I complete the setup by posting my toes on a bench positioned behind me and straightening my back.

2) Keeping my back perfectly flat, I relax my upper body and lower my chest toward the floor. It is important to mention that I use my core muscles to prevent the dumbbells from rolling away from the start position. Once I reach the bottom of the push-up, my shoulders are positioned below my feet, which places the majority of my body weight on my arms.

3) Contracting my pectoral and triceps muscles, I push my torso away from the floor by extending my arms. Once I lock out my elbows at the top of the movement, I can continue with more repetitions or finish the set.

LEGS ELEVATED UNSTABLE PUSH-UP

In this sequence I demonstrate how to increase the difficulty of the push-up by decreasing the stability of your base. Just as with the previous technique, you elevate your legs to distribute the majority of your body weight onto your arms, but instead of placing your feet on an immovable object, you place them on a physio ball. To make the exercise even more challenging, you grip the sides of a BOSU ball. While it is possible to grip dumbbells in this exercise, they only roll forward and backward or side-to-side, depending upon how you position them. The BOSU ball shifts in all directions, which challenges both your shoulders and pectoral muscles to stabilize your body as you perform the movement. Although this is still classified as a body weight exercise, it is an extremely challenging one.

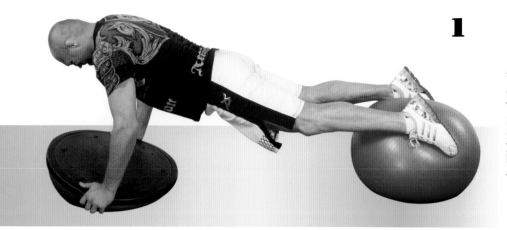

1

To set up this technique, I grip the sides of a BOSU ball with my hands, wrap my feet around the sides of a stability ball positioned behind me, and straighten my body. It is important not to begin your push-ups until you have found your balance and all edges of the BOSU ball are off the floor.

2

Relaxing the muscles in my arms, I lower my torso toward the BOSU ball. To keep my back stable and flat during the descent, I isometrically contract all of my core muscles.

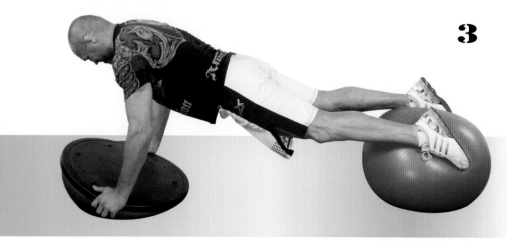

3

Contracting my pectoral and triceps muscles, I push my torso away from the BOSU ball by extending my arms. It is important to mention that when performing exercises such as this one on unstable surfaces, slower movements are often better.

PUSH-UP WITH FLEX BAND

While it is true that the benefits of the body weight push-up quickly plateau, there are numerous ways to add resistance. I've covered how to elevate your legs and use unstable hand/feet positions to make the push-up more difficult, but perhaps the easiest way to increase the challenge is to use a flex band looped over your back. The tension on the band adds resistance throughout the entire range of motion, with it peaking at the top of the movement, and depending upon the thickness of the band, you can approach loads similar to your max effort bench press. You get all the difficulty of the standard barbell pushing movement, and because you're still pushing your body away from something rather than pushing something away from your body, you increase your ability to stabilize your core. One of the best things about this exercise is that you can throw a flex band in your gym bag and get a workout on the road, which is vital to the modern MMA athlete.

After securing a flex band around my upper back, I place my hands on the floor slightly more than shoulder width apart, place my toes on the floor behind me, and straighten my back.

Relaxing my arms, I bend my elbows and lower my chest down to the floor. Notice how I keep my back completely straight.

Once my chest touches the floor, I push my torso away from the ground by extending my arms. As my torso elevates, the band stretches, increasing tension. This forces me to use the muscles in my core to stabilize my ascent. It also makes it more difficult to lock my elbows out at the top of the movement.

HORIZONTAL PLANE

PARTNER PUSH-UP

In this sequence I demonstrate the partner push-up, which allows you to take advantage of having a partner available to increase the difficulty and efficiency of your workout. If you look at the photos below, you'll notice that both the person on the bottom and the person on top are performing push-ups. With the top person's hands elevated, the majority of his weight is transferred to his feet, which allows him to perform a slightly easier version of the body-weight push-up. However, the person on the bottom performs one of the most difficult push-ups available. With nearly the full body weight of the partner on top resting on his back and head, it turns the push-up into a very challenging movement. It is important to note that there are several variations of this exercise. In the sequence below, both athletes tax their core muscles and their upper-body muscles in the same workout. If this proves too challenging, there are a couple of easier variations. The first is the "top only" push-up, where only the person on top executes a push-up. This is a light upper-body workout for the man on top, as well as a good core workout for the person on bottom, as he must use his core muscles to stabilize his lower back and head from dipping under the pressure of the man on top. Another method of utilizing this drill is the "bottom only" push-up. This provides a very moderate core stabilization workout for the person on top, while the person on bottom gets a maximal effort workout. These variations are good to have in your arsenal because not every athlete will be strong enough to execute the "bottom" push-up.

BOTTOM PUSH-UP

Jake and Lance assume the partner push-up position. Jake has his hands and feet on the floor with his back flat in the push-up position. Lance has his feet on the floor, his right hand on Jake's head, and his left hand on Jake's lower back.

As Jake begins to lower his chest to the ground, the majority of Lance's body weight shift onto his back. This makes Jake's push-up progressively more difficult. Notice Lance keeps his arms straight and his back flat as Jake drops toward the floor.

Jake contracts his triceps and pectoral muscles, elevating his torso until his arms are straight and he reaches the top of the push-up position.

TOP PUSH-UP

Lance and Jake both begin in the push-up position. Jake's hands and feet are flat on the ground, while Lance is perpendicular to Jake's body with his right hand on Jake's head and his left hand on Jake's back. Notice how Jake's arms are not straight, but rather bent.

Lance lowers himself down by flexing his elbow joint and dropping his chest down toward Jake's back. As Lance lowers his body weight, Jake must isometrically contract his transverse abdominis muscle to keep his back stable. At the same time, he isometrically contracts the splenius muscles in his neck to keep his head from dipping under Lance's weight.

Lance contracts his triceps and pectoral muscles, reversing his movement and elevating his torso until he reaches the top of the push-up position. Note that Jake keeps his arms flexed throughout the entire movement. This makes the act of core stabilization much more challenging, as well as taxes his arms. This is a much more advanced support position. For less developed athletes, keeping the arms straight throughout the movement is perfectly acceptable.

STAGGERED PUSH-UP WITH MEDICINE BALL

In this sequence I demonstrate how to perform a staggered push-up with a medicine ball. If you look at the photos, you'll notice that I begin with one hand resting on top of the medicine ball and my other hand on the ground. This is already an unstable position as my muscles are stretched at different angles and lengths. Once I drop my body down and then return to the starting position, I switch to the opposite side. To accomplish this, I momentarily place both hands on top of the medicine ball, giving me only three points of base. In addition to challenging my core muscles to resist spinal rotation, I must also be very coordinated with my movements. With my hands essentially overlapped on the top of the ball, I must be careful how I transfer my weight as I shift to the opposite side. Although this is still just a body weight push-up, the added challenges to my stability and coordination make it a much harder push-up to complete.

To set up this exercise, I place my left hand on the floor, place my right hand on the top of a medicine ball, place my toes on the floor behind me, and straighten my body. Notice how my hands are currently spread slightly more than shoulder width apart.

Relaxing my arms, I bend my elbows and lower my chest toward the floor. Notice how even though my hands are at different heights, I utilize my core muscles to keep my back perfectly flat.

Flexing my pectoral and triceps muscles, I push my torso away from the ground by extending my arms. It is important to note that due to the different angles of my arms, each side of my body is getting a slightly different workout during my ascent.

Shifting my body weight toward my right side, I place my left hand on top of the ball next to my right hand. It is important to notice that although a portion of my left hand is on top of my right, I have not completely covered it, as it would make removing my right hand from the ball too difficult.

Once my left hand is firmly on the medicine ball, I remove my right hand and place it on the floor to my right. Again, notice how my arms are spread roughly at shoulder width.

As I lower my torso toward the floor, I keep my body perfectly straight by contracting my core muscles. From here, I will increase my elevation and return to the opposite side for another repetition.

ELEVATED TORSO EXPLOSIVE PUSH-UP

The push-up variation demonstrated in this sequence is similar to the elevated torso push-up shown earlier. By gripping a barbell supported in a power rack, you elevate your torso and shift weight onto your legs. However, instead of executing a standard push-up, you explode upward from the bottom push-up position so that your torso rockets backward and your hands leave the bar. As you come back down, you grab the bar again and bend your arms to absorb your falling weight. When you reach the bottom of the push-up, you explode upward for another repetition. Although this version may seem pretty basic, it is very challenging and requires a baseline level of athletic ability. You need coordination to catch the bar, core strength to keep your spine straight throughout the movement, and of course a powerful upper body to propel your torso upward. Just as with the elevated push-up variation shown earlier, you can progressively lower the bar toward the ground to increase the difficulty level of the exercise.

To set up this exercise, I fix a barbell a few feet off the ground in a squat rack. Notice how the bar is held in place by strong pins—this is very important because you don't want the bar moving as you drop down to catch your body weight. Next, I grip the bar at slightly wider than shoulder width, place my toes on the ground behind me, straighten my back, and lower my chest down to the bar by bending my elbows and pulling my shoulder blades together.

Explosively flexing my pectoral and triceps muscles, I push my torso away from the bar and release my grips so my body can elevate farther than my arms would allow. However, I keep my arms positioned in front of me so I can regrab the bar during my descent. It is important to notice that despite my explosive movement, I have kept my back perfectly straight.

As my body descends, I catch the bar in my hands slightly more than shoulder width apart, bend my elbows, and allow my arms to absorb the force of my plummeting body weight. From here, I can explode upward into another repetition or finish my set.

ELEVATED LEG PLYOMETRIC PUSH-UP

In this sequence I demonstrate an elevated leg push-up variation that incorporates an explosive plyometric movement to increase difficulty. If you look at the photos below, you'll notice that I begin the exercise with my feet resting on a bench behind me, and my hands on the ground in the standard push-up position. However, I have positioned an Olympic bumber plate between my arms. To perform the exercise, I lower my torso toward the mat just as I would when performing a standard push-up. Once I have completed my descent, the nature of the exercise changes. The goal is to reposition my hands on either side of the weight plate, which is accomplished by exploding my body upward so that my palms leave the ground. As my body begins to fall, I move my hands inward and catch myself on the sides of the plate. I use my arms to absorb the impact, drop down for another push-up, and then explode upward again. As my palms leave the sides of the plate, I move my hands outward and catch my body. It is important to mention that this is a much more challenging plyometric push-up than the one shown in the previous sequence. With your legs elevated, the majority of your body weight is positioned over your hands, which requires your upward explosions to be much more powerful. Personally, I recommend beginning with the previous variation until you have adequately built up your strength.

To set up this exercise, I place my hands on the floor on either side of a weight plate, place my toes on a bench positioned behind me, and straighten my body.

Relaxing my arms, I lower my torso toward the plate.

At the bottom of the movement, I drive my torso upward by explosively flexing my pectoral and triceps muscles. Due to my powerful contraction, my hands lift off the floor as my arms fully extend, allowing me to quickly pull my hands toward one another and grip the edges of the weight plate.

4

Relaxing my arms, I lower my torso toward the weight plate beneath my chest.

5

At the bottom of the movement, I drive my torso upward by explosively flexing my triceps and pectoral muscles. Due to my powerful contraction, my hands lift off the weight plate as my arms fully extend, allowing me to me to quickly move my hands toward the outside of my body and place them on the floor. From here, I will continue the exercise for a set number of repetitions.

ELEVATED LEG PLYOMETRIC PUSH-UP (OPTION 2)

If you are training in a gym that does not have benches or weight plates, it is just as easy to perform the elevated leg plyometric push-up using a kicking shield and a plyo box.

1) To set up this version of the exercise, I place my hands on the floor to either side of a kicking shield, place my toes on a plyo box positioned behind me, and straighten my body.

2) When I reach the bottom of the push-up position, I drive my torso upward by explosively flexing my pectoral and triceps muscles. Due to my powerful contraction, my hands lift off the floor as my arms fully extend, allowing me to quickly pull my hands toward one another and grip the edges of the kicking shield. From here, I will explode back upward and reposition my hands back on the mat.

PLYOMETRIC PUSH-UP WITH MEDICINE BALL

Earlier in this sequence I demonstrated how to perform a staggered push-up with a medicine ball. The technique shown here is similar in that you begin by placing one hand on the mat and one hand on top of the ball. The primary difference is in how you shift from one side to the other. Instead of doing a regular push-up, placing both hands on top of the ball, and then moving your opposite hand down to the mat, you explode upward from the push-up position so that both hands leave the surfaces they are resting upon. While suspended, you move the hand formerly on the medicine ball to the ground and the hand formerly on the ground onto the medicine ball. This turns the medicine ball push-up into a plyometric movement. You still need to powerfully contract your core muscles to keep your back flat and stable, but you must also use your pectoralis major and triceps to generate a much more powerful upward explosion to bring both of your hands off of their resting surfaces. It is important to mention that the coordination aspect of this exercise is much greater.

To set up this exercise, I place my left hand on the mat, place my right hand on the top of a medicine ball, spread my legs slightly more than shoulder width apart, place my toes on the mat behind me, and straighten my body. Next, I relax my arms and dip my torso slightly toward the mat.

Once I have reached the bottom of the movement, I elevate my torso by explosively contracting my pectoral and triceps muscles. At the same time, I shift my body weight toward my right side. Since my left hand is positioned lower than my right hand, it lifts into the air first, allowing me to pull it toward the medicine ball.

As my right hand lifts off the medicine ball due to my upward explosion, I do two things at once—I shift my right hand toward the mat to my right and I place my left hand on the top of the medicine ball. As my weight descends, I let my arms absorb the impact. Once again I am in the starting position, only on the opposite side. Immediately I dip my torso slightly toward the mat.

At the bottom of the movement, I powerfully extend my arms. As my right hand leaves the mat, I begin pulling it toward the medicine ball.

As my left hand leaves the surface of the medicine ball, I do things at once—I shift my left hand to my left and place it on the mat and I place my right hand on top of the medicine ball.

PLYOMETRIC PUSH-UP WITH LATERAL OBSTACLE

In this sequence I demonstrate a plyometric push-up variation that focuses more on lateral movement. If you look at the photos below, you'll notice that I begin the exercise in the push-up position with a weight plate positioned to the side of one hand. As I explode upward, I push my body to the side, jump my arms over the weight plate, and then reposition my hands on the opposite side. To absorb the impact, I bend my arms and lower myself back down into the push-up position. Lateral push-ups such as this one are great for challenging your body. Moving side to side rather than straight up and down places different stresses on your chest and shoulder muscles. It's no better or worse than the other plyometric push-ups previously demonstrated, just different. It is important to mix different types of movements into your program to prevent from plateauing or developing muscular imbalances. It is important to mention that although I am using a very shallow weight plate in this scenario, you can progressively increase the height of your hurdle as you get stronger.

To set up this exercise, I place a weight plate on the floor, position my hands shoulder width apart to the left of the plate, place my toes on the ground behind me, and straighten my back. Once I have the proper positioning, I bend my elbows outward and lower my torso toward the floor.

Powerfully contracting my pectoral and triceps muscles, I push my torso upward and toward my right side. Due to the speed generated with my extension, my hands leave the floor and my body shifts toward my right side. It is important to notice that my entire body is moving toward my right side, not just my arms.

As my hands land on the floor with the plate on my left side, I bend my elbows to absorb the impact. Once I have reached the bottom of the movement, I will explode upward and laterally again and return to the opposite side.

FRONTAL PLANE

ROLLING TRICEPS

Rolling triceps is a great strength-building tool for the triceps and shoulder muscles. Although it is possible to use substantial load for the exercise, I tend to use it more as a supplemental movement to my pushing routine. It's great for bringing up any weak spots in your shoulders and putting some extra volume on the triceps muscles. If you look at the photos below, you'll notice that there is a forward rolling movement in the exercise, which also tends to cause the muscles of the back to come into play. Below Jake demonstrates the exercise on the ground for simplicity, but it can also be executed on a bench to allow for a little extra range of motion during the final stages of shoulder flexion.

To begin the exercise, Jake lies on his back, bends his knees slightly, grips a dumbbell in each hand, and then positions the dumbbells to either side of his head with his elbows facing upward.

Jake flexes his posterior deltoids and latissimus muscles in order to extend his shoulders forward, bringing his arms down until his triceps are flat on the ground at his sides. Notice that his elbows are still bent and now the dumbbells are off the ground and balanced over his arms.

Jake now flexes his triceps muscles, allowing his elbows to extend. This forces the dumbbells upward. As Jake's arms reach the end of the motion, he locks out his elbows and slightly pauses in the top position. Notice that Jake's palms are still facing each other. This is the optimal hand positioning to allow the shoulders to move in their natural range of motion.

Jake now relaxes his triceps, slowly lowering the dumbbells back down until his triceps are flat on the ground once again.

As soon as Jake's triceps touch the ground, he fires his anterior deltoid muscles to flex his shoulder joints and roll the dumbbells back into the starting position next to his head. This is one complete rep of the exercise.

DUMBBELL TRICEPS EXTENSION SERIES

The dumbbell triceps extension is another supplemental movement that I use in my strength building routine. Many of the exercises previously shown tax your triceps, but this one allows you to exclusively isolate this important muscle. In the sequences below, I demonstrate three variations of this technique. None is better than the others. I recommend trying them all and seeing which one works best for you.

STANDING DUMBBELL TRICEPS EXTENSIONS

1 2 3

1) Standing upright, I grip a dumbbell in each hand so that my palms are facing each other and then pull them up onto my shoulders. It is important to notice that my elbows are pointing toward my front rather than my sides.

2) Slightly bending my knees, I contract my triceps muscles and extend the dumbbells vertically. Notice how at the top of the movement my palms are still facing one another.

3) Relaxing my triceps, I lower the dumbbells back down onto my shoulders.

STANDING ONE-ARM DUMBBELL TRICEPS EXTENSIONS

1 2 3

1) Standing upright, I grip a dumbbell in my right hand so that my palm is facing inward and then place it on my right shoulder. It is important to notice that my elbow is positioned to the front rather than the side.

2) Slightly bending my knees, I contract my right triceps muscle and extend the dumbbell vertically.

3) I relax my right arm and lower the dumbbell back down to my shoulder.

FRONTAL PLANE

LYING DUMBBELL TRICEPS EXTENSIONS

1) To set up this exercise, I lie flat on my back, bend my knees, place my feet on the floor, grip a dumbbell in each hand, and then position the dumbbells to either side of my head. Notice how my elbows are pointing toward the ceiling. 2) Flexing my triceps, I extend my arms vertically. It is important to mention that my elbows did not move from the previous step. 3) Keeping my elbows vertical, I lower the dumbbells back down to the sides of my head, completing one repetition. Although this exercise can also be performed while standing, it becomes easier to cheat using your legs. When lying down, you are forced to isolate your triceps muscles.

DIPS

In this sequence I demonstrate the bench dip, which is another excellent exercise for isolating your triceps muscles. If you look at the photos below, you'll notice that I establish a narrow grip on the edge of the bench behind me and then move my body straight down and back up. By utilizing this form, I remove the workload from my chest and shoulders and place it on my upper arms. It is important to mention that although I have my feet resting on the ground, which requires my triceps to overcome only a fraction of my body weight, you can increase the load placed upon your triceps by elevating your legs onto a second bench positioned to your front.

1) To set up this exercise, I sit my butt on the width of a bench, cup my palms over the edge of the bench slightly less than shoulder width apart, scoot my butt off the edge of the bench, and straighten my legs out in front of me. It is important to notice that instead of moving my butt far away from the bench, I keep it close to the edge.

2) I bend my elbows and lower my butt straight down. Once my triceps are roughly parallel with the floor, I have reached the bottom of the movement. Again, notice that my back is positioned very close to the edge of the bench. This removes the weight of your body from your shoulders and places it on your triceps.

3) Flexing my triceps muscles, I straighten my arms and push my body back to the starting position.

TRICEPS DIPS

While the bench dip previously shown is a great downward pressing movement for beginners, it only uses a fraction of your actual body weight as resistance and tends to be outgrown relatively quickly by trained athletes. If you should find this to be the case, the triceps dip variation shown below comes in very handy. It is identical to the bench dip in that the arms are directed downward, and then the triceps and anterior deltoid muscles contract to move your back up to the starting position. However, unlike the bench dip, your hands support your entire body weight. This means that 100 percent of your body weight is being utilized for resistance, making it a much more powerful movement. Although the triceps are the primary movers in this exercise, it is possible to lean your weight slightly forward, causing the pectoral muscles to be activated as well. If triceps dips prove too difficult to perform at least several repetitions, it is possible to wrap a flex band around your body and attach it to the top of the rack to assist with your upward movement. Conversely, if your body weight is insufficient resistance, a flex band can be wrapped around your body and attached to the bottom of the rack to add increasing difficulty as you ascend. It is also possible to increase your load by attaching a weight plate around your waist.

1 Jake begins the movement with his arms extended straight down and his hands gripping the dip handles. These handles extend perpendicular from a rack heavy enough to support the weight of the athlete. Additionally, Jake's legs are hanging in the air, causing his arms to support his entire body weight.

2 Jake flexes his elbow joints. This moves his torso straight down, putting stress on the anterior deltoid muscles as well as the triceps. In this position Jake can also choose to lean forward substantially, which will increase the load placed upon his pectoral muscles.

3 Jake now flexes his triceps, causing his torso to elevate. With his arms locked out at the top of the movement, he has completed one repetition.

HANDSTAND PUSH-UP

In this sequence I demonstrate the most difficult variation of the body-weight push-up—the handstand push-up. Unlike many of the push-up exercises already demonstrated, the core muscles taxed in this movement are not your chest or triceps, but rather your shoulders. Turned completely upside down with all of your weight on your arms, you're basically doing an over-the-head shoulder press. For the majority of athletes, this is a near max movement. It is a rather simple exercise to execute because it requires no equipment, but the downside is that standing on your hands and performing a push-up can be very difficult to stabilize. Personally, I like to have a partner stabilize my legs to increase my balance, but this is just as easily accomplished by resting your back against a wall.

1) I begin by standing face-to-face with my training partner a few feet apart.

2) I bend forward and place my hands on the mat at shoulder width.

3) Shifting the weight of my body onto my hands, I push off the mat using my feet, causing my legs to move above my torso and into my training partner's hands.

4) Once my body is completely vertical and my training partner has stabilized my legs, I bend my elbows and begin slowly lowering my head toward the mat.

5) Just prior to my head touching the mat, I force my body to rise by contracting my triceps and shoulder muscles. If needed, my partner can assist by pulling upward on my ankles.

6) As I reach the top of the movement, my partner releases my ankles and I drop my feet back to the mat. To prevent blood from quickly rushing from my head and possibly causing me to pass out, I stand up slowly.

PUSH PRESS

The overhead press shown previously is excellent for building your shoulder muscles, but when you isolate any one muscle group in such a manner, you are forced to use lighter loads, which is less than ideal for overall mass gain and strength development. The push press is one of the best ways to increase the load on the barbell while executing the overhead press. The two exercises are very similar. In both you flex your shoulders upward and extend your elbows, moving the bar straight overhead. However, the push press is not a strict shoulder movement. Instead of keeping your body erect, you dip your legs slightly and then drive upward in synch with your elbow extension. This gives extra momentum to the barbell as it moves overhead. While this might seem like cheating, using full-body effort is mandatory for moving heavy loads. Using your legs to assist in moving the barbell past the sticking point allows your shoulders and upper arms to attain much more volume than with strict overhead movements. This leads to greater stress on the shoulders and upper arms, which in turn leads to increased size and strength gains. Since the push press can be loaded relatively heavy, it should be used more as a primary pushing movement, which means it should be executed before your lighter pressing movements that involve high repetition. When you combine the push press with the standard overhead pressing movements previously demonstrated, you will achieve a great upper-body workout that will increase strength, size, and power in your upper body.

1) Jake begins the exercise holding a barbell across the front of his shoulders with his hands underneath the bar. His feet are together in a shoulder-width stance and his head is slightly back to allow a clear path for the barbell to move upward. 2) Jake bends at the knees very slightly. This will allow him to utilize his lower body to accelerate the bar upward. This step differentiates the push press from other strict overhead pressing movements. 3) As Jake's hips drive forward, he begins extending his elbows to force the bar upward. The momentum of his leg drive, combined with the flexion of his medial deltoids, accelerates the bar overhead. Jake now has the bar locked out in the overhead position. 4) Jake now relaxes his deltoids and triceps, allowing the barbell to drop back to his shoulders. At this point he will either rebend at the knees to drive the barbell upward for another rep or set the bar on the ground and move on to another exercise.

OVERHEAD DUMBBELL PRESS SERIES

In this sequence I demonstrate several variations of the overhead dumbbell press. The primary muscles being taxed are those of your shoulders, but your upper arms and upper back are responsible for stabilizing the dumbbells as you complete your repetitions and receive a moderate workout as well. Although the various versions shift the focus slightly from one muscle to another, the basic movement remains the same. Standing on one leg can force the core muscles to activate as the weight attempts to drive you toward your missing point of base, while performing this technique on a BOSU ball can assist your sense of balance and increase proprioceptive ability. Personally, I like to use overhead dumbbell exercises as assistance movements to heavier pressing motions or to rehab shoulder injuries. However, to minimize your risk of damaging your shoulder girdle, do not attempt to lift maximum loads. If you're a fighter, you'll receive a lot more benefit by sticking to lighter weights and higher repetitions.

OVERHEAD DUMBBELL PRESS

1) Standing upright, I grip a dumbbell in each hand, elevate them up to my shoulders, and flare my elbows out to my sides. 2) I extend my arms vertically. 3) Relaxing my shoulders, I lower the dumbbells back down to the starting position.

ONE-LEG OVERHEAD DUMBBELL PRESSES

1 **2** **3**

1) Standing upright, I grip a dumbbell in each hand, elevate them up to my shoulders, and flare my elbows out to the sides. Next, I shift my weight onto my right leg, find my balance, and then elevate my left foot off the floor.

2) Maintaining my balance on my right leg, I extend my arms vertically.

3) I relax my shoulders and lower the dumbbells back down to my shoulders.

ONE-LEG SINGLE-ARM DUMBBELL PRESSES

1 **2** **3**

1) Standing upright, I grip a dumbbell in my left hand, elevate it up to my shoulder, and then flare my left elbow out to the side. Next, I shift my weight onto my left leg, find my balance, and then lift my right foot off the mat.

2) Maintaining my balance on my left leg, I extend my left arm upward.

3) Relaxing my left shoulder, I lower the dumbbell back down to the starting position.

OVERHEAD DUMBBELL PRESS ON BOSU BALL

FRONTAL PLANE

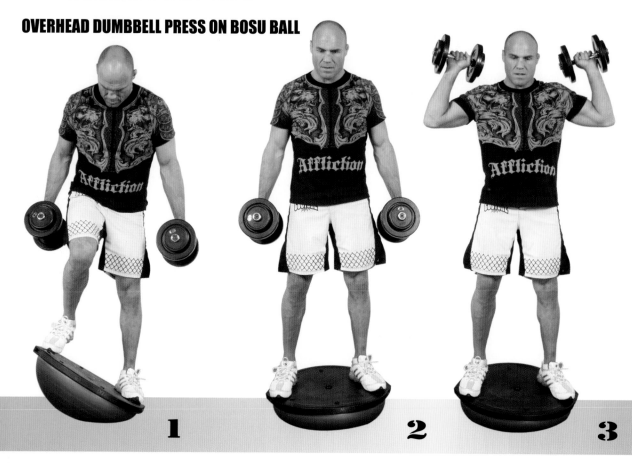

1 **2** **3**

4 **5**

1) I grip a dumbbell in each hand so that my palms are facing toward my body. Next, I step my left foot on the far edge of the BOSU ball. Once my foot is stable, I step my right foot on the opposite edge.

2) I redistribute my weight so that both edges of the BOSU ball are off the floor.

3) I elevate the dumbbells up to my shoulders.

4) Maintaining my balance, I extend my arms upward.

5) Sill maintaining my balance, I lower the dumbbells back down to my shoulders.

ALTERNATING DUMBBELL FRONT RAISES

Athletes with shoulder injuries will often begin to feel pain during overhead pressing movements first, but as the damage in their shoulders accumulates, they will also begin to experience problems with horizontal pressing movements. If you are such an athlete, performing the dumbbell front raise is an excellent alternative to the standard bench press. Just like with the bench press, this exercise activates the anterior muscle fibers of the deltoid muscles, but you can experience gains using a lot less weight, which most of the time translates to less pain. A large part of being a good fighter is being aware of your own body and analyzing which exercises cause you pain and eliminating or replacing them can drastically increase your longevity in the sport. However, it is important to note that alternating dumbbell front raises are not just for injured athletes. If you are injury free, it is a great exercise to supplement your overhead or horizontal pressing movements.

Jake begins this exercise in the standing position with a dumbbell in each hand and his arms hanging to his side. His hands have a pronated grip on the dumbbells, with his hands facing backward.

Jake begins the exercise by flexing his deltoid muscles in his right arm, causing flexion in the shoulder joint and his arm to move vertically in front of his body.

Jake now lowers the dumbbell by relaxing his deltoid muscles. At this point, Jake will switch arms and repeat the motion on his left side.

DUMBBELL LATERAL RAISE

While overhead pressing is a great way to train your shoulders, not all athletes are capable of performing this movement, especially in MMA where shoulder injuries are very common. The shoulder is a very complex joint, capable of moving in more than ten different articulations, all of which are used heavily in fighting. Your shoulders are utilized when punching, clinch fighting, jockeying for takedowns, and fighting on the ground. This overuse can cause wear and tear on the shoulder joints, and performing overhead presses might very well make these injuries worse. If you are one of the many athletes with shoulder problems, instead of ignoring the entire muscle group in your workouts, you must simply work around your injuries. In this sequence Jake demonstrates the dumbbell lateral raise, which is a simple shoulder abduction exercise where you elevate your arms to the side of your torso. It allows you to tax your shoulders without the accompanying pain many fighters experience with overhead pressing exercises.

Jake begins this exercise in the standing position with a dumbbell in each hand and his arms hanging to his side. His hands have a neutral grip on the dumbbells, with his palms facing his body. This neutral grip is important to allow the shoulder joint to move in a natural path as the arms abduct away from the body.

Jake flexes his medial deltoids, raising his arms laterally until his hands reach shoulder height. It is important to stop the movement at shoulder height to prevent shoulder impingement.

Jake now lowers the dumbbells by relaxing his deltoid muscles. If doing this movement as a rehabilitation exercise for a shoulder injury, slow movement and light weight is recommended.

SECTION FOUR
UPPER-BODY PULL

Pulling exercises can be categorized as movements in which your arms start in a position away from your body and then move toward your torso in a concentric motion. This can be accomplished by moving your arms closer to the centerline of your body, which is referred to as adduction, or by pulling your hands closer to your torso on a flat plane of motion by flexion of your arm joints. Simply put, anytime you grab something and bring it nearer to your body, you are utilizing a "pulling" motion. Basic examples of this would be rowing a boat or pulling a lever.

The muscles targeted by pulling exercises are mainly located in your upper back. The middle and lower trapezius, rhomboids, latissimus dorsi, and teres major and teres minor muscles all play big roles during pulling exercises. However, the muscles of the shoulder joint, including the anterior, lateral, and posterior deltoid muscles can be activated by different pulling movements as well. Depending upon the angle of your movement, even your biceps brachii muscles of your upper arms and the pectoralis major muscles of your chest can assist in your pulling motion. While the upper back plays the biggest role, heavy pulling movements will cause stress in nearly your entire upper body.

For all athletes, pulling exercises are essential in their routine. To have a balanced physique, you need equal amounts of pushing and pulling exercises. If one set of muscles overpowers another, you will begin to suffer from structural weaknesses. In addition to increasing the likelihood of injuring yourself during training, you will also most likely suffer from degraded sports performance. However, some sports tend to focus on either pulling or pushing motions more than the other. For example, Olympic rowers spend the majority of their time pulling the oars toward their body and offensive lineman in football spend the majority of the game using their arms to push their opponents away from them. Despite this fact, balancing their routine to include equal parts of pushing and pulling is vital for injury avoidance.

As a mixed martial artist, neither pushing nor pulling dominates your movement patterns while in the cage. The broad array of techniques you must learn to be successful in the sport requires you to employ many different muscle patterns, movements, and joint angles. However, this is not to say that certain aspects of an MMA fight don't emphasize pulling over pushing. When grappling on the mat, pulling is a much more dominant movement than pushing. For example, when you gain control of your opponent's wrist, attempting to push it away from your body is often futile. Much like pushing on a rope, your opponent's arm will most likely bend in the middle rather than move your opponent away. However, pulling on his wrist will usually have a much better result. As his arm straightens, you can move his upper body in the direction you choose. In order to make use of overhook control, a collar tie, or a double underhook body lock, you must have well-developed pulling muscles. For me, coming from a Greco-Roman wrestling background, having a strong upper back and the ability to pull my opponent toward me while tied up in the clinch or in top control on the ground has been an important aspect in my ability to control a fight.

To help you develop the ability to execute a powerful and sustained pulling force, I demonstrate some of my favorite methods to exercise the muscles of my upper back and arms in this section. I start by offering the horizontal pulling movements I use in my routine. I demonstrate several horizontal rows, including barbell and dumbbell variations that allow you to increase external load. I demonstrate different grip variations, and how to add difficulty to the horizontal row using various tools, including flex bands and a Swiss ball. I even show single- and double-arm rowing movements. The reason I start with horizontal pulling movements is because I use them heavily when fighting. When jockeying for position in the clinch or on the ground, the majority of my pulling movements are initiated in front of my body and then finalized by pulling my arms to my chest. Whether it's sucking my opponent's hips toward me in the clinch or locking down overhook control from the guard position, the majority of my pulling effort in a fight happens on a horizontal plane. As a result, I have made horizontal pulling movements the bread and butter of my upper-body pulling routine.

Next, I switch gears and cover vertical pulling movements, which are initiated with your arms overhead. Although there tend to be very few overhead pulling motions in the sport of MMA, generalized strength-and-conditioning work in this movement pattern is extremely beneficial because it builds upper-body strength and size. Remember, the whole purpose of general physical preparation is to build your body up in all aspects to better prepare it to perform in your sport of choice. Vertical pulling is a necessary tool to build your foundation of general physical preparation, and I offer several exercises to help you fulfill this movement pattern.

In this section I offer you all the exercises you need to develop strength and endurance in the muscles used for pulling. This increased power and stamina will directly translate into a more powerful clinch, more control while on the mat, decreased fatigue when grappling with your opponent, and an overall improved game. When you combine this chapter with the previous one on pushing movements, you will have all the tools needed to develop your upper body to elite status.

BENT-OVER BARBELL ROW

In this sequence I demonstrate how to perform the bent-over barbell row. Although the muscles of your upper back and shoulders are the primary movers, the muscles of your arms, lower back, and legs also come into play. Aside from being an excellent full-body exercise, the bent-over row is also simple to set up. It makes matters easier when you can load the barbell on a bench or squat rack, but it can just as easily be placed on the ground. However, it is extremely important that you utilize proper form when performing this movement. If you look at the photos below, you'll notice that as I bend forward at the waist, I keep my back perfectly straight and pull the bar upward into my abdomen. If you allow your back to arch or you pull the weight up to your chest, you increase the chance of injuring your spine. To limit your risk, I recommend starting with light weight until you are familiar with the movement.

HORIZONTAL PLANE

1 Standing with my feet spread approximately a foot apart, I grip a barbell at shoulder width, bend my knees, move my hips backward, and bend forward at the waist. It is important to notice that my torso is angled forward at roughly a forty-five-degree angle.

2 Contracting the muscles in my upper back, I pull the barbell straight up into my abdomen. Notice how there is no curvature in my back and that my knees are still bent.

3 Relaxing the muscles in my upper back, I lower the barbell back down to the starting position.

HORIZONTAL PLANE

BENT-OVER BARBELL ROW WITH SUPINATED GRIP

The only difference between this exercise and the previous one is how I establish my grip. Instead of assuming a pronated grip with my palms facing toward my body, I establish a supinated grip with my palms facing away from my body. The upper back is still the primary muscle group targeted, but due to my inverted grip, the muscles in my upper arms become slightly more involved. Personally, I add this exercise into my rowing routine every once in a while to shock my body.

| **1** | **2** | **3** |

Just as in the previous version of this exercise, I stand with my feet spread approximately a foot apart, grip a barbell at shoulder width, bend my knees, move my hips backward, and bend forward at the waist. However, instead of gripping the bar so my palms are angled toward me, I grip it so my palms are facing away from me.

Contracting my upper back and biceps muscles, I pull the bar upward into my abdomen.

Relaxing my upper back and upper arms, I lower the bar back to the starting position.

BENT-OVER DUMBBELL ROW

In this sequence I demonstrate the bent-over dumbbell row. If you look at the photos below, you'll notice that it looks almost identical to the bent over barbell row. With my knees slightly bent, I bend forward at the waist and pull the dumbbells upward into my abdomen. Although using a different implement to perform the exercise might seem like a minor change, it alters the position of my shoulder joints. By gripping dumbbells instead of a barbell, I can establish a neutral grip with my palms facing one another, which places less stress on my shoulders. It also becomes impossible for one side of my body to perform more of the work, giving both sides of my body an equal workout. Personally, I like to perform the bent-over dumbbell row when I'm nursing an upper-body injury, to rebuild a weak muscle, when I simply don't have access to a barbell, or to switch up my routine to keep from plateauing in my workouts.

1

2

3

Standing with my feet close together, I grip a dumbbell in each hand, bend my knees, move my hips backward, and bend forward at the waist. It is important to notice that in this rowing exercise I grip the weights so my palms are facing one another.

Keeping my back straight and my knees bent, I contract the muscles in my upper back and pull the dumbbells upward along the side of my body. Notice how by keeping my palms facing one another my shoulders flare out at the top of the movement.

Relaxing my arms and upper back, I lower the dumbbells back to the starting position.

BENT-OVER DUMBBELL ROW WITH FLEX BAND

The exercise demonstrated in this sequence is exactly the same as the previous exercise—the only difference is that I use a flex band to increase resistance in the movement. After performing the standard dumbbell row for a period of time, it is possible to lift very heavy loads, and not all gyms are equipped with heavy dumbbells. If you run into this problem, employing a flex band is an excellent way to continue to challenge yourself.

To set up this exercise, I loop a flex band around one dumbbell, fasten it to a sturdy object at ground level in front of me, and then loop it around a second dumbbell. Next, I stand with my feet close together, grip a dumbbell in each hand, bend my knees, move my hips backward, and bend forward at the waist. As with the previous exercise, is important to notice that I have gripped the weights so my palms are facing each other.

Contracting the muscles in my upper back and arms, I pull the dumbbells upward and toward the outside of my body. As the dumbbells rise, the flex band stretches, increasing the resistance.

Relaxing the muscles in my upper back and arms, I lower the dumbbells back down to the starting position.

BENT-OVER T-BAR ROW

The T-bar row is different from many other rowing exercises in that instead of lifting an entire barbell off of the ground, you only lift one end. The other end is run between your legs and fixed on the floor behind you. Although you will experience similar results as from other rowing exercises, due to the narrow grip, the emphasis with the T-bar row moves slightly away from your latissimus muscles toward the middle of your back. Your rhomboids, traps, deltoids, and even biceps become more heavily engaged in the movement. In addition, your grips are also challenged. If you look at the photos below, you'll notice that instead of gripping the barbell, I wrap a towel around the barbell and then grip both ends of the towel, which allows me to tax my grips by performing high repetitions. The longer your hands must fight to hang on to the towel, the more grip strength you develop.

1

2

3

After securing one end of a barbell to the floor using a heavy dumbbell, I step over the opposite end, wrap a towel around the top of the bar, and then grip the towel in both of my hands. Next, I bend slightly at the knees and hips, causing my torso to tilt forward.

I contract my upper back and biceps muscles, pulling the loaded barbell to my upper abdominals. Notice how my hands move toward the outside of my body, allowing for a fuller range of motion.

Once the plate touches my abdominals, I relax my biceps, allowing my arms to drop back to full extension.

SINGLE-ARM DUMBBELL ROW WITH BENCH SUPPORT

In this sequence I demonstrate how to perform a single-arm dumbbell row while supporting yourself on a bench. If you look at the photos below, you'll notice that my posture is slightly different than when performing two-handed standing rows. By bracing my body on the bench using my free hand, I can bend more forward at the waist without the risk of injuring my back. This brace also removes many of the supporting muscles that come into play when rowing from the standing position, allowing me to focus on developing the muscles of my upper back and working arm. If you reach a plateau when performing standing rows, this is a great exercise to mix things up.

1 To set up this exercise, I place my left knee and left hand on a bench, place my right foot on the floor toward the outside of my body, and grip a dumbbell in my right hand. It is important to mention that my back is perfectly parallel with the floor. If you allow your back to arch during the movement, you risk injuring your spine.

2 Keeping my back level, I contract the muscles of my upper back and right arm and pull the dumbbell up to my chest. It is important to notice how my right palm is facing the inside of my body and I've kept my right elbow tight to my right side.

3 Relaxing my upper back and right arm, I lower the dumbbell back to the starting position. After doing a set number of repetitions, I will switch to the opposite arm.

SINGLE-ARM DUMBBELL ROW WITH SWISS BALL SUPPORT

The exercise shown here is exactly same as the previous technique—the only difference is that instead of supporting my body by placing my free hand on a stable bench press, I place it on the unstable surface of a Swiss ball. This minor change alters the exercise from an isolation movement back to a full-body workout. The upper back and working arm are still taxed the heaviest, but with this version every other muscle in the body must isometrically contract to fix your torso in place and stabilize the movement.

To set up this exercise, I place my right knee and hand on the top of a stability ball, place my right foot on the floor behind the ball to increase my balance, position my left foot on the floor off to my side, and grip a dumbbell in my left hand. Before beginning the exercise, I will establish a somewhat solid base.

I contract the muscles of my upper back and right arm, lift the dumbbell toward my chest, and keep my left elbow tight to my side. To avoid losing my balance and rolling off the ball, I use all the muscles in my body to stabilize my position.

Relaxing my upper back and left arm, I lower the dumbbell back to the starting position. Once I have completed a set number of repetitions, I will switch to the opposite arm.

HORIZONTAL BODY WEIGHT ROW

In this sequence I demonstrate the horizontal body weight row, which is a little different than the other horizontal rowing movements previously offered. With all of the other exercises, your body remained stationary while you pulled an implement toward you. In this exercise, the implement remains stationary and you pull your body toward it. While in theory this may seem the same, these two methods build strength very differently. Learning to move your body more efficiently is extremely beneficial in MMA. In a fight, there are many scenarios where you need to move your body into your opponent, such as when you sit up into your opponent from guard or move toward him to secure a clinch position while on your feet. By performing body weight rows, you develop the type of strength needed to control the fight.

Positioning myself underneath a squat rack, I grip the barbell overhead at slightly wider than shoulder width. Once accomplished, I place my feet on the floor and straighten my body.

As I contract the muscles in my upper back and pull my chest up to the bar, I keep my heels on the ground and flex my core muscles to prevent my back from dipping in the middle.

I relax my arms and lower my body back to the starting position.

SINGLE-ARM HORIZONTAL BODY WEIGHT ROW

In this sequence I demonstrate a one-arm variation of the previous exercise, which comes in handy when your body weight alone no longer provides enough resistance for the two-arm version. In addition to allowing you to double the resistance, it also has some very practical benefits for MMA due to it being a single-arm movement. When in a fight, you seldom perform the same action with both arms at the same time. For example, it is common to secure a single collar tie while striking with your opponent. To prevent him from striking you with his free hands, you must use your collar tie to pull your body close to his, which in turn allows you to establish a dominant clinch position. Performing the single-arm horizontal body weight row will allow you to develop this type of strength.

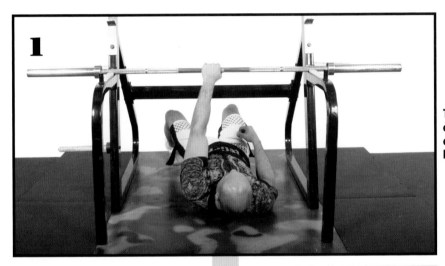

To set up this exercise, I secure a barbell an arm's distance off the floor in a squat rack. Next, I lie underneath it, grip the center of the bar with my left hand, and straighten my body.

Contracting the muscles of my upper back and left arm, I pull my chest up to the bar. Due to my off-centered grip, my core muscles are challenged to keep my spine from twisting or dipping in the middle.

I relax my left arm and lower my body back down to the starting position.

HORIZONTAL PLANE

PARTNER ROW

The movement involved in the partner row is very similar to the movement of the horizontal row shown in the previous technique, but instead of using a barbell, you use a training partner, which comes in handy when a gym isn't available. The exercise is mutually beneficial to both participants. While the person on the bottom develops his latissimus and trapezius muscles through performing the rowing movement, the person on top must isometrically contract his hamstrings, glutes, lower back, upper back, and core to stabilize the rowing movement. Switching positions after a set number of repetitions allows you to work your upper back and develop total-body stabilizing strength.

To begin the exercise, Lance lies on his back and Jake stands over him. Notice how he has one foot on either side of Lance's body. Next, Lance reaches up and grabs Jake's wrists, and Jake braces his body to support the weight.

Lance dynamically contracts his latissimus, rhomboids, biceps, and trapezius muscles in order to pull his back off the ground. Jake isometrically contracts his posterior chain to support Lance's body weight as he moves upward.

After reaching the top of the movement, Lance relaxes his arms and upper back and lowers his back toward the floor. Jake continues to isometrically contract his posterior chain to support Lance as he descends. If this variation is too difficult, it's possible for the athlete on the bottom to execute the row from his butt rather than his feet. This will increase the leverage the arms have to move the torso, and reduce the amount of total weight rowed by the person on the bottom.

STANDING ROW WITH FLEX BANDS

In this sequence I demonstrate how to perform a standing row using a flex band. Although it can be difficult to perform heavy lifts with this exercise, the flex band provides a smooth resistance as it stretches, making it a relatively gentle workout for the upper body. If you have a shoulder or elbow injury, it's a great exercise to perform to slowly work back into the mix. It's also an excellent exercise to perform at the end of a workout to add a little more volume to your pulling routine.

1

To set up this exercise, I wrap the flex band around the vertical bar of a squat rack, grip each end of the band in one hand, and then walk backward until all slack in the band is removed. Notice how my knees are bent, my back is straight, and I'm leaning slightly back.

2

Maintaining a neutral grip on the flex band, I pull my arms toward my body by contracting the muscles of my upper back and arms.

3

Relaxing my arms, I allow the flex band to pull my arms away from my body until I have reached the starting position.

PULL-UP WITH PRONATED GRIP

The pull-up is an extremely powerful exercise because it recruits nearly every muscle in your upper body. When you establish a wide grip on the bar as I do in the sequence below, the primary movers will be your latissimus dorsi, traps, and rhomboids, but if you choose a slightly narrower grip, your pectoral and biceps muscles can be powerful movers as well. Those with weak upper bodies can experience massive gains by including pull-ups into their routine. There is little need for including any other fancy vertical pulling exercises—progressing in the pull-up can give you all the results you want from your vertical pulling movements.

1) I place a barbell on the top rung of a squat rack, establish my grips slightly wider than shoulder width, and then bend my knees so that my body does not touch the floor. It is important to notice that my palms are facing away from my body, which places the emphasis of the workload on my back. **2)** I powerfully contract my latissimus dorsi muscles and pull my body straight up until my chin is positioned over the barbell. **3)** Relaxing my arms, I lower my body back down to the starting position.

PULL-UP WITH SUPINATED GRIP

In this sequence I demonstrate a pull-up with a supinated, or inverted, grip. Instead of grabbing the bar so that your palms are facing away from you, as you did in the previous exercise, you grab the bar so that your palms are facing toward you. This removes much of the workload from your back and places it on your arms, primarily your biceps. This variation is no better or worse than the previous one—it's just different. As I mentioned before, it is important to constantly switch up your workout routine to prevent from plateauing.

1) I place a barbell on the top rung of a squat rack, establish a grip slightly narrower than shoulder width, and curl my legs back at the knees to prevent my body from touching the floor. It is important to notice that in this version, my palms are facing toward me, which shifts the emphasis to my arms. **2)** I powerfully contract my lat and biceps muscles and pull my body straight up until my chin is positioned above the bar. **3)** Relaxing my arms, I lower my body back down to the starting position.

LYING DUMBBELL PULL-OVER

The dumbbell pull-over is a great strength-building tool for the muscles of the upper back and shoulders. It adds volume to the trapezius, rhomboid, and deltoid muscle groups. While it's a great motion to develop the upper back, as well as help bring up any weak spots in your shoulders after your main pulling exercises are completed, it puts the shoulders in a position of great mechanical inefficiency. Because of this, I tend to perform it using lighter weight and as more of a supplemental movement to my pulling routine. In the sequence below, I demonstrate how to perform the dumbbell pull-over with your back on a bench to allow for a full range of motion.

To set up this exercise, I place my upper back across the width of a bench, place my feet on the floor in front of me, wrap the web of each thumb around the pole of a dumbbell, and then extend my arms directly over my chest.

1

I rotate my shoulders back and relax my triceps, allowing my elbows to bend. With this movement, the dumbbell rotates, moving over my head and toward the floor.

2

I rotate my shoulders forward and contract my triceps muscles, bringing the dumbbell back over my head. By extending my arms fully I'm now holding the weight directly over my chest once again.

3

FRONTAL PLANE

ROPE CLIMB

While the pull-up is possibly the best overall pulling exercise for developing your upper-body, it can't match the benefits of the rope climb for developing the muscles of your upper arms. The closer you position your arms toward your centerline when conducting pulling exercises, the more your arms become involved. The same is true when you establish a neutral grip with your palms facing each other. As you can see in the photos below, the rope climb requires a very narrow, neutral grip, making the arms a very important mover in the exercise. In addition to challenging your biceps muscles, the rope climb increases grip strength as well, which is extremely important in the sport of MMA. When looking at the photos, it is important to notice that I do not use my feet to help climb the rope as they do in the army. This would defeat the purpose and shift much of the workload away from the arms. Instead, I let my feet dangle below me. By performing the rope climb in this manner, you will most likely experience a dramatic strength increase in your arms.

1) I stand next to the rope fastened to the ceiling and grip it above my head using my right hand.

2) Maintaining a solid grip, I contract my right biceps muscle and pull my entire body upward. This allows me to move my left hand over my right and establish a higher grip on the rope. Notice how I do not use my legs to help me climb.

3) I powerfully contact my left biceps and pull my body upward. This time, I move my right hand over my left to establish a higher grip. It is important to note that while pulling yourself up, your entire body weight will be supported with a single arm.

4) I continue to alternate my grips and pull myself upward until I reach the top of the rope. Once accomplished, I must reverse my movement and slowly lower myself back toward the mat. It is important to mention that the eccentric motion is very taxing on your upper arms, and the constant gripping is extremely challenging on your lower arms.

BICEPS CURLS

The biceps curl is an isolation exercise that focuses on the flexion of the elbow joint, which is accomplished by contracting your biceps brachii. While biceps curls should play a relatively small role in your routine, its benefits should not be overlooked. Isolation exercises of this nature force the entire load of the movement onto a single muscle. This puts a great amount of stress onto that muscle, causing localized growth. Sometimes after an injury, focusing on a single muscle can be beneficial for rehab purposes. Personally, I add biceps curls in at the end of my routine to add extra volume to the upper body, and I use lighter weights with higher repetitions. This allows me to increase the strength in my upper arms without placing much stress on the rest of my body.

DUMBBELL CURL

Jake begins in the standing position with a dumbbell in each hand and a neutral grip. Even though the biceps curl can be done while sitting, it's better to stand because it keeps the entire body active while the arms are in motion.

Jake flexes his elbows by contracting his biceps while at the same time externally rotating his shoulders. This places more tension on the biceps muscles, allowing them to fully contract at the peak of the movement.

Jake relaxes his biceps muscles and allows his elbows to extend. At the same time, he internally rotates his shoulders and allows his hands to return to a neutral grip.

 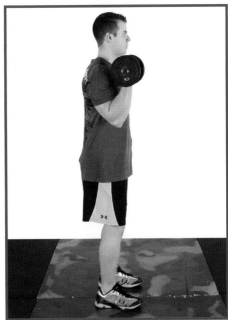 

FRONTAL PLANE

ALTERNATING DUMBBELL CURL

Jake begins in the standing position with a dumbbell in each hand and a neutral grip. However, in this exercise he will flex one arm at a time, allowing each arm to work independently of each other.

Jake contracts his right biceps while externally rotating his right shoulder. He curls the dumbbell in his right hand until it reaches his shoulder.

Jake now lowers the right dumbbell by extending his right elbow joint. As it returns to his side, he mirrors the motion on the left side of his body, curling the left dumbbell. This single-arm motion isolates each individual biceps even more, as 100 percent of your focus is dedicated to a single biceps on each repetition.

BARBELL CURL

The biceps curl can also be done with a barbell instead of dumbbells. To perform the exercise, Jake grabs a barbell with both hands, assumes a supinated grip, and curls the barbell up to his shoulders. Because each biceps is working in unison to move the same implement, the total weight on the barbell curl is heavier than individual dumbbell curls. However, this comes at the expense of less isolation to the individual biceps muscles.

SECTION FIVE
CORE

Both the upper and lower body are capable of powerful movements in their own right. But for maximum power development, the upper and lower body need to work in unison and combine their effort. For this to happen an athlete needs to have an extremely powerful core. The term core is used to describe the muscles surrounding the midline, or spinal column, of the body. Muscles generally associated with core strength are the rectus abdominis (the abs), the obliques (side abs), the transverse abdominus (TVA), and even the erector spinae (the spinal erectors). These muscles are challenged with preventing undesired midline flexion or rotation. Simply put, having a powerful core is necessary in order to transmit force. Your core muscles perform a function similar to the driveshaft in your car. They allow the power generated in the "engine" to be transmitted to the "wheels." If you have a solid core, it will allow movement generated in your legs to be transferred up the body to your arms and vice versa.

The carryover is obvious for an MMA fighter. The entire stand-up game revolves around having a powerful midsection. As often mentioned in this book, the power for any strike begins in the legs and travels upward. However without a strong midsection, you will be unable to transmit the force generated in the legs upward into the fists or elbows. The same is true of many wrestling maneuvers. For a double-leg pick-up, the legs must transmit power up the body, allowing the arms to lift your opponent off the mat. But without a powerful core, as your legs drive upward, your torso will simply fold in the middle, preventing you from lifting your opponent and compromising the takedown.

The muscles of the core also serve another purpose. Aside from stabilizing the spine and preventing midline flexion or rotation, the core muscles can also initiate movement in the lumbar and thoracic spinal column. The abs,

obliques, and spinal erectors can be fired to actively move the spine in various directions. Spinal extension, flexion, lateral flexion, and rotation are all movements powered directly by the core muscles. This is another critical aspect of the core that is vital to performance in MMA. Sitting up in the guard for a kimura is one situation in which the abs initiate spinal flexion. Without a powerful set of abs, any attempt you make to sit up in guard and begin an attack will be nullified by your stronger opponent. Another example is the hip throw. Before completing a hip throw you must turn your hips into your opponent by powerfully contracting your oblique muscles to rapidly twist your hips.

Keeping these two competing but opposite goals in mind, the training of the core muscles must be approached from these two different angles. The first section of this chapter focuses on using the core to initiate movement in the four articulations previously mentioned (flexion, extension, lateral flexion, and rotation). The chapter starts with the quintessential abdominal flexion exercise, the crunch. After I explore several crunch variations with increasing intensities, I move on to more challenging ab flexion exercises. Some of the exercises become more challenging as I move a higher percentage of my own body weight with my abs, as in the V-up, while in other exercises I use an external load to challenge my abs, such as a medicine ball. In some exercises shown in this section, I do a variation of both, as in the decline sit-up with medicine ball.

The next section focuses on spinal rotation and lateral flexion. These two movements are often overlooked in many athletes' core training programs, but they are of critical importance. I begin with simple rotational movements, demonstrating several body-weight exercises one can use to develop the oblique muscles, such as the scorpion and the windshield wipers. I then move on to various weighted movements such as Russian twists using different objects to vary the intensity. After covering many different ways to train the rotational movement of the core, I demonstrate lateral flexion exercises. Again I start the section with the simplest body-weight movements, such as oblique crunches, and then escalate the intensity with heavy-loaded movements as the section comes to a close.

The next section in this chapter spotlights movements that resist spinal flexion and rotation. All of these movements have a single goal in mind: to keep the spine as neutral as possible throughout the exercise. This means that the back will be neither flexed nor extended. It will be in its natural position throughout the techniques, regardless of the amount of weight it's being forced to support. Much like the previous section, I begin showing various positions utilizing only my body weight to load my core muscles. This is one type of training that will humble many athletes. It's quite common to find extremely strong fighters unable to hold simple body-weight core exercises, such as the plank or the superman, for long periods of time. Although there is very little movement involved, exercises such as these very rapidly fatigue your core muscles and leave you trembling after a short period of time. I show many progressions of these simple exercises, allowing you to increase the intensity until you finally move on to using an external load. This section closes with several variations of the most difficult ab exercise around, the ab wheel roll out. This simple tool can train the abs in ways unmatched by other methods. And with a simple change in foot placement, this single core exercise can go from being a rep movement to being a max-effort movement.

The human spine is broken down into three different sections. While the bottom two portions of the spine, the lumbar and the thoracic, were thoroughly covered in the prior sections, there is another portion we've yet to cover. The cervical spine, or the neck, is another pivotal section of the torso that needs developing. As I mentioned in the previous sections, midline stability is a necessary element for a healthy, successful fighter. And without stability in the neck joint, your hard work developing the rest of your body will be in vain. While it may seem like a relatively small area to focus on, it is subject to a huge amount of strain in each fight. On the defensive side of the coin, the majority of the strikes in MMA are focused on the head. Each time a punch, kick, elbow, or knee lands to the head, the neck must absorb the impact. A strong neck is the most important physical asset for having a strong "chin." On an offensive slant, the head is the critical "third arm" used in

clinch situations as well as on the ground. A great wrestler will always use his head to control his opponent and push him into the desired position. Fighting for head position is one of the most important elements to winning the clinch fight, and without a strong neck, you will be vulnerable to having your head coerced into an inferior position.

To build a powerful neck and complete the chain of spinal stability, the final section in this chapter aims to realize more powerful neck muscles. There are literally dozens of different muscles attached to the base of the spine and involved in neck and cervical spine articulations. However the sternocleidomastoids, the scalene muscles, and the splenius muscles are the prime movers of the neck joint. In this section I will show some of the exercises I use to keep my neck strong while at the same time keeping my cervical spine healthy and pain free. Just like in the previous sections, I begin with body-weight movements. The section starts with the simple wrestler's bridge variations used in high school wrestling gymnasiums all throughout the country. Then the section progresses to externally loaded movements used to increase the strength and power of the neck. My coach, Jake Bonacci, shows several different possible ways to use weight plates to train the neck in flexion, extension, and lateral flexion. Remember that the neck is just another section of the spine and needs to be trained the same way as the abdominal muscles. Elements both of resisting movement and initiating movement must be duplicated in training in order to increase the overall strength of the neck joint in a balanced, healthy manner.

While it often goes unnoticed, the core is the most used muscle grouping in any fight. Every movement, whether standing or on the mat, must utilize the core to keep the spine stable and to effectively transfer force where it's needed. It's easy to overlook the core during your strength training sessions, but it's absolutely necessary to train these muscles in order to fight to your full potential. This section goes over some of my favorite, and some of the best, exercises available for developing your core.

ABDOMINAL CRUNCH

The abdominal crunch is the most basic spinal flexion training movement, but it is also one of the safest. If you look at the photos below, you'll notice that your lower back stays supported on the floor throughout the duration of the movement, which leaves little chance of spinal hyperextension. This is a big risk factor when performing un-supported sit-ups and can result in injury to the spinal column. While the abdominal crunch is a great exercise and standard in many strength-and-conditioning routines around the world, it does have its limitations. With only a small percentage of the body being elevated off the ground in each repetition, the impact on the abdominals is minimal. However, by raising your feet off the ground, it makes the movement more challenging as your abdominals must not only raise your upper body off the floor, but also isometrically support your elevated legs. Despite the limitations, the abdominal crunch has a place in my workout routine. I use the exercise as a part of my warm-up and perform them in high repetition during drilling sessions to build endurance in my core.

To begin the exercise, Jake lies on his back, places his hands on the sides of his head, and elevates his legs to make the movement more challenging.

Jake flexes his abdominals and raises his upper back off the ground until his elbows touch his legs. Note that he does not raise his lower back off the floor, as it would present a high degree of risk in lumbar spinal hyperextension.

Jake relaxes his abdominals and lowers his upper back down to the floor. Even as his upper back touches down, his transverse abdominals are still working to keep his legs steady in the air. This maintains the intra-abdominal pressure in between reps, keeping Jake's spine safe and injury free.

LEG SCISSOR CRUNCH

Crunches are an excellent way to train your abdominal muscles, but for many people they are too easy to perform. Personally, I like to do my crunches in conjunction with a leg scissor to increase the work load placed upon my abdominals. To accomplish this, I'll straighten my legs out in front of me, keep one leg hovering a few inches off the floor, elevate the other one vertically, and then perform my crunch into my elevated leg. Utilizing this form has several benefits. By extending my legs, my abdominals are not only tasked with pulling my shoulders forward, but also holding my legs off the ground, which adds more difficultly. And by raising one leg upward, my oblique muscles are tasked with preventing my spine from twisting as I perform my crunch. Although this is an exceptional exercise, it's slightly advanced. If you are new to abdominal training, I recommend starting with the normal crunch where both of your feet are flat on the floor.

Lying flat on my back, I place my hands on the sides of my head, extend my right leg, lift my right heel off the mat, and elevate my left leg vertically by flexing my hip.

Flexing my abdominal muscles, I elevate my shoulder blades off the floor and pull my chest toward my left knee. Notice how my upper back is rounded and my lower back remains on the ground.

I drop my shoulders to the mat and lower my left leg so that my heel is suspended a few inches off the mat. At the same time, I elevate my right leg vertically by contracting my right hip flexors.

I repeat the crunching motion by flexing my abdominals, lifting my shoulders off the floor, and pulling my chest toward my right knee. By switching sides, the oblique muscles on both side of my body are taxed as they prevent my torso from twisting as my shoulders elevate.

CRUNCH ON SWISS BALL

In this sequence I demonstrate how to add difficulty to the crunch by incorporating a Swiss ball and flex band. The normal crunch is primarily a contraction of the abdominal muscles, but when you perform the same movement on an unstable surface such as the Swiss ball, your entire core is forced to flex statically to stabilize your back. Once you get comfortable with this new exercise, you might find that you need added resistance. An excellent way to accomplish this is to hold one end of a flex band in your hands and have your training partner hold the other while standing behind you. As you move forward and away from your partner, the tension increases on the band, adding resistance to the crunch. Depending upon how much resistance you need, your opponent can stand closer or farther away. There are many situations in MMA competition that require both dynamic and isometric contractions of the core muscles, making exercises such as this one extremely beneficial.

1

I lie on my back on top of the Swiss ball, place my feet flat on the floor, and put my hands on the sides of my head. Notice how my legs are bent at a ninety-degree angle.

2

Flexing my abdominal muscles, I lift my shoulders off the Swiss ball. As I execute the crunch, my obliques and hips statically flex to prevent my body from rolling off the ball.

3

I relax my abdominal muscles and lower my shoulders back onto the Swiss ball. It is important to mention that I do not hyperextend my back as I come down. The instant my back is straight, I retighten my abdominal muscles to prevent my spine from curving backward.

FLEX BAND–RESISTED CRUNCH ON SWISS BALL

1 I lie on my back on a Swiss ball, place my feet flat on the floor, and grip the ends of a flex band in my hands. In this scenario, my training partner stands behind me and holds the flex band taut, but it is also possible to secure it around an immovable object.

2 I contract my abdominal muscles and lift my shoulders off the Swiss ball. As my torso rises, the tension in the flex band increases, adding difficulty to the movement. Notice how I position my arms out in front of me to prevent the band from digging into my neck.

3 Relaxing my abdominal muscles, I lower my shoulders back down and return to the starting position. Notice how there is no backward curvature in my spine.

CRUNCHES WITH THAI PAD

In this sequence I demonstrate an old-school crunch exercise. While the movement is the same as the traditional crunch, having your training partner whack your stomach with a Thai pad at the top of each repetition totally changes the game. To prevent from getting the wind knocked out of you, you must maximally contract your abdominal muscles with every crunch. If you get lazy and fail to flex your abdominals tight, you will be in for some unpleasantness. Personally, I feel this is a very practical exercise for fighters because it not only builds core strength, but it also prepares you physically and psychologically for absorbing punishing body shots. For decades boxers and Muay Thai practitioners have utilized this exercise to toughen up their midsection, and it works just as well for mixed martial artists. It is important to note that while it is possible to use a focus mitt for this exercise, I recommend a sturdy Thai pad. Considerably heavier, it mimics a punch rather than a slap.

1 Lying on my back, I cross my legs, elevate my feet off the floor, and place my hands on the sides of my head. My training partner kneels by my side with the Thai pad positioned above my abdomen.

2 I contract my abdominal muscles and lift my shoulders off the floor. At the top of my crunch, my training partner slams the Thai pad down into my stomach. To absorb the impact, I keep my abdominals flexed tight.

3 I relax my abdominals and lower my shoulders back down to the floor.

V-UP

The V-up is one of the most challenging body-weight abdominal exercises available. When performed correctly, your abdominals are forced to lift nearly your entire body weight off the floor. Although it is a simple movement, it requires a tremendous amount of strength. If you are not a well-conditioned athlete, I recommend building up your abdominal muscles using some of the other techniques in this section before incorporating the V-up into your training regimen. The key to success with this exercise is utilizing proper form, and this is can be very difficult to accomplish for beginners. Note that in the photos I alternate between touching the inside of my toes and the outside of my toes with the tips of my fingers. This forces me to achieve maximum depth as I reach across my body and touch the sides of my feet, rather than just simply touching the tips of my toes. I alternate positions simply to prevent my body from adapting to one movement pattern. In exercises like this, a small amount of variation can go a long way to prevent the body from adapting too quickly. As I alternate grips, the muscles fire in a slightly different pattern, making the exercise more challenging from rep to rep.

Lying flat on my back, I extend my arms over my head and straighten my legs.

Contracting my abdominal and hip flexor muscles, I elevate my legs and arms vertically. At the top of the movement, I touch the outside of my feet with my fingers. Notice how I keep both my arms and legs perfectly straight.

After touching my toes, I relax my abdominal muscles and slowly lower my legs and arms.

I once again contract my abdominal and hip flexor muscles to elevate my legs and arms vertically. This time, I touch the inside of my feet with the tips of my fingers.

PIKE

Although the V-up is an excellent abdominal and hip flexion exercise, the obliques are not challenged because there is no side-to-side movement. To ensure your obliques get a proper workout, it's good to add the pike into the mix every once in a while. If you look at the photos below, you'll notice that this is accomplished by elevating one leg and touching your toes with the fingers of your opposite hand. In order to bring your foot and fingers together in this fashion, you must slightly twist your torso, which employs your obliques. The exercise doesn't place as much strain on your abdominals because you're not elevating both arms and legs off the floor at the same time, but the oblique workout you receive makes up for this weakness. As long as you employ this exercise with the other techniques demonstrated in this section, your abdominal training won't be lacking.

1 I lie flat on my back, straighten my arms above my head, and extend my legs.

2 I elevate my right leg and left arm by contracting my abdominal and right hip flexor muscles. As I bring my fingertips toward my toes, my obliques contract to twist my torso slightly to the right.

3 I relax my abdominal muscles and slowly lower my right leg and left arm, returning to the starting position.

4 I switch sides by elevating my left leg and right arm. It is important to notice that I keep my left arm outstretched over my head to create an additional load on my rectus abdominis muscles.

5 I lower my left leg and right arm, completing one repetition.

STRAIGHT-LEG SIT-UP WITH MEDICINE BALL

In this sequence I demonstrate a simple sit-up variation that utilizes external weight. If you look at the photos below, you'll notice that I keep a medicine ball elevated above me as I perform my sit-up, which provides added resistance for my abdominals to overcome. You'll also notice that I employ a straight-leg position rather than a bent-leg position to counterbalance the weight of the medicine ball. If you keep your legs bent, you won't have the leverage needed to reach the sit-up position. Although it is possible to substitute a dumbbell for the medicine ball, I do not recommend it. The exercise requires you to suspend the weight over your face, and if it should fall during your repetitions, a medicine ball is a lot more forgiving than a metal dumbbell.

With a medicine ball in my hands, I lie flat on my back, extend my legs, and straighten my arms above me. Notice how the ball is positioned directly above my chest.

Flexing my abdominal muscles, I perform a sit-up by lifting my shoulders and back off the floor. Notice how I keep the medicine ball positioned over my chest.

Reaching the top of my sit-up, my abdominals are fully contracted and my body has formed an L-shape. To maintain my balance, I have positioned the medicine ball directly over my head and hips.

Relaxing my abdominal muscles, I slowly lower my shoulders back to the floor and position the medicine ball above my chest.

ABDOMINAL FLEXION

VERTICAL MEDICINE BALL PASS

In this sequence I demonstrate a handy abdominal exercise that requires a medicine ball and a training partner. To perform this exercise, stand back-to-back with your partner, pass the ball to him over your head, and then receive the ball from between your legs. The challenge is to overcome the weight of the medicine ball while extending and contracting your abdominals. Once you have completed a set number of full circles with the ball, it is important to reverse the direction so that both you and your partner have a chance to pass the ball over your head and under your legs. Personally, I like doing this drill before or after a training session when I'm already paired up with a partner and we both feel like doing some supplemental abdominal work.

1 I stand back-to-back with my training partner with approximately a foot and a half of space between us. I'm holding a medicine ball in front of my body using both of my hands

2 I bend backward, extend my arms over my head, and pass the medicine ball to my training partner's waiting hands.

3 After my training partner receives the ball, I begin bending forward at the waist and lowering my arms.

4 I contract my abdominals, bend forward at the waist, and reach my arms between my legs to receive the ball from my training partner. Notice how I have kept my legs straight.

5 In control of the medicine ball again, I return to the starting position by extending my abdominals and straightening my body. After doing a set number of repetitions, we will switch directions.

DECLINE SIT-UP WITH MEDICINE BALL TOSS

In this sequence I demonstrate an exercise that helps you develop more explosive force in your abdominals. While it takes a bit of equipment—a training partner, a medicine ball, and a decline bench—it's one of the more effective ways to increase the power of your core muscles. If you look at the photos below, you'll notice that the base movement is a decline sit-up. Although decline sit-ups are an extremely challenging movement, catching a medicine ball on your decent turns it into a strenuous plyometric movement. The goal is to absorb the weight of the medicine ball using your abdominals, and then immediately rebound upward and toss the ball back to your partner. Unlike other abdominal training methods, this exercise doesn't increase the endurance or isometric potential of your abdominals. It is geared toward increasing the power and speed at which your abdominals can contract. Due to the demanding nature of this technique, it should only be employed after you've developed a base level of core strength. If you cannot perform the exercise without hyperextending your back, you aren't ready to include it in your regimen.

1 I assume the sit-up position on a decline bench and position my arms out in front of me. My training partner stands before me with a medicine ball in his hands.

2 I begin lowering my shoulders toward the bench. This action cues my training partner to toss the ball to me. To receive it, I elevate my arms and position my palms out.

3 As I catch the ball, my abdominal muscles powerfully contract to absorb the additional weight. Rather than pause as I receive the medicine ball, I continue a smooth descent by lowering my shoulders toward the bench.

4 I lower my back to the bench and move the medicine ball toward the back of my head.

5 Without hesitating at the bottom, I powerfully contract my abdominals, elevate my shoulders to the upright position, and move the medicine ball in front of my body.

6 Using my forward momentum, I release the ball and toss it into my training partner's hands. It is important to note that this pass is more like a shot-put than a basketball pass. Instead of my arms doing the work, I use my abdominals to generate the momentum that carries the ball through the air and to my partner.

PARTNER SIT-UP

In this sequence I demonstrate an exercise that challenges the core muscles of both you and your training partner. To perform this drill, jump guard on your standing training partner, have him wrap his arms tightly around your legs, drop back until you assume an extreme decline position, and then sit-up into his body. Once accomplished, return to your feet and catch your partner as he jumps guard on you. In addition to getting an excellent abdominal workout while doing your decline sit-ups, you also get an intense workout while playing the part of the pillar. To keep from falling over as your partner does his sit-up, you must isometrically contract your entire body. Personally, I like doing this exercise before or after practice when I am already paired up with a training partner. However, to prevent injury and ensure you both get an adequate workout, it is important that your partner be similar in weight.

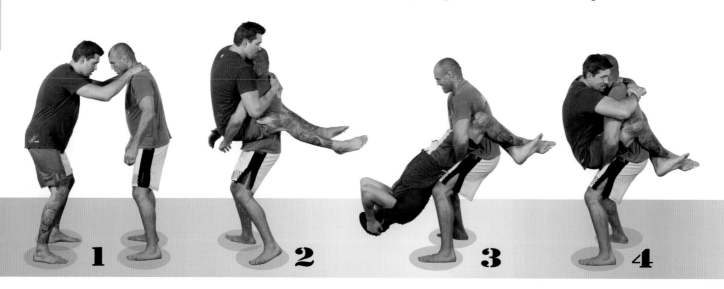

1) Standing face-to-face with my training partner a few feet apart, he places his hands on my shoulders and prepares to jump guard by bending his knees. 2) As I brace for the impact, my training partner jumps into me and wraps his legs and arms around my body to catch himself. Immediately I hook my arms around the back of his legs to support his weight. 3) As I clasp my hands together around the back of my partner's legs, he unhooks his arms from around my body and lowers his shoulders toward the mat. To counterbalance his weight, I flex every muscle in my back, legs, arms, and core. It is important to notice that my partner does not allow his spine to bend backward. 4) Using his abdominal muscles, my partner elevates his shoulders up to mine and then wraps his arms around my body to support his weight. 5) I release my control over my training partner's hips and he drops his feet to the mat, returning to the starting position. Immediately I place my hands on his shoulders and prepare to jump guard. 6) I jump into my training partner and wrap my legs around his body. To support my weight, he hooks his arms around the back of my legs. 7) With my training partner supporting my weight, I release control of his shoulders and lower my shoulders slowly toward the mat. It is important to note that I contract my abdominal muscles to prevent my spine from bending backward. 8) I powerfully contract my abdominal muscles and perform a sit-up to elevate my shoulders up to my training partner's shoulders. Once accomplished, I wrap my arms around his body to support my weight. We will continue alternating this exercise until we reach a set number of repetitions.

BENCH-SUPPORTED LEG LIFT

In this sequence I demonstrate an exercise that allows you to train your abdominal muscles without bending your back, which is ideal if you have spine problems. When performed correctly, your abdominals flex in the same way as when you do crunches. The only difference is that instead of keeping your legs in a fixed position and bending your torso, you keep your torso in a fixed position and bend your legs. When studying the photos below, it is important to notice that I have positioned by butt off the end of the bench and at no point do I drop my legs below my torso. Both of these details are imperative for receiving an adequate workout. It is also important to note that the legs are not nearly as heavy as the torso. To receive the same type of workout as when you do crunches, you might need to perform additional repetitions.

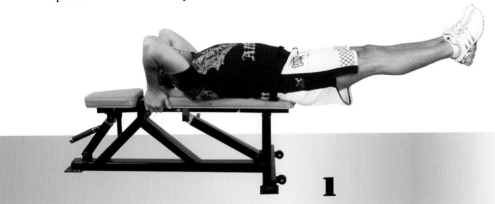

1

Lying flat on a bench press with my butt hanging off the end, I grab the sides of the bench above my head with my hands and extend my legs perfectly straight. It is important to note that because there is nothing holding up the weight of my lower body, I statically contract the muscles of my back to prevent my legs from dipping below my torso.

2

I elevate my legs to the vertical position by contracting my abdominal muscles.

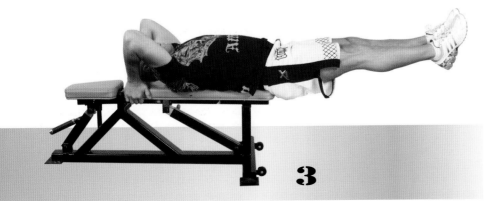

3

I relax my abdominal muscles and lower my legs to the horizontal position. Again, it is important to notice that I do not allow my legs to dip down below my torso. This is an excellent workout for people with back injuries because your spine is not forced to move during the entire exercise. All movement is located at the hip joint.

SINGLE-ARM-SUPPORTED LEG LIFT

This is a variation of the leg lift shown in the previous sequence. The movement is the same—you lie flat on a weight bench and flex your abdominals to raise your legs vertically. The only difference here is that you hold the bench with one hand rather than two, which causes your torso to naturally twist as you elevate your legs. To prevent this twisting action and keep your spine stable, you must flex you oblique muscles. In addition to making the leg lift more challenging, it also saves time by combining your abdominal and oblique work into one exercise. Just as with the previous leg lift variation, it is important to position your butt off the end of the bench and not drop your legs below your torso.

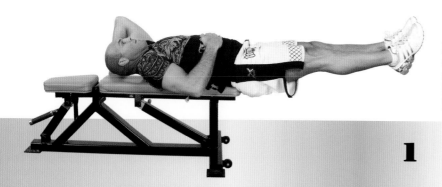

Lying flat on a bench press with my butt hanging off the end, I grab the left side of the bench above my head using my left hand and place my right hand on my abdomen. To prevent my legs from dipping below my torso, I statically contract my spine.

1

I elevate my legs by dynamically flexing my abdominal muscles. Due to the uneven support, my torso attempts to twist to the side as my legs rise. To keep my spine stable, I contract my oblique muscles.

2

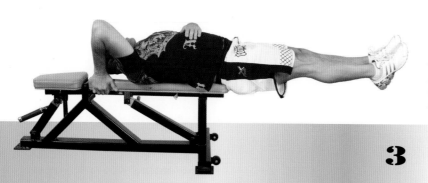

I lower my legs to the horizontal position, grab the right side of the bench using my right hand, and then place my left hand on my abdomen. This ensures that the oblique muscles on both sides of my body are taxed. From here, I will elevate my legs once again.

3

SEATED RUSSIAN TWIST

In this sequence I demonstrate a trunk rotation exercise that strengthens your abdominal and oblique muscles. The movement is simple. Sitting on your butt, you cross your legs at the ankles, elevate your legs off the floor, and then move a medicine ball from one side of your body to the other. Although your obliques are responsible for the twisting of your torso, what makes this exercise really challenging is the fact that your feet are elevated off the mat. When you have your legs on the mat, they stabilize your entire body, making twisting movements much easier to accomplish. When you lift them off the mat, that stabilization isn't there. Not only does this make moving the medicine ball from one side of your body to the other more difficult, but it also requires your rectus abdominis muscles to support the weight of your legs. I highly recommend adding this exercise into your training regimen because it makes you more powerful in twisting movements, which are heavily utilized in fighting. You twist when your throw punches and kicks, and you twist when executing a number of sweeps and submissions on the mat. The more powerful you become at twisting your body, the more success you will have in fighting.

1 Sitting on my butt, I cross my legs at the ankles and then elevate them off the floor. At the same time, I grip a medicine ball in both hands and position it to my left side by twisting my torso.

2 Contracting my right oblique muscles, I twist my torso, move the medicine ball over my legs, and position it on my right side. Notice how my legs are still straight and my feet are off the floor.

3 I contract my left oblique muscles, move the medicine ball over my legs, and reposition it on my left side. This completes one repetition.

ROTATIONAL

HORIZONTAL MEDICINE BALL PASS

In this sequence I demonstrate a partner drill that develops your oblique muscles. To perform this drill, stand back-to-back with your partner and pass a medicine ball back and forth. Instead of delivering the ball to him over your head, as demonstrated in an earlier exercise, you twist your torso and deliver it to the side. Although your obliques are tasked with both the passing and receiving of the ball, to get the most out of this exercise, it is good to switch directions. This can be done either after a set number of reps or a set amount of time.

1

I'm standing back-to-back with my partner a few feet apart. I'm holding a medicine ball in front of my body using both of my hands.

2

I twist my torso in a clockwise direction by contracting my right oblique muscles. At the same time, my training partner twists in a counterclockwise direction. As our hands come together, I pass him the medicine ball.

3

Immediately after passing off the ball, I begin rotating my torso in a counterclockwise direction while my training partner rotates his torso in a clockwise direction.

4

Continuing with our rotations, my training partner passes the medicine ball back to me as our hands come together.

5

After I receive the medicine ball, I contract my right side obliques and once again begin rotating my torso in a clockwise direction.

6

I pass the ball off to my training partner, completing one repetition. After a set number of repetitions, we will reverse the direction to train both obliques equally.

STANDING RUSSIAN TWIST

This exercise is very similar to the previous one. From a standing position, I rotate my torso from side to side, causing my oblique muscles to contract. However, instead of passing a medicine ball off to a partner, I utilize a weight plate and perform the movement solo. While the medicine ball partner drill allows me to do a high number of repetitions due to the minimal weight and the rest period between the passing and receiving of the ball, this solo exercise allows me to dramatically increase the weight I'm holding, which in turn increases oblique strength. Personally, I feel it is important to do both types of drills. Developing stamina is important because in most fights you need to employ twisting movements hundreds of times, both while throwing strikes on your feet and while executing techniques on the ground. However, it is just as important to be explosive in your twisting movements when executing certain techniques, such as bridging escapes.

1) Standing with my feet shoulder width apart, I grip a weight plate and position it in front of my body by extending my arms. Notice how the center of the plate is positioned directly in front of my chest.

2) Contracting my left oblique muscles, I rotate my torso and move the plate in a counterclockwise direction.

3) As I reach the end range of my twisting motion, I relax my left oblique muscles, contract my right oblique muscles, and move the plate in a clockwise direction by twisting my torso.

4) Continuing with my clockwise rotation, I reach the end range of my twisting motion. I will now continue going back and forth until I complete a set number of repetitions.

SCORPION

The abdominals are an important muscle group to train, but you don't always have to use heavy resistance to get a good abdominal workout. In this sequence I demonstrate the scorpion, a simple spinal rotation movement that only requires the weight of the lower body for resistance. Much like other spinal twisting exercises, the scorpion primarily relies on the oblique muscles to power the movement. However, because your legs travel up and laterally, there is also some lower-body involvement to raise your legs, as well as hip flexor involvement in twisting your hips. This makes the scorpion not only a great exercise to work out your oblique muscles, but also a great exercise to warm up your posterior chain and hip flexors. Generally I will use the scorpion near the beginning of my routine to work my core and warm up my hips in preparation for the upcoming power movements. If you look at the photos below, you'll notice that Jake demonstrates two versions of the scorpion. The first is the front version, and the second is the back version. While both variations utilize the obliques to power the movement, the articulation of the hips and the assisting muscles is different. Both variations are useful, so it's best to mix them both into your training routine.

FRONT SCORPION

Jake begins the scorpion lying flat on his stomach with his arms to his side and his legs extended straight back.

Jake initiates the movement by flexing his left glute muscle to raise his left leg off the ground. As he does this, he contracts his oblique muscles to twist his hips and adduct his left leg across his lower back. As his weight shifts, he uses his hands as a base to prevent his upper body from twisting as well.

Jake continues his hip rotation movement until his left leg comes all the way across his body and touches the floor on his right side. In this position his hips are fully twisted to his right and his left foot is on the ground. Jake's hands are still wide to provide a base of support for his upper body.

4

Jake now reverses his movements by pulling his left leg back to the left side of his body, returning to the start position.

5

Jake now performs the scorpion on the opposite side by using his obliques to twist his hips and slowly move his right leg across the midline of his body.

6

Jake's right foot touches the ground on the left side of his body. From here, he will reverse the movement until his legs are once again parallel. This is one complete repetition.

ROTATIONAL

OPTION TWO (FACE-UP SCORPION)

1

Jake begins on his back with his legs straight and his arms extended perpendicular to his body.

2

Jake initiates the exercise by raising his right leg off the floor and twisting his hips until his left leg travels across his body. This movement employs his oblique muscles.

3

Jake continues twisting his hips until his right leg touches the floor on his left side. Notice how both of his shoulders are still flat on the floor.

4

After Jake's foot touches the floor, he begins to reverse the movement by contracting his obliques and twisting his hips in the opposite direction. He keeps his leg extended as it moves back across his body. This provides resistance to his core muscles, forcing them to flex on both the concentric and eccentric motions.

5

Jake lowers his right leg to the floor, returning to the start position.

6

Jake now begins to initiate the scorpion in the opposite direction. He raises his left leg off the ground, contracts his obliques, and begins twisting his hips toward his right.

7

Keeping his leg extended, Jake touches his left foot to the floor on the right side of his body. Notice how he keeps his leg at a perpendicular angle to his body to provide maximum resistance. From here, he will reverse his movements by twisting his hips in the opposite direction and returning to the starting position.

WINDSHIELD WIPERS WITH BARBELL

In this sequence I demonstrate another rotational exercise to challenge your obliques. Lying flat on your back with your legs elevated, you move your legs from one side of your body to the other by rotating your hips. When first starting out, you might want to flatten your arms out to your sides to stabilize your torso. However, over time you should work toward the variation demonstrated below, which involves holding a barbell above your body as you perform the exercise. In addition to being tasked by the side-to-side movement of your legs, your obliques are also challenged with stabilizing your torso and balancing the weight held in your hands.

Lying flat on my back, I grip a barbell in my hands and elevate my arms and legs vertically. Notice how I have my grips at approximately one and a half times my shoulders' width.

Keeping my legs straight and my feet together, I lower my legs toward my left side. To counterbalance my weight, I twist my body slightly toward my right side. It is important to notice that I do not let my feet touch the floor. This requires more control and effort from my oblique muscles.

I contract the oblique muscles on my right side and return my legs to a vertical position. At the same time, I straighten my torso so the barbell is once again horizontal.

I contract my left oblique muscles and slowly lower my legs toward my right side. To counterbalance my weight, I twist my torso slightly toward my left side. Again, it is important to notice that I do not let my feet touch the floor.

I contract my left oblique muscles and elevate my legs back to the vertical position. This completes one repetition.

OBLIQUE CRUNCH

In this sequence I demonstrate the least-challenging oblique exercise in this section. To perform it correctly, lie on your back with your feet on the ground, crunch your body forward to elevate your shoulders off the floor, and then contract your oblique muscles to pull your upper body from one side to the other. Instead of twisting your body, you simply reach your hands toward your heels one at a time. While it is somewhat elementary, it is an excellent exercise to prepare you for some of the more intense side-to-side movements demonstrated in this section.

Lying on my back, I place my feet on the floor, reach my hands down my sides, and elevate my shoulders off the mat by contracting my abdominal muscles.

Keeping my shoulders elevated off the floor, I contract my left oblique muscles and touch my left heel with the tips of my fingers. By touching my heel with each repetition, I can gauge the depth of my movement.

I relax my left oblique muscles and contract my right ones as I touch my right heel with the tips of my right fingers.

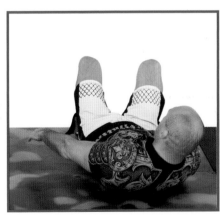

SIDE BEND WITH DUMBBELL

In this sequence I demonstrate how to train your oblique muscles using a side bend. The goal is to load weight onto one side of your body to get your shoulder to dip toward the floor, and then use the oblique muscles on the opposite side of your body to overcome the weight and straighten your posture. Personally, I like to use dumbbells for this exercise because they are compact and easy to grip. In addition to this, most gyms also have a broad assortment of dumbbells, which allows you to adjust your load during a set without having to add or subtract plates. However, it is important to mention that this is not an exercise where you want to lift as much weight as possible. To experience the best results, you want to kept the weight relatively light, execute higher repetitions, and focus on keeping your back perfectly straight. If your spine bends forward or backward during its execution, you increase your chances of injury.

1

Standing with my feet slightly less than shoulder width apart, I grip a dumbbell in my right hand and position my left arm straight down my side. Notice how my back is perfectly straight.

2

I relax my core muscles and allow the dumbbell to slowly pull my right shoulder toward the floor. Instead of hunching forward, I have bent at the waist.

3

I lower my left shoulder and straighten my posture by dynamically flexing my left oblique muscles. This completes one repetition. After a set number of reps, I will switch the dumbbell to my left hand and repeat the process.

SUITCASE DEADLIFT

This exercise is different from the side bend in that instead of moving your torso by dynamically contracting your oblique muscles, you isometrically contract your oblique muscles to prevent your torso from moving. They both train your oblique muscles, just in a different way. If you look at the photos, you'll notice that I squat down and lift a heavy weight positioned at my side. With the weight offset, it attempts to pull one shoulder downward as I increase my elevation. Instead of letting that happen, I keep my torso upright and stable by powerfully contracting my oblique muscles. The primary goal of the core muscles is to keep your spine stable, and this exercise increases your ability to accomplish this. Although this is a good enough reason to make the suitcase deadlift a regular part of your training regimen, it also increases your grip strength and taxes the muscles in your legs and back.

I position myself to the side of a barbell loaded with weight, squat down by bending my knees and hips, grip the center of the barbell in my right hand, and position my left hand at my side. Notice how both of my shoulders are on the same level and my back is not curved.

I stand straight up, lifting the barbell using my right hand. As the weight lifts off the ground, the barbell attempts to pull my right shoulder toward the mat. To keep my spine straight, I powerfully contract my left oblique muscles.

I lower the barbell to the floor by bending my knees and hips. It is important to mention that I keep my left oblique muscles isometrically contracted during my descent to keep my back straight. After a set number of repetitions, I will switch to the other side and lift the barbell using my left hand.

ALTERNATING TWO-POINT PLANK

As I mentioned, one of the most important functions of the core muscles is to keep the spine stable. The best way to train this function is to stabilize the spine in extremely challenging positions, which is what you accomplish in the exercise demonstrated in this sequence. If you look at the first photo below, you'll notice that I am balanced on my feet and forearms. With my two points of base being at the extreme ends of my body, my back naturally wants to dip down in the middle. By challenging myself to keep my back flat for a set period of time, I become stronger at keeping my spine stabilized. This exercise is known as the standard plank, and if it isn't challenging enough, you can add the two-point plank into the mix. This is accomplished by balancing on an opposite arm and foot. This adds twisting force to your torso, which you must resist as well. Personally, I like to hold the standard plank for a set period of time, switch to the two-point plank on my left arm, return to the standard plank, and then execute the two-point plank by balancing on my right arm. This is a challenging body-weight exercise that makes your obliques and transverse abdominis more adept at resisting spinal flexion, which makes you less prone to injury.

To perform the standard plank, I place my forearms on the floor so that my elbows are directly below my shoulders, straighten my body, and support the weight of my lower body on my toes. It is important to note that in order to keep my back level, I am isometrically flexing my transverse abdominal muscles.

To make the standard plank more challenging, I elevate my right arm and left leg off the floor. This imparts a twisting force on to my torso, which I resist by flexing my oblique muscles. The goal is to prevent my back from dipping in the middle by keeping it perfectly level. I will hold this position for several seconds before returning to the standard plank position.

3

I return my right forearm and left foot to the mat and reestablish the standard plank position. I will hold this position for several seconds before moving into another two-point plank.

4

I elevate my left arm and right leg off the floor, forcing me to once again balance on two points. Again, the goal is to keep my back perfectly level.

SIDE BRIDGE

The side bridge is another isometric exercise that challenges your oblique and abdominal muscles to support your torso. Much like the plank exercise demonstrated in the previous sequence, the goal is to keep your back straight and prevent it from dipping in the middle. The primary difference between the two exercises is that they work your core from different angles. If you look at the photo below, you'll notice that I balance my weight on one arm and leg. This tends to be rather challenging for beginners. If you are unable to keep your back straight, placing both feet on the floor makes the exercise considerably easier. If that is still too difficult, base on your knees instead of your feet.

I assume the side bridge position by placing my right forearm and right foot on the floor, straightening my body, and elevating my left arm vertically. To keep my back straight and support my spine, I flex my oblique muscles. Although I have chosen to make this exercise more challenging by elevating my left arm and resting my left foot on top of my right foot, if you find this too difficult, drop your left arm to your side and place your left foot on the floor next to your right foot.

PLANK WITH LOAD TRANSFER

When the two-point plank becomes too easy to execute, switch to the plank with load transfer demonstrated in the sequence below. Just as with the two-point plank, your rectus abdominis is forced to flex isometrically to prevent your back from dipping in the middle. However, the instant you use your free hand to move a weight from one side of your body to the other, your base becomes unstable, which induces a rotational force upon your torso. To prevent your torso from twisting, your core muscles are taxed even greater. The goal is to slowly and smoothly transfer the weights over your posted arm without letting your back dip. If you need to resort to fast or jerky movements in order to accomplish this goal, you are most likely using too much weight. Once you have moved a set number of weights across your body, post your opposite arm on the mat and move them back.

I assume the three-point plank position by posting my left forearm and both feet on the floor. To begin the load transfer, I reach my right arm across my body and grip one of the weight plates positioned on my left side.

Gripping the weight plate in my right hand, I slowly move it over my left arm and place it on my right side. It is very important to note that throughout this movement I keep my back perfectly straight.

Once I have moved a set number of plates from my left side to my right side using my right hand, I change sides. I accomplish this by posting my right elbow on the floor, reaching my left arm across my body, and gripping a weight plate positioned to my right side using my left hand. From here, I will transfer the weights back to my left side.

I transfer the weight plates back to the left side of my body using my right hand. Again, I keep my spine stable and straight throughout the exercise.

PLANK ON SWISS BALL

As you already know, the plank exercise is designed to strengthen the core muscles that are responsible for stabilizing the spine. In this sequence, I take the exercise one step further by supporting myself on the unstable surface of a Swiss ball, which requires my transverse abdominis to work doubly hard to keep my back straight and stable. To make the exercise even more challenging, I have my training partner kick the Swiss ball once I secure my position. His intent is not to kick the ball out from underneath me, but rather to destabilize the Swiss ball if I become too balanced. It is important to note that this is the most challenging version of the body-weight plank. If you are new to this exercise, I recommend practicing the previous versions before incorporating this exercise into your training regimen.

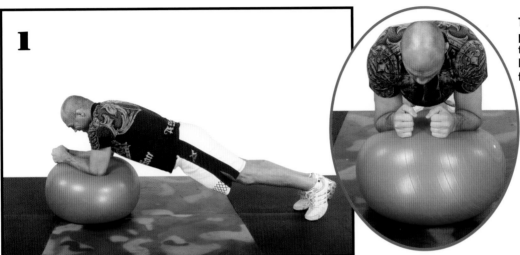

To assume a four-point plank position, I place my forearms on top of a Swiss ball, straighten my back, and plant my toes on the floor.

My training partner recognizes that I have stabilized my position and cocks his right foot back.

My training partner lightly kicks the front of the Swiss ball to destabilize it. This changes the position of my body relative to the position of the ball, forcing my core muscles to contract to keep me balanced.

SUPERMAN

The superman is a unique exercise used to increase the core's ability to resist spinal deflection. Most standard isometric core exercises, like the plank, support the body at the far ends and attempt to prevent spinal deflection in the middle. The superman is the exact opposite. In this drill the body is supported directly on the core, and the far ends of the body are raised off the ground, supported only by the power of the midsection. This small difference has a profound effect on the focus of the exercise. While exercises like the plank and the bridge mostly activate the abdominals and the transverse abdominals, the superman also strongly activates the spinal erector muscles to help keep the arms and legs elevated. This adds another element to spinal stability. In the ideal situation, you want your abs and the spinal erector muscles to be equally adept in resisting spinal flexion, and performing this exercise on a regular basis in addition to the other isometric core exercises will help move you in that direction. With time, you will increase your core strength and decrease your chances of injury.

To begin the drill, Jake lies flat on the ground and extends his arms straight over his head with his legs straight back.

Flexing his erector spinae muscles, Jake elevates his chest off the ground. At the same time, he contracts his glutes to raise his legs off the floor and contracts his deltoids to raise his arms off the floor. At this point, his transverse abdominals must remain contracted to stabilize his spine and maintain the position. To get the full benefits of this drill, he will hold this position for several seconds.

OPTION 2

In this sequence Jake demonstrates the alternating superman, which is a less demanding version. To begin, Jake lies on the ground with his arms extended overhead and his legs straight behind him.

Jake flexes his left glute to raise his left leg off the ground, while at the same time flexing his right deltoid to raise his right arm off the ground. His other arm and leg remain on the ground to help stabilize the position. Jake will hold this position for several seconds. It is important to mention that by raising a single arm and leg, Jake reduces the overall weight supported by his core, making the movement less challenging. This is a good option for less conditioned athletes.

Now Jake alternates the movement, raising his right leg and left arm into the air while leaving the right arm and left leg on the ground for support. Again, he contracts his spinal erector muscles in this position to raise his chest off the mat. Ideally, in this position his back would remain perfectly flat as he raises his chest, despite his alternating arm and leg body position. Jake will hold this position for several seconds before alternating again.

AB WHEEL ROLLOUT

The ab wheel rollout is perhaps one of the best methods for taxing your core muscles. When you perform this exercise, both functions of your abdominals are trained—your rectus abdominis is forced to dynamically flex to pull you up from the extended position, and your transverse abdominis isometrically contracts to prevent your spine from dipping. Even when posted on your knees it is an extremely challenging movement because of the instability of the wheel and your extreme lack of leverage when your arms are extended. However, if the workout becomes too easy, you can increase the load and decrease your leverage by posting on your feet, but this is far too strenuous for most people. One of the best things about this exercise is that it can be performed by those who have back problems. With your back remaining flat through the duration of the movement, it won't aggravate old injuries. I strongly recommend adding this exercise into your regimen because it's one of the most functional and challenging abdominal workouts available.

1

I post on my knees and grip the handles of the abdominal wheel. Notice how I'm bent slightly forward with the wheel centered under my chest.

2

I allow my body weight to push the ab wheel away from me. To prevent it from rolling away too quickly, I slowly extend my abdominal muscles.

3

Once my arms are fully extended, I powerfully flex my transverse abdominal muscles to stop the motion of the wheel. Notice how my back is flat and my spine stabilized.

4

I dynamically contract my abdominal muscles and reverse the movement of the wheel. As it draws toward me, I pull my hips back underneath my body. It should be noted that while the ab wheel rollout is primarily an abdominal exercise, the act of stabilizing the implement also taxes the arms and shoulder girdle.

5

Continuing to contract my abdominal muscles, I return to the resting position. Notice how my weight is on my knees and the ab wheel is once again centered under my chest.

LATERAL AB WHEEL ROLLOUT

This is a variation of the ab wheel rollout that incorporates side-to-side movement to activate the oblique muscles as well as the abdominal muscles. The exercise has the same strong points as the traditional ab wheel rollout—it forces the abdominals to contract both dynamically and isometrically, and your spine remains in a safe, neutral position throughout the movement. The upside to this exercise is you can train both your abdominals and obliques without having to reset your body and move to a different position.

1) I post on my knees and grip the handles of the abdominal wheel. Notice how I'm bent slightly forward with the wheel centered under my chest.

2) I allow my body weight to push the ab wheel away from me. To prevent it from rolling away too quickly, I slowly extend my abdominal muscles.

3) Once my arms are fully extended, I powerfully flex my transverse abdominal muscles to stop the motion of the wheel. Notice how my back is flat and my spine stabilized.

4) I dynamically contract my abdominal muscles and reverse the movement of the wheel. As it draws toward me, I pull my hips back underneath my body and return to the resting position. Notice how my weight is on my knees and the ab wheel is once again centered under my chest.

5) As I begin another roll out, I pull my left arm in slightly. This causes the wheel to turn toward my left side as it rolls away from me.

6) As my arms become fully extended, I contract my abdominals to stop the movement of the wheel.

7) To return to the starting position, I not only have to contract my abdominal muscles, but also my right oblique muscles.

8) I begin another rollout, but this time I pull my right arm slightly in, causing the wheel to turn toward my right side.

9) At full extension, I contract my abdominals to stop the movement.

10) To return to the starting position, I dynamically contract my abdominal and left oblique muscles. By going in three directions with this movement—forward, left, and right—I work my abdominals equally in every direction. From here, I will restart the movement once again.

FORWARD NECK BRIDGE

The forward neck bridge, is an old-school exercise used to increase the strength and stamina of the muscles in charge of moving the neck. The premise of the forward neck bridge is to post on your head and use your neck muscles to support the weight of your body. This strengthens the muscles controlling the neck, causing the atlantooccipital and atlantoaxial joints to become more stable over time. Like many core-strengthening movements, the body weight of a fighter is generally ample resistance to get a suitable workout with the forward neck bridge, which makes it an ideal neck warm-up or strength-and-conditioning finisher after a hard wrestling workout. The lack of sharp joint angles at the neck, as well as its ease of progression, makes the forward neck bridge a good exercise for those who haven't tried bridging before. While this movement may be hundreds of years old, it's still a great tool for building neck strength in a fighter.

Lance begins the forward neck bridge by assuming the all-fours position and placing his forehead on the floor.

Keeping his hands on the floor, Lance extends his legs and raises his knees off the floor. This transfers more of his body weight onto his head, which causes the sternocleidomastoid muscle to contract isometrically to hold the position.

After Lance stabilizes the position, he removes his hands from the ground. This forces even more of his body weight onto his neck. In this position, he will slowly flex and extend his neck joint, rolling backward and forward on his head. This changes the angle of the neck joint, allowing the muscles to be strengthened over a larger range of motion.

After holding the forward neck bridge for a period of several seconds, Lance places his hands back on the ground to stabilize himself.

Lance slowly lowers his knees back to the floor to remove pressure from his neck.

BACKWARD BRIDGE

While the forward neck bridge is a great tool for developing your neck, it only works your neck joint at one angle. In order to develop your neck symmetrically, you want to incorporate the backward bridge demonstrated below into your routine. The base movement is the same as the forward neck bridge, except instead of performing it while looking down at the ground, you perform it while looking up toward the ceiling. This utilizes the posterior fibers of the sternocleidomastoid muscle, as well as the splenius muscle group. The downside to this technique is that it causes extreme hyperextension of the neck joint, which can cause injuries to the cervical spine in certain athletes. The back bridge was originally used by wrestlers to prevent their shoulders from being pinned to the mat in competition, so many utilized this exercise regardless of pain, as the added neck strength could mean the difference between a win and a loss. However, for MMA, where the neck bridge is not a crucial movement needed to survive a match, it should be trained in progression. Start with the forward neck bridge from the knees and advance into the back bridge in a safe and controlled manner as your neck strength develops.

Lance begins the exercise lying on his back. His feet are flat on the ground, his arms are over his head, and his hands are flat on the ground.

Lance bridges up, driving his hips off the ground. As he rolls his neck backward, his body weight is supported not only by his feet and hands, but also his forehead.

After he stabilizes the position, Lance raises his hands off the floor. This transfers the weight from his upper body onto his neck. In this position Lance will slowly roll his head backward and forward to develop neck muscles in a larger range of motion.

After he holds the position for a set period of time, Lance places his hands back on the floor to stabilize himself before letting go of the position.

With his weight primarily on his hands and feet, Lance can now take the pressure off his neck. He drops his hips back down and returns to the starting position.

BENCH BRIDGE

While bridging is an incredibly useful tool to develop the muscles in your neck, as mentioned in the previous technique, the backward bridge can place a large amount of stress on the atlantooccipital joint in your neck. However, with the addition of a standard bench into the exercise, you can get all the strength-building advantages and eliminate the severe hyperextension on the neck joint. If you look at the photos below, you'll notice that instead of placing the back of your head on the ground, you place it on the top of the bench. Just as with the previous exercise, you bridge your hips off the ground, using your neck and your feet to support your body weight. Again, the motion is nearly identical to the standard backward bridge, but the spine stays in perfect alignment throughout the duration of the exercise. In addition to making it easier for athletes with prior neck injuries to execute the bridge, this variation also makes it safer to utilize external weights to increase the load. These two factors make the bench bridge an excellent isometric exercise for both beginning and advanced athletes.

To prepare for the bench bridge, Lance sits on the floor, rests his neck on a bench behind him, and holds a medicine ball to his chest to add external resistance.

To initiate the exercise, Lance drives his hips forward, raising his hips off the floor. As his groin elevates, his body weight transfers onto his neck.

Once Lance's torso is parallel with the floor, he holds himself in the bridge position for several seconds. While gravity is attempting to pull his midsection downward, his sternocleidomastoid and splenius muscle groups must contract to keep his spine in a natural, straight position.

After several seconds, Lance lowers his body back to the floor.

As Lance comes back to the resting position, he can either repeat the movement or move on to the next exercise. Since the position is extremely stable, it's easy to increase the external resistance with this exercise by switching the medicine ball for a dumbbell, a weight plate, or even a barbell.

NECK HARNESS

As mentioned previously in this chapter, the muscles surrounding the spinal column have two jobs. The first one is to resist twisting and deflection of the spine, and the other is to initiate it. While the various bridges already shown do a great job of training the neck to resist deflection and rotation, it is also just as important to train the neck to initiate movement, and utilizing the neck harness is one of the best ways of accomplishing this. The neck harness is essentially a head strap with a chain hanging off the bottom, which allows you to secure a weight plate to the end of the chain. Once you have the external resistance attached, moving your neck forward and backward builds strength in the sternocleidomastoid and splenius muscles. It is important to mention that not much weight is needed in this exercise due to the small size of the muscles controlling the neck.

Jake begins the exercise by placing the neck harness over his head. A short length of chain is dangling from the bottom hoop and Jake has attached a weight plate to it. Jake has his hips back and his chest up, with his head slightly ahead of his hips. This will allow him to achieve a full range of motion.

Jake relaxes his splenius muscles, allowing flexion in the atlantooccipital joint. This lowers his head forward, bringing his line of sight toward the ground.

Jake's neck is in full flexion. His chin is at his chest and he is looking toward the ground.

To bring his head back to the upright position, Jake flexes the muscles of the splenius and the posterior sternocleidomastoid, which extends his neck and brings his head back to the upright position. Jake will continue this exercise for the desired number of sets and reps.

LATERAL NECK RAISES

The neck harness is an ideal tool for loading the head and providing resistance for neck training, but it only works in two directions—flexion and extension. However, the neck has many articulations that it moves through, and simple forward and backward movement is insufficient to fully exercise the neck joint. The lateral neck raises demonstrated in this sequence allow you to add resistance to lateral motion of the neck, strengthening it in all four ranges of motion. While it is possible to use the neck harness for this type of exercise, the weight attachments tend to get caught up on your shoulders and arms, making it less efficient. By adding weight manually as demonstrated below, you eliminate that interference. When you combine this exercise with the neck harness and the bridging motions, you will develop the muscles of your neck and make your cervical spine stronger and less prone to injury.

To begin the exercise, Jake lies on his side on a bench. His head is hanging off the top of the bench, and he has a weight plate held to the right side of his head. This allows his neck a full range of motion while supporting his body weight. Note: Jake has a towel in between the plate and his face, as a heavy plate pressing into the soft tissue of your face can be very distracting.

Jake relaxes his neck, allowing his head to drop toward to the floor. As his head abducts away from the midline of his body, he has to be sure to hold onto the plate tightly with his right hand to ensure it doesn't slide off his head.

To raise his head back into the neutral position, Jake flexes his splenius capitis and sternocleidomastoid muscles, which reduces the neck joint angle and brings the spine back into straight alignment.

Jake continues the upward movement, flexing the neck laterally until his head is abducted away from the midline of the body in the other direction.

To bring his head back down into the neutral position, Jake relaxes his splenius and sternocleidomastoid muscles. He will continue this lateral motion for a set amount of reps before turning onto his other shoulder to ensure an equal workout on both sides of his neck.

PART TWO
SPORT-SPECIFIC TRAINING

While generalized strength-and-conditioning training is important to your success as an MMA fighter, it will only take you so far. Developing a solid base of strength allows you to execute your techniques with power and accuracy, but if you lack technique, gaining more strength is futile. As a fighter, strength and conditioning are simply tools to ensure that you are able to execute your techniques with precision, regardless of the circumstances on the mat. Whether it's the fifth round of a grueling title fight or you're attempting to double-leg an opponent with a fifty-pound advantage, you cannot allow a lack of physical ability to prevent you from executing your technique. While strength and conditioning should carry you into the fifth round with plenty of gas in the tank, technique is still the driver. As a result, this second part of the book focuses on sport-specific training.

Sport-specific training is any type of training that closely mimics the movements of your sport and is performed to make you stronger or more skilled in that particular movement. There are several characteristics that make sport-specific training different from general physical preparation. The first characteristic has to do with the movement. Sport-specific training must duplicate an actual motion in your sport. In MMA this can be as specific as practicing a single punch repeatedly to develop the mechanics or practicing your entire takedown arsenal during a wrestling session. While the focus can be either very narrow or somewhat broad, the motions used in a particular exercise must be identical to the motions used in the actual fight.

The second characteristic is the range of motion. Without a complete range of motion, your sport-specific training will fail to transfer effectively to the actual fight. Much like in basketball where every free throw is practiced with follow-through, you must commit the same amount of ef-

fort in your drills as you do when performing the technique you are mimicking. For example, when you practice a takedown, you need to change levels and complete your penetration step on each shot. If you get lazy and fail to complete the level change, this bad habit will carry over into your fight. To ensure increased power development, you must follow through, just as you would when executing techniques in the ring.

The third characteristic that defines sport-specific training is the contractile force. The motion you are drilling must mimic the power requirements of the actual sport motion. For example, to effectively increase the power and efficiency of your lead hook, it needs to be drilled with knock-out power in training, either on the heavy bag or in sparring. If you practice your lead hook with less than maximum effort, the power of your hook will decrease over time. By training your body to only punch lightly, that low level of contractile force will be remembered and executed by your body when you get into the cage.

These three characteristics, movement pattern, range of motion, and contractile effort, need to be mimicked in order for the central nervous system to adapt and increase your ability to execute the movements accurately, powerfully, and efficiently. The central nervous system is the controller for all the movement in the human body. Anytime you want to move, the central nervous system, or CNS, is responsible for telling the correct muscles to fire in order to execute the desired movement. The CNS is capable of evolving in the same way that muscle groups are capable of evolving. Consistent stress on a target, followed by periods of recovery, will yield development in that target area. Just like consistent arm training will make your arms grow, consistent development of movement patterns will cause CNS adaption. The more you repeat a movement, the more efficient your CNS becomes at performing that movement. When you spend time developing a sport-specific movement, your CNS will deactivate muscles not needed to execute that movement and simultaneously allow the muscles that are necessary to contract with maximum force. This is the key component to sport-specific training's adaptation. Again, each time a movement is repeated, the body becomes more efficient at that particular movement. However, this only applies if the drill mimics the actual sporting movement, range of motion, and contractile effort. If any of these conditions are not met while drilling, then the sport-specific training will be suboptimal.

While it's obvious that sport-specific training can be a very broad subject, it's possible to break it down into manageable segments. All sport-specific movements must include the three characteristics outlined above, but each drill can have varying levels of specificity. For example, sparring is the closest you can get to an actual MMA fight. To make it as similar as possible, you would use the same rules, the same equipment, the same time frame, and the same intensity as an actual MMA match. While training in this manner is 100 percent sport specific, sparring at full speed for hours every day would be a very poor use of training time. Not only would you most likely get injured, but you would also not have opportunities to practice the weaker techniques in your arsenal. On the other end of the spectrum is sport-specific strength training, which is aimed solely at increasing strength or stamina in a certain movement, but not necessarily improve your fighting technique in that movement. An example of this would be drilling sit-ups from the guard. While sitting up from the guard is an important movement necessary to execute different sweeps and submissions, it is just as important to drill the actual sweeps and submissions. Performing hundreds of sit ups from the guard will improve the strength of your abs and make you more proficient at sitting up, but it won't necessarily improve your sweeps and submissions.

Between the extremes of sport-specific strength training and sport-specific sparring lies sport-specific drills, which is where you are allowed to practice a technique on a partner without resistance. This helps ingrain perfect movement patterns into the central nervous system without your partner wildly flailing or trying to escape.

All three types of training, sport-specific strength, sport-specific drills, and sport-specific sparring are all necessary for the development of a fighter, but they need to be done in the proper ratios to be effective. While sport-specific strength movements are good for developing power in

unique motions that are otherwise hard to duplicate in the weight room, the bulk of my strength development comes from general physical preparation. So while sport-specific strength movements are good tools for certain goals, because I'm an advanced athlete, I tend to use them very little in my program. However, a beginner with a lower level of general physical preparation will see great benefits from simple sports drills designed to increase strength or stamina.

The bulk of my sport-specific training revolves around drilling and situational sparring. Drilling, generally the first half of my sessions, is my chance to learn new movements and techniques or simply to refine the movement of an old technique. Each drill is an opportunity to focus the CNS and become more efficient at a particular movement. After a technique has been learned and the motor patterns ingrained, it's good to do situational sparring to test that technique. This is a situation where you and a partner begin in a specific position and battle for the upper hand. While you actually contest one other, neither of you goes 100 percent. It is important to mention that there should always be a sense of control in your situational sparring sessions. For me, situational sparring generally takes up the last half of my MMA practice sessions.

Full sparring is the last element of my training camps. This is when my training partners and I begin in a neutral position and go hard in an effort to best one another. Whether we are engaging in boxing, kickboxing, grappling, or full MMA, the intent is to approach the sessions as if we were actually competing in a contest against each other. The goal is not to learn or develop a new technique, but rather to win the sparring session using all available tools. This type of training is not as frequent as drilling or situational sparring, as it tends to be much harder on the body, but it is necessary to prepare yourself for the rigors of an actual MMA match. In an effort to make hard sparring sessions as safe as possible, my partners and I generally use heavier gloves and padding than we would use in an MMA contest.

Different types of sport-specific training have different places in each of my training camps. When a fight is several months out, I like to practice new material. This is the point in time where I'll learn new techniques or tune up old techniques. This keeps me evolving as a fighter and is a big component to my continued success. Having new strengths in each fight makes it hard for my opponents to prepare for our match. As fight time draws closer, maybe four to twelve weeks away, I'll incorporate a lot of drilling and situational sparring in my sport-specific sessions. This is my chance to ingrain a movement pattern into my CNS, and test that new movement against resisting opponents. Generally these drills and sparring sessions will be geared specifically to counter my opponent in the upcoming fight. For instance, if I'm competing against a strong boxer that I intend to take-down, my drills and sparring will be focused on taking the fight to the mat while absorbing the least amount of punishment possible. Around a month out from a fight, I will begin to focus on hard sparring to get mentally and physically prepared to stand up to the challenge of a game opponent trying to defeat me. This is the last stage in my training camps, but it needs to be tapered off at the correct time, as full sparring can be very rough on the body and I want to enter the fight in peak physical condition. In the same situation where I'm preparing to fight a boxer I want to take to the mat, I will instruct my training partners to attempt to keep the fight standing during our sparring sessions. Their goal is to use their entire bag of tricks to keep the fight on the feet, while I will use any tool necessary to force it to the ground.

Strength, speed, and power are great athletic abilities, but they are useless unless paired with technique. Sport-specific training is what allows you to learn, refine, and perfect various techniques in every aspect of the fight game. In the upcoming sections I cover my strategy for developing sport-specific training exercises in each different area of the fight game, as well as which movements I focus on during various stages in my training camp.

SECTION ONE
SPORT-SPECIFIC STANDING

Although MMA fighters as a whole are evolving and becoming more rounded by the day, most MMA combatants still consider themselves more proficient in one martial art or another. Those coming from a strong boxing or kickboxing background are generally more capable in the standing position, while those with a wrestling, judo, or jiu-jitsu base are more proficient on the ground. Due to the differences in these two elements of training, as well as the different skill sets of coaches in the mixed martial arts world, sport-specific training sessions are often broken down into striking and grappling.

All fights start in the standing position. Whether you are a primarily a wrestler, striker, or jiu-jitsu player, you need to train specific techniques from the standing position in order to win a fight. A wrestler's goal is often to execute a takedown and claim the top position on the ground; a striker's goal is often to keep the fight standing and deliver damage using his hands and legs; and a dedicated jiu-jitsu practitioner's goal is often to drag his opponent to the ground to lock in a submission hold. Without ability in the stand-up department, none of these game plans is feasible. In order to be proficient in MMA, you cannot be a one-sided fighter. You must spend a portion of your training time training from the standing position. As a result, I demonstrate some of my favorite drills that I employ in my camps to train my stand-up techniques.

While there are many different techniques shown in this chapter, it should be noted that my primary goal is not to explain the technical aspects of the drills, as that was covered in my previous book *Wrestling for Fighting*. The goal is to demonstrate the actual drills and positions that I utilize in my training caps to help prepare for an upcoming fight. As your fight draws nearer, learning new techniques should not be your goal. Instead, you want to focus on de-

veloping a game plan and sharpening existing technique. This section closely follows that philosophy. All the drills and techniques shown are designed to either improve an existing technique or drill an important series of movements that will be needed in your fight.

The beginning of the section focuses on sport-specific strengthening. While the general physical preparation sections shown earlier in the book will increase overall strength, the movements at the beginning of this chapter aim to improve strength and power within a certain movement. While this strength may not carry over into other areas of a fight, if it can improve upon a weakness in your stand up game, then it is a good investment of time. First, I demonstrate how to improve upon the power of punches, kicks, knees, and wrestling takedowns. Not only are these the most important elements of a standup fight, but they are also the techniques that will directly benefit from improved power. If you are able to specifically increase the power in either your striking or your takedowns, you will directly improve your fighting ability. As you will see, by using varying methods of resistance, it's possible to vastly improve your power in the standing position.

After I demonstrate various ways to improve power in both striking and takedowns, I move into wrestling drills. The majority of them were taught to me at the beginning of my wrestling career to help me improve and perfect various motions. The goal of all these movements is the same—utilize perfect motion for several repetitions with a partner to ingrain wrestling movement patterns into your central nervous system. In addition to demonstrating my favorite clinch, body lock, double-leg, and single-leg takedown drills, I also demonstrate drills that will help you hone your defense against these techniques. By practicing these movements over and over during training camp, the execution of these movements becomes automatic. The goal is to train them so frequently that the moment you consciously recognize an advantageous position, your brain automatically sends signals to your body to execute the takedown. As a lifelong wrestler, these drills have been an important part of building my foundation.

Next, I move on to combinations. I demonstrate combination drills that allow you to keep the fight standing and damage your opponent and also that allow you to damage your opponent and then transition the fight to the ground. Whether you consider yourself primarily a striker or a grappler, I strongly recommend incorporating both into your routine because you never know where a fight will take you. If you are a striker and get caught with an unlucky punch, using a striking combination to set your opponent up for a takedown might be your only chance of survival. Conversely, if you are a grappler but are unable to take your opponent to the mat, having a host of combination movement patterns ingrained into your CNS can come in very handy.

The drills shown in this section have been essential in assisting with my fight preparation. They've come in very handy for refining technique and developing game plans, but by no means is the section comprehensive. There are hundreds, if not thousands, of drills out there that will help you improve upon your standup abilities. However, the contents of this chapter, combined with boxing, kickboxing, wrestling, and MMA sparring, will help you increase your effectiveness and perfect your stand up abilities.

MEDICINE BALL PUNCH

In this sequence I demonstrate a drill to increase the power of your straight punches. Instead of simply throwing a medicine ball against a wall using my arm, I mimic the mechanics of a cross as much as possible. If you look at the photos below, you'll notice that I begin in my fighting stance and then rotate my hips and pivot on the ball of my rear foot, just as I do when I throw a cross. When you perform drills to increase punching power using dumbbells, you must decelerate toward the end of the movement in order to keep from hyperextending your arm. However, in this drill you release the medicine ball as your arm becomes fully extended, which allows you to accelerate all the way through the movement, making it similar to an actual punch. It is important to note that this drill taxes your central nervous system more than it does your muscles. Even though you may still have energy after dozens of repetitions, as your central nervous system becomes fatigued, your form will most likely break down. For the best results, do one repetition at a time with 100 percent explosive effort and then rest for one to three minutes before conducting your next repetition. This break gives your central nervous system time to recover and ensures that you develop your power rather than stamina.

| I begin in my fighting stance with my left foot forward. To prepare for the drill, I hold a medicine ball in the palm of my right hand. | I mimic the mechanics of a cross by shifting my weight to my left foot, pivoting on my right foot, turning my hips, and extending my right arm. I continue to accelerate the ball forward until it leaves my hand. | After the medicine ball hits the wall and bounces back toward me, I catch it in my right hand. However, to get the most out of this drill, I will allow my central nervous system to rest between one and three minutes before performing another repetition. |

MEDICINE BALL PUNCH FROM KNEES

Punching drills such as the previous one shown tend to be very hip and leg dominant. Although the power for your straight punches should originate from your legs, the muscles of your upper body come into play as you follow through with your punch. By including the abdominal, back, and arm exercises demonstrated earlier in the book, you will increase the strength of your upper body, which leads to more powerful punches. But as I have mentioned, it is very important to include sport-specific workouts into your regimen. By performing the medicine ball punch from your knees, you remove your legs and hips from the picture, allowing you to isolate the upper body muscles utilized when throwing punches. Just as with the standing version of this exercise, you will make the most gains by performing each throw with 100 percent explosive effort and then resting between one and three minutes before your next repetition.

I place a towel on the floor and then rest my knees on top of it. To prepare for the drill, I grip a medicine ball in the palm of my right hand.

I mimic the mechanics of a cross by twisting my hips and extending my right arm. It is important to mention that I continue to accelerate the ball until it exits my hand. With both of my knees planted firmly on the floor, my abdominals, back, and arm become the dominant movers in the exercise.

After the ball bounces off the wall, I catch it in my right hand. However, I will wait between one and three minutes before completing my next repetition. This will allow me to fully recover and execute all my reps with 100 percent power.

BAND-RESISTED STRAIGHT PUNCH

In this sequence I demonstrate a flex band drill that allows you to increase your punching power and speed. If you look at the first photo below, you'll notice that I grip the ends of the band in each hand, wrap the band around my upper back, and then assume my fighting stance. Once accomplished, I alternate between throwing jabs and crosses. As the band stretches, the resistance applies an overload to your muscles, causing your central nervous system to recruit more muscle fibers to straighten your arm. This increases the efficiency of your central nervous system, which in turn leads to quicker and harder punches. Using a band for punching drills has several advantages over using weights. When you perform punching drills using dumbbells, you increase your punching power through overload, but the dumbbells pull your arm downward, altering your punching mechanics. If you attempt to fix this problem by performing dumbbell punching drills while lying on your back, you are unable to employ your hips, which also affects the mechanics of your punches. The flex band doesn't use weight to provide resistance—it uses tension. And with that tension being applied in the opposite direction of your punch, it causes no deformation of your punching mechanics. The nice part about this drill is that by looping the band around your upper back instead of hooking it on a fixed object, you can alternate between jabs and crosses, which saves time. The only downside to this drill is that the band will come out of place when you attempt to throw looping punches.

To set up this drill, I grip a flex band in both of my hands, loop the band around my upper back, and then assume my fighting stance. Notice how both of my hands are up, just as they would be in a fight.

I throw a jab with my lead hand, causing the band to tighten and add resistance to the movement.

As I retract my jab, I shift my weight onto my lead leg, pivot on my rear foot, rotate my hips in a counterclockwise direction, and throw a cross. Again, the band tightens as my arm extends, adding resistance to the movement.

PARTNER-ASSISTED BAND PUNCHES

In this sequence I demonstrate a variation of the previous flex band punching drill. Instead of wrapping the band around my upper back, I grip it in one hand and have my training partner hold the opposite end while standing behind me. Although this only allows me to train one arm at a time, it has its benefits. Having your training partner hold the opposite end tends to make the exercise more stable than when you loop the band around your upper back. No longer having to worry about the band sliding upward and snapping you in the back of the neck, you can concentrate on executing proper form. In addition to this, partner-assisted band punching also eliminates the pressure the band places on your back when performing the regular band-assisted punches. While this pressure is hardly noticeable when performing high repetitions with a relatively thin band, it can cause chaffing as you become stronger and increase the band thickness.

To set up this drill, I grip one end of a flex band in my right hand and then assume my fighting stance. My training partner grips the opposite end of the flex band and takes up position directly behind me. Notice how there is currently no slack in the band.

I throw a right cross by shifting my weight onto my left leg, pivoting on the ball of my right foot, rotating my hips in a counterclockwise direction, and extending my right arm. As my hand moves away from my body, the tension in the band increases, providing resistance to my muscles.

I pull my right arm back into my fighting stance. From here, I have a couple of options. If my goal is to increase my punching stamina, I will immediately execute another repetition. If my goal is to develop my punching power, I will rest between one and three minutes before executing another repetition at 100 percent effort.

BAND-RESISTED KNEE STRIKES

In this sequence I demonstrate how to increase the power of your knee strikes by adding resistance using a flex band. If you look at the first photo below, you'll notice that I secure one end of the flex band to a stationary object behind me, wrap the other end around the bottom of my rear shin, and then walk forward to remove slack from the band. Once accomplished, I drive my rear knee forward into my imaginary opponent's abdomen. As my knee extends, the tension on the band increases, forcing my central nervous system to recruit more muscle fibers than when performing the same movement without resistance. In turn, this leads to more powerful knee strikes. Once you complete a set number of repetitions with your rear knee, remove the flex hand from your rear leg, wrap it around your lead leg, and then perform an equal number of lead knee strikes.

| To set up this drill, I attach one end of the flex band around my right ankle, secure the opposite end of the band to a fixed object behind me such as a power rack, and then assume a traditional Muay Thai stance by standing with my left foot in front of my right and my hands held high. | I throw a straight rear knee by elevating my right knee upward, slightly rotating my hips in a counterclockwise direction, and then driving my knee forward into my imaginary target. | Keeping my guard high, I pull my right leg back into my fighting stance. From here, I have a couple of options. To work my stamina, I will immediately execute another repetition. To increase my power, I will rest between one and three minutes before performing another repetition at 100 percent effort. |

BAND-RESISTED DOUBLE-LEG

In this sequence I demonstrate a flex band drill that allows you to develop a more powerful double-leg takedown. To set up the drill, you slide into a flex band harness and have your training partner hold the opposite end while standing behind you. Once accomplished, you throw a cross, drop your elevation, shoot forward for your imaginary opponent's legs, and then return to your fighting stance by increasing your elevation. Just as with the band-resisted strikes shown previously, the band stretches as you shoot forward, increasing resistance. To complete the movement, your central nervous system recruits more muscle fibers than when performing the movement without any resistance, making your double-leg takedowns more explosive. Instead of walking backward after your first repetition, have your partner walk forward. This allows you to execute one repetition after another without any breaks. The nice part about this drill is that is allows you to mimic the exact mechanics of the actual double-leg takedown, which is extremely important when performing sport-specific drills.

To set up this exercise, I climb into a flex band harness and then assume my fighting stance. Behind me, my training partner grips the handles on the opposite side of the flex band. Notice how there is currently no slack in the band.

To set up a double-leg takedown just as I would in a fight, I begin by shifting my weight onto my left leg, rotating on the ball of my rear foot, turning my hips in a counterclockwise direction, and throwing a right cross. While it is possible to skip the cross, it is just as important to practice the setups to your takedowns as the takedowns themselves.

After throwing the cross, I pull my right arm back into my stance and execute a level change. I accomplish this by taking a small step forward with my left foot, bending both knees, and dropping my hips straight down. Notice how my torso is still vertical and my eyes are still pointing forward. At this point in the exercise, the band is stretched tight, providing added resistance to my shot.

To close in on my imaginary opponent's legs, I drop my lead knee down to the mat, pull my right leg forward, and plant my right foot next to my left knee. At this point, the band provides an extreme amount of resistance, forcing me to maximally contract the muscles in my hips and legs to finish the double-leg takedown.

Now that I have control of my imaginary opponent's legs, I increase my elevation by straightening my legs and lifting my hips. Having returned to the start position, my partner walks forward to remove the tension on the band and I prepare to execute another repetition.

SHOULDER BLADE CAGE WALK-UP

When your opponent establishes the top ground position, a lot of times he will attempt to pin your shoulders up against the cage. This dramatically limits your mobility, making it hard to cut angles off to his side and set up submissions or evade his ground and pound assault. All MMA fighters find themselves in this horrible predicament at one time or another, and it is important that you train to escape this situation. While it is possible to place your hands on the mat and push your body back up to the standing position, this exposes your head and completely destroys your defense against strikes. A much better option is to return to the standing position by walking your shoulders up the chain link. With both of your arms still free, you can use them to tie your opponent up and prevent him from throwing damaging strikes. However, walking your shoulders up the chain link requires a lot of energy. To keep from completely gassing out in a fight using this maneuver, it is important that you train it on a regular basis using the drill demonstrated in this sequence. In this particular drill, I walk up the cage solo, but once you get comfortable with the movement, it can be beneficial to add resistance using a medicine ball or having a training partner in your guard.

To set up this exercise, I squat down and place my back against the cage. Notice how my legs are bent and my feet are positioned slightly in front of my body. If you've watched the UFC, then you've seen many fighters end up in this exact position with an opponent in their guard.

I tilt toward my left side and raise my right arm, causing my right shoulder blade to move upward. To prevent it from falling back down, I drive my heels into the mat and push my right shoulder blade into the cage wall.

With my right shoulder blade locked to the fence, I tilt toward my right side and elevate my left arm. After my left shoulder blade has moved upward, I pin it to the cage by driving off my heels. It is important to mention that if you fail to pressure your back into the cage by driving off your heels, your back will slide downward, negating your hard work.

I continue climbing up the cage one shoulder at a time.

Once I have reached the upright position, I have completed my first repetition. From here, I will drop back down and once again begin climbing my shoulders up the cage wall.

CAGE WALK-UP WITH RESISTANCE

The drill demonstrated in this sequence is almost identical to the previous one—the only difference is that here I add resistance to my cage walk-up by holding a medicine ball in my arms. As I mentioned, it is important for your sport-specific exercises to be as close to the real thing as possible. When in a fight, your opponent will not allow you to simply stand up. He will provide as much resistance as possible to hold you on the ground, so it is important to train to fight that downward pressure. Of course holding a medicine ball does not provide nearly as much resistance as an opponent using all of his body weight to keep you pinned, but it is a step in the right direction. Once you can perform the cage walk up with a medicine ball with relative ease, the next step is to perform the drill with a training partner in your guard, providing mild downward resistance.

1) To set up this exercise, I rest my butt on the ground, press my back up against the cage, and position my feet on the mat in front of me. To add resistance, I clutch a medicine ball in my arms. 2) I tilt to my right side and elevate my left arm and shoulder blade. Once accomplished, I pin my left shoulder to the cage by driving my heels into the mat. 3) Pivoting on my left shoulder blade, I lean toward my left side and elevate my right arm and shoulder. Once accomplished, I pin my right shoulder to the cage by driving off my heels. 4) As I continue to crawl my shoulders up the cage, I walk my feet underneath my body to increase my leverage. 5) Once I reach the upright position, I have completed one repetition. From here, I will drop my butt back down to the mat and repeat the exercise for a set number of repetitions.

FLEX BAND SHOULDER THROW

As you're probably starting to gather, it is extremely important to train your primary fighting movements over and over to increase your power and stamina. In earlier sequences I demonstrated how to train your punches and knee strikes using a flex band, and in this sequence I demonstrate how to use a flex band to train your shoulder throws. While there is no substitute for the real thing, it can be difficult to find a training partner that is willing to be tossed painfully to the mat hundreds of times in a row. It can also be difficult to maintain proper form when performing numerous repetitions with the full body weight of a training partner. This drill solves both dilemmas. If you look at the photos below, you'll notice that I tie one end of a flex band to the cage, grip the opposite end in both of my hands, execute a step back, and then twist my body and perform the same shoulder throw movement I would in a fight. As the band stretches during my movement, it provides the same type of resistance as when throwing a real opponent. But with the resistance being much less than the weight of a body, I can execute a much higher number of repetitions.

1) To set up this drill, I tie one end of a flex band to the cage and grip the opposite end in my hands. Before starting the exercise, I establish my fighting stance while facing the cage. 2) As I begin rotating my shoulders in a counterclockwise direction, I begin executing a back step by moving my left foot behind my right foot. Notice how these actions cause me to turn into the flex band. 3) I place my left foot next to my right foot, come up onto the ball of my right foot, and continue to rotate my body in a counterclockwise direction. At the same time, I begin raising my arms just as I would when throwing an actual opponent. 4) Continuing my clockwise rotation, I position the flex band over my right shoulder, drive my hips backward, and bend forward at the waist. As my torso lowers and my shoulders roll, I generate forward momentum. If I were executing this technique against a person, his arm would be in the same position as the flex band and my rotation would drive him over my hips and toward his back. 5) After executing the powerful hip drive to initiate the shoulder roll, I relax and allow the tension in the band to pull me back into the upright position. 6) To reduce the tension in the flex band, I rotate my body in a clockwise direction and return to the starting position. From here, I can execute another repetition or switch to my opposite side.

BEAR CRAWL AND FROG HOP DRILL

In this sequence I offer a warm-up drill that gets blood flowing to the muscles and joints, which makes the more high-impact work such as takedown practice and sparring safer and easier to execute. To perform this drill, stand face-to-face with your training partner, drop your level, bear crawl between his legs, stand up behind him, and then reverse your direction by executing a frog hop over his back. As you turn back to face your partner, he drops his level and executes the same movements. Although there are many drills to warm-up the body, I like this one in particular because it's a full-body movement that warms up every muscle group and joint. In addition to getting a workout when you are the mover, you also get a workout when you play the role of pillar. As your partner goes under your legs and over your body, you must isometrically contract your legs and back to keep from falling over. It's important to mention that this drill doesn't play a major roll it my workout—it's just a quick warm-up to get ready for the more powerful dynamic movements that follow.

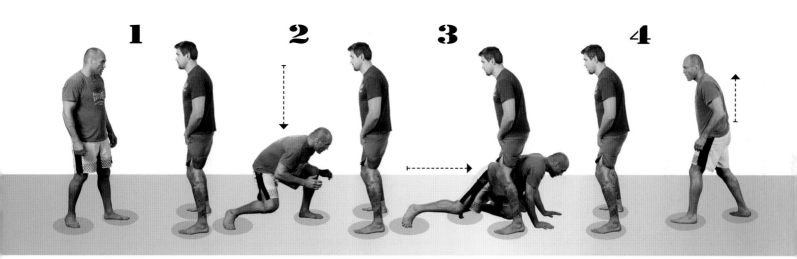

1) I assume my fighting stance and stand face-to-face with my training partner a few feet apart. Notice how he is standing with his feet spread wide. 2) As if I were shooting in for a takedown, I drop my level by bending at the knees and lowering my hips. To make it easier for me to move between my training partner's legs, I lean forward more than normal. 3) I roll forward onto my left knee, plant my hands on the mat, and then bear crawl between my partner's legs. 4) Once I have crawled through my partner's legs, I stand up and turn to face his back. 5) My training partner bends forward, which will allow me to leap frog over his back. 6) I move forward, place my hands on my partner's back, and then drive off of my legs and leap over his body. It is important to mention that I keep my hands on his back for as long as possible to help guide my body over his. 7) I land on the mat in front of Neil. 8) I turn to face Neil. From here, I will spread my legs and he will complete one repetition. We will go back and forth like this for a certain number of repetitions or a set amount of time. The goal is to continue with the exercise until both of your bodies are warm.

ARM DRAG DRILL

The arm drag is a classic wrestling move that allows you to pull your opponent off balance and gain access to his back, which in turn allows you to secure back control or execute a takedown. Just like punches and kicks, it's a movement that you must train your muscles to execute, and there is no better way to accomplish that than to practice this arm drag drill. However, it is important to mention that the goal of this drill is not to complete a takedown, but rather execute one arm drag after the next. If you look at the photos below, you'll notice that I accomplish this by executing an arm drag and off balancing my opponent, and then returning to the start position and performing an arm drag on my opponent's opposite arm. By performing the drill in this manner, you can achieve a lot of repetitions in a short period of time.

1 To set up this drill, my training partner and I stand face-to-face with our left foot forward. As he reaches his right hand for my left collar, I cup my left hand over his wrist and swat it downward. Practice this movement slowly at first, and then increase your speed as you become more proficient with it.

2 As I swat my partner's hand down and toward my right side using my left hand, I reach my right arm across my body and grip his right triceps. It is important to establish a firm grip on the triceps because it is what will allow you to pull your training partner off balance.

3 To finish the arm drag, I pull my training partner's right arm toward my right side using my triceps grip and wrap my left arm around his waist. At the same time, I step my right foot forward to add power to the tug and close off all space between our bodies. From here, I am in a great position to execute a number of takedowns or secure control of his back.

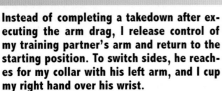

4 Instead of completing a takedown after executing the arm drag, I release control of my training partner's arm and return to the starting position. To switch sides, he reaches for my collar with his left arm, and I cup my right hand over his wrist.

5 As I push my training partner's arm down and toward my left side, I reach my left arm across my body and establish a triceps grip. Again, this movement should be practiced slowly when warming up, and then slowly increase your speed as the drill goes on. The goal is to create a rhythm with the drill, moving from one arm drag to the next.

6 To complete the arm drag, I pull my partner's arm across my body using my left triceps grip and wrap my right arm around his waist. At the same time, I step my right foot forward so that we are shoulder to shoulder. From here, I will return to the start position and execute another repetition on my opposite side.

BODY LOCK LIFT DRILL

In this sequence I demonstrate how to practice lifting your opponent off the mat from the body lock position. If you look at the photos below, you'll notice that I begin with an overhook and underhook, and my partner begins with an overhook and underhook, making it a neutral position. Once our locks are both established, we take turns lifting each other up off the mat. However, it is important to mention that we do not keep our hips square with one another. When it is my turn to perform the lift, I acquire a dominant angle of attack by stepping off to his side prior to initiating the lift. This allows me to pull his hips into mine and provides me with the leverage needed to effortlessly lift his body upward. When it is my training partner's turn to perform the lift, he does the exact same thing. Once you have your training partner's feet off the mat, executing a takedown is as simple as rotating his body over your hips to disrupt his balance and then slamming his back down to the mat. The most difficult part of the technique is to acquire the proper angle and perform the lift, which is why this drill leaves out the actual takedown. While becoming a master at completing takedowns is extremely important, you will never get the chance to employ those finishes unless you take the time to master the setups.

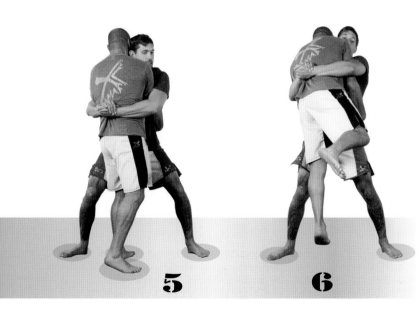

1) To set up this drill, I wrap my right arm underneath my training partners left arm, wrap my left arm over his right arm, and then clasp my hands together in the small of his back. At the same time, my partner wraps his left arm over my right arm, hooks his right arm underneath my left arm, and locks his hands together in the small of my back. With both of us having one overhook and one underhook, it is a neutral tie-up position. 2) To dominate the neutral clinch, I pull my partner's hips toward me using my hands, shattering his base. At the same time, I lower my hips, step my right leg around to the outside of his left leg, and angle my body off to his side. The combination of these actions provides me with a dominant angle of attack and will allow me to lift his body upward with ease. 3) Having lowered my hips below my partner's hips and angled my body off to his side, I pop my hips forward, straighten my legs, and pull his body upward. Once I have him in the air, I could easy corkscrew his body and complete the takedown, but instead I will lower him back to the mat so we can continue with the lifting drill. 4) After lowering my training partner to the mat, we return to the neutral clinch by squaring our hips up with one another. 5) My training partner pulls my hips into his to shatter my base, lowers his hips, steps his right leg to the outside of my left leg, and circles around to my side to acquire a dominant angle of attack. 6) To complete the lift, my training partner pops his hips forward, straightens his legs, and pulls me upward off the mat. Performing this drill for repetitions has several advantages. In addition to becoming more efficient at acquiring a dominant angle of attack and hefting your opponent off his feet, it is also a great way to condition your legs, hips, back, and arms.

DOUBLE UNDERHOOK SWING DRILL

When you establish a double underhook body lock on your opponent, you not only limit his ability to attack, but you also create a broad array of takedowns at your disposal. However, the majority of these takedown options require you to lift your opponent up off that mat, and this can be a very tiring endeavor. Performing this drill on a regular basis is an excellent way to prepare your body to perform this movement over and over in a fight without losing steam. If you look at the photos below, you'll notice that instead of lifting my opponent upward off the mat and then setting him back down, as I did in the earlier body lock lifting drill, I lift him up and then swing his body from side to side. As his body moves off to my right side, I bump my right knee into his hips to sweep his lower body out from underneath his upper body. Once accomplished, I am in the perfect position to dump his back down to the mat, but for the sake of the drill, I swing him to my left side instead and perform another knee bump. By cutting out the actual takedown, I can perform one repetition after the other without removing my partner's body weight from my arms, leading to a physically taxing workout.

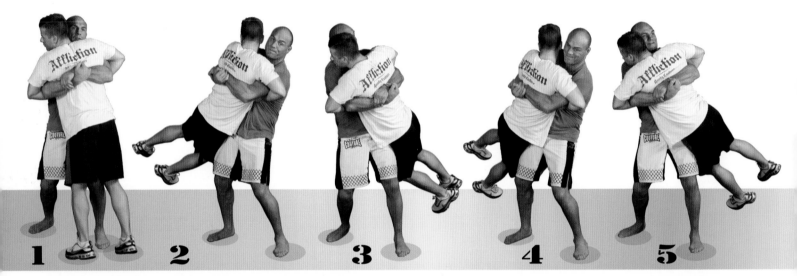

1) To set up this drill, I secure a double underhook body lock by wrapping my arms underneath my partner's arms and then clasping my hands together behind his back. Next, I step my left leg between his legs and pull his torso into my body. This helps elevate his hips above my hips, which in turn will make it easier to lift him up off the mat.

2) As I straighten my legs and lift my training partner up off the mat, I lean toward my left side and rotate my hips in a clockwise direction. The combination of these actions forces my partner's legs to my right.

3) I reverse directions by leaning toward my right side and rotating my hips in a counterclockwise direction. This causes my partner's legs to swing toward my left side. Once accomplished, I thrust my left leg forward to block his legs. If my goal was to complete the takedown, I would rotate toward the right, keep his legs blocked, and then drop him down to the mat. With his lower body on one side and his upper body on the other, he would not be able to catch himself. However, for the sake of the drill, I end with the knee bump.

4) Rather than finish the takedown by forcing Jake to the mat, I remove the blockade of my leg as I swing him toward my right side.

5) As I move my partner's legs toward my left side, I once again thrust my left leg forward to block his legs. By performing this drill back and forth, I not only become more proficient with the knee block takedown, but I also develop the muscles of my legs, hips, back, and arms.

HEADLOCK THROW DRILL

The headlock throw is a great technique to employ when you're having a difficult time establishing deep underhooks on your opponent. But just like the body lock lift, to become fluid with the headlock throw you must train the movement repeatedly. Although it can be beneficial to execute the throw full speed and powerfully dump your training partner down onto a crash pad, it is rough on his body and requires long breaks between repetitions. Instead of following through with the throw in this drill, you pull your training partner's body over your back and allow him to land on his feet. Next, you use your headlock control to help him back up to the standing position. The nice thing about this drill is that when your opponent stands, he is in a perfect position to execute a headlock throw on you, allowing you to take turns throwing one another without any breaks between repetitions. In addition to ingraining the movements involved in the headlock throw into your subconscious, the drill is also an excellent fully-body workout.

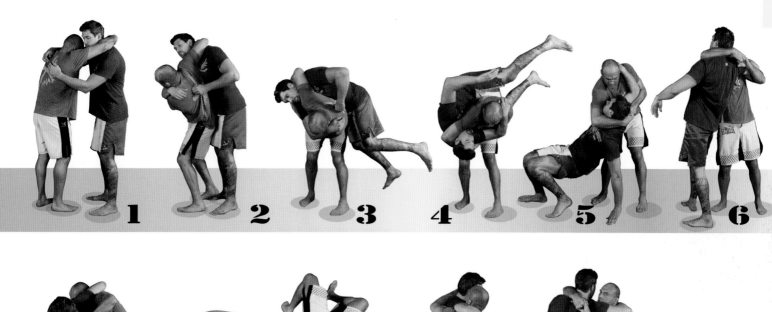

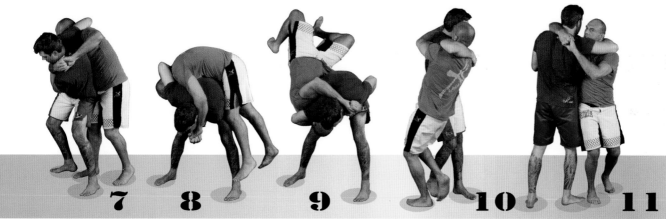

1) To set up this drill, my training partner and I once again establish a neutral clinch position. However, in this scenario I wrap my right arm around the back of his head and my left arm underneath his right arm, and he wraps his right arm around the back of my head and his left arm underneath my right arm. 2) I execute a back step by rotating my hips in a counterclockwise direction, pivoting on the ball of my left foot, stepping my right foot across my body, and lowering my hips. At the same time, I hook my right arm around the back of my partner's neck and clasp my hands together. To gain the leverage to pull him over top of me, I position my hips lower than his hips. 3) With the headlock position secured, I drive my hips back into my partner's body, rotate my hips in a counterclockwise direction, and bend forward at the waist. Notice how this pulls him over my hips and lifts his feet off the mat. 4) As I continue with my rotation, my training partner rolls over my hips and toward his back. 5) As I cast my partner over my hips, I release the pressure of the throw, allowing him to land on his feet. To prevent him from falling to his back, I keep my headlock grip locked tight. 6) Using my headlock grip, I help pull my partner back to the upright position so we can continue the drill with minimal breaks. 7) With my partner and I still in the neutral tie-up position as he returns to his feet, he immediately takes his turn to perform the headlock throw by executing a back step. Again, notice how his hips are positioned below mine and that he has closed off all space between our bodies. 8) Continuing to rotate his body in a counterclockwise direction, my partner forces me to trip over his hips and my feet to lift me off the mat. 9) As I fall toward my back, I outstretch my legs to prepare for the landing. Notice how my partner maintains his headlock grip to prevent me from falling to my back. 10) I land on my feet, and my training partner uses his headlock grip to help pull me back into the upright position. Once again, we are in a neutral tie-up position. 11) Once we have returned to the start position, I immediately begin my next repetition by executing a back step. From here, we will go back and forth for a set amount of time or a set number of repetitions.

BICEPS PUSH DOUBLE-LEG DRILL

Throughout my career, the double-leg takedown has been one of the primary techniques that I utilized to sweep my opponents off their feet and put them on their back. Like most takedowns, it is not a technique that you can become proficient at overnight. It requires thousands of repetitions to learn the proper mechanics and develop a powerful shot. While practicing double-leg takedowns on a training partner should certainly be a part of your weekly routine, it can be a painful experience for both the man on top and bottom. If I had finished every double-leg I ever performed in practice, it's possible that I would not have been able to keep fighting into my mid-forties. This drill is an excellent way to practice your double-leg takedowns without putting you and your training partner through constant abuse. If you look at the photos below, you'll notice that I tie up with my partner in the clinch, drop my elevation, obtain control of his legs, and then heft him upward off the mat. However, instead of completing the takedown by dropping him down to the mat and landing on top of him in side control, I place him gently back on his feet and execute another repetition. It's a perfect example of smart training—you're still working the muscles involved in executing double-leg takedowns, as well as ingraining the mechanics involved into your mind, but you're forgoing the most painful part of the technique to ensure your longevity. Personally, I like to execute five or ten repetitions and then switch and have my partner work his takedowns.

1) To set up this drill, I stance face-to-face with my opponent and secure inside biceps control. Notice how my elbows are positioned underneath my partner's arms. This will allow me to lift his arms upward and attack the lower half of his body. 2) I use my biceps ties to elevate my partner's arms upward. Once accomplished, I drop my elevation by bending my knees and sinking my hips, step my right foot to the outside of my partner's left foot, and move my head toward my right. 3) With my hips positioned below my partner's hips, I can effectively secure the double-leg position. I accomplish this by wrapping my arms around the back of his legs, pressing my left ear against his left ribs, and pulling his body into mine. 4) With a secure grip on my partner's legs, I thrust my hips forward and lift his feet up off the mat. From here, I could easily complete the takedown by driving his torso toward my left side using my head and pulling his legs toward my right side using my arms, but the goal of this drill is to do repetitions of the lift, so I will lower my partner back to his feet and return to the start position.

RUNNING THE PIPE SINGLE-LEG DRILL

After the double-leg, the single-leg takedown is perhaps the most common takedown in MMA. And out of all the various ways to finish the single-leg, running the pipe is probably the most versatile. In the sequence below I demonstrate a drill that teaches you the mechanics of running the pipe without completing the takedown, which allows you to perform one repetition after another without putting wear and tear on your own and your training partner's body. If you look at the photos below, you'll notice that I start in the high-single position, and then off-balance my partner by taking a circular step back with my lead foot and driving my head into his shoulder. However, instead of using this pressure to drive my opponent to his back as I would in a fight, I allow him to hop circularly on his grounded foot to reestablish his base and balance. Once we return to the start position, I again take a circular step back with my lead foot and drive my head into his shoulder. After completing a set number of repetitions, I will then complete the takedown before giving my opponent my leg and allowing him to perform the drill.

To acquire the high-single position, I cup my hands together behind my partner's knee, pull his leg up between my legs, and position my head against the right side of his head.

To shatter my partner's base, I step my left leg back and begin rotating my hips in a counterclockwise direction.

Still rotating my hips in a counterclockwise direction, I step my left foot circularly across the mat. At the same time, I drive my head into the side of my opponent's head to further shatter his base. To prevent from falling over, my partner hops on his grounded leg.

To perform another repetition, I rotate my hips in a counterclockwise direction and again slide my left foot circularly across the mat. To maintain his balance, my partner hops on his grounded foot. Performing this drill on a regular basis makes you much better at positioning, and it also increases your training partner's balance.

DEFENDING THE SINGLE DRILL

When your opponent establishes the high-single position, there is a good chance that he will attempt to complete the takedown by running the pipe. The best way to prevent him from accomplishing his goal is to develop flawless balance while on one leg. A perfect example of a fighter with excellent single-leg defense is BJ Penn. In many of his fights his opponents establish the single-leg position, but as they burn energy trying to haul him to the mat, he simply maintains his balance by hopping on one foot. Eventually, he either breaks his opponent's grips and frees his leg or his opponent gets tired and releases his leg voluntarily. But have no misconceptions—developing this type of balance takes a lot of practice, and the drill demonstrated below is an excellent way to get that practice. If you look at the photos, you'll notice that I start by giving my training partner my lead leg so he can assume the high-single position. During the drill, his goal is to rotate his body and use his head to shatter my balance and complete the take-down, and my job is to maintain my balance by hopping on one foot while at the same time using my hands to break his grips. If my partner should manage to force me down to my back, we restart the drill in the standing position. If I should break his grips and escape the position, we do the same thing. I highly recommend incorporating this drill into your regimen. A lot of fighters focus so much on offense, they forget about defense, which often gets them into serious trouble in fights. When you take the time to master defending against the pipe-run finish, you shut down your opponent's first option to complete the single-leg takedown and force him to switch to an alternate takedown, which often provides the time and space you need to escape the position.

To set up this drill, I allow my training partner to establish the high-single position by clasping his hands together behind my left knee, pulling my leg up between his legs, and driving his head into the left side of my head. Before he begins working for the takedown, I grab his left wrist with my right hand.

As my partner works to off-balance me and complete the takedown, I hop on my grounded leg and use my right hand to try and break his grip.

My training partner continues to try to off-balance me, and I continue to maintain my balance by hopping on one foot. The more time you spend practicing this position, the better you will get at preventing your opponents from running the pipe and completing the single-leg takedown.

THROWING DUMMY SUPLEX

One of the hardest parts of learning to finish a suplex is that very few training partners are willing to be dumped on their head in order to help you improve your takedown ability. Unfortunately, when executing a powerful slam, there can be no hesitation on the follow through or you will ruin the technique. To get the work you need, it can be beneficial to invest in a throwing dummy. A throwing dummy is simply a weighted heavy bag that's in the rough shape of a human. The dummy can be thrown over and over again, allowing you to practice your slams will full commitment without worrying about causing damage to a training partner.

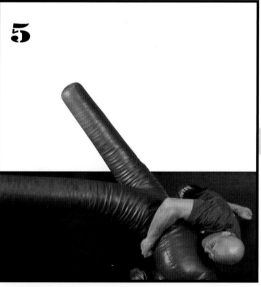

1) I set the throwing dummy on its stomach, squat down over top of it, and secure a waist lock. 2) With my grip attained, I begin to stand up. I post my feet on the mat and extend my legs to pull the dummy up off the mat. 3) With my grip tight around the dummy's waist, I pull it to my chest while exploding upward. It is important to note that I am generating the momentum for the throw as I elevate my hips, making it vital that this step is done with speed. 4) With the dummy vertical, I twist my hips and arch my back, pulling the dummy over top of my body in a horizontal position. This is an extremely explosive movement and must be done very quickly. 5) I slam the dummy's head into the mat over my left shoulder. This prevents us from clashing heads as we go down and also causes my body weight to crash into the dummy rather than into the mat. This can be an extremely devastating maneuver against a real opponent. 6) Maintaining my waist lock, I twist my hips, come onto both knees, and retake the top position. From here, I can easily stand back up and suplex the dummy again. I will repeat this technique for the desired amount of reps or time.

JAB/CROSS/JAB/CROSS/SPRAWL/KNEE COMBO DRILL

Almost any combination can be turned into a fantastic conditioning drill, but the goal is to choose combos that are realistic in a fighting scenario. In this sequence, I throw a jab, a cross, a jab, another cross, execute a sprawl, pop back up to my feet, and then deliver a knee strike to the midsection. This is a very realistic combination because after throwing four punches at your opponent, there is a good chance that he will shoot in for a takedown. To block his shot, you execute a sprawl. Once you've stuffed his takedown attempt, your opponent will most likely attempt to work back to his feet, which allows you to throw a knee strike to his midsection. Of course you won't encounter this exact scenario in every fight, but by training this type of realistic combination on a regular basis, you increase your reaction speed and become more adept at stringing your techniques together. If you look at the photos below, you'll notice that my training partner is holding a medicine ball instead of focus mitts. Personally, I like using a medicine ball in this drill for several reasons—it provides more resistance, which makes it closer to hitting an actual body; the surface area is a lot smaller, which forces you to have pinpoint accuracy with your strikes; and it is positioned along your opponent's centerline, which eliminates the bad habit of throwing your straight punches off toward the sides.

To begin the drill, my training partner holds a medicine ball to his chest and I establish my fighting stance in front of him. It is important to notice how my partner is holding the ball. To leave a gap for me to throw punches at, he has hooked his right arm underneath of the ball and his left arm over the top of the ball.

Keeping my right hand elevated to protect my face, I throw a jab at the center of the ball.

As I pull my left arm back into my stance, I rotate my hips in a counterclockwise direction and throw a cross at the center of the ball.

I pull my right hand back into my stance, rotate my hips in a clockwise direction, and throw another jab.

Rotating my hips in counterclockwise direction, I come up onto the ball of my right foot and throw another cross.

After throwing four punches in a real fight, there is a chance your opponent will attempt to counter with a takedown. With the goal of making my drills as realistic as possible, I execute a sprawl by shooting my legs back, dropping my hips straight down, and placing my hands on the mat. Notice how I keep my head facing forward.

Immediately after executing the sprawl, I pop back up to my feet, shift my weight onto my left leg, and throw a powerful straight rear knee strike into the medicine ball. As I do this, notice how I throw my right arm behind me to generate power for the strike and use my left arm to protect my face from any counterpunches.

After landing the knee strike, I pull my right leg back into my stance and square my hips with my training partner's hips. From here, I will continue the drill for a set number of repetitions.

COUNTER LOW KICK ON SHIELD DRILL

In this sequence I demonstrate a conditioning drill that Muay Thai practitioners have used for centuries. Standing in front of a training partner holding a kicking shield, you alternate between throwing rear leg round kicks to the outside of his lead leg and lead leg round kicks to the inside of his lead leg. Including this drill into your training routine increases your coordination, does wonders for your conditioning, and develops your hip flexor muscles, which in turn allows you to throw more powerful and accurate kicks. While this drill can certainly be performed on a heavy bag, I personally like using a training partner. If you look at the photos below, you'll notice that I have my training partner begin each repetition by throwing a cross at my face. As his fist sails toward me, I step my lead foot to the outside of his rear leg to avoid his punch and acquire a dominant angle of attack, and then throw my first kick before he can pull his hand back into his stance and reestablish his base. Adding this punch into the drill forces you to develop your timing and utilize proper form. If you do perform this drill on a heavy bag, it is important to visualize an opponent standing before you, and then take that outward step with your lead foot as his imaginary punch comes at you. Getting lazy with your kicking drills is an excellent way to develop bad habits, which can lead to a lot of pain in a real fight.

1) To set up the drill, I assume my fighting stance and my training partner holds a kicking shield over his left thigh. Notice how we are just a few feet apart, which is the distance low kicks are most effective. **2)** My training partner initiates the drill by throwing a cross with his right hand. The instant I see his shoulder move, I step my left foot to the outside of his right foot and slightly shift my head toward my left side. It is important to notice that the toes of my left foot are pointing at a forty-five-degree angle in relationship to my opponent and I have kept my guard high to protect my face. **3)** As my training partner misses his cross due to my outside slip, I rotate my hips in a counterclockwise direction and throw a low kick to the outside of his lead leg. Notice how I keep my left hand up to protect my face and extend my right hand into my partner's body to gauge distance. **4)** After landing the kick, I pull my right leg behind me and reestablish my fighting stance. Immediately my partner shifts the kicking shield from the outside of his lead leg to the inside of his lead leg. **5)** The instant my partner has the kicking shield in place, I rotate my hips in a clockwise direction and throw a lead round kick to the inside of his lead leg. Notice how I keep my right hand up to protect my face and extend my left arm to gauge distance. **6)** After landing the kick, I pull my left leg back into my stance and take a small step backward to disengage. From here, my partner will shift the kicking shield back to the outside of his lead leg and I will perform another repetition.

MID KICK ON SHIELD DRILL

This drill is similar to the previous one in that I alternate between throwing round kicks with my rear and lead leg. However, instead of low kicks to my training partner's legs, I throw them to his midsection. Unlike the low kick drill, your training partner must use both of his hands to hold the kicking shield in place, which eliminates his ability to start each repetition with a cross. While this takes away a bit of realism from the drill, it is still better than performing it on a heavy bag because your training partner can point out any weaknesses in your form. Have him inform you if you are failing to step your lead foot to the outside of his rear leg prior to initiating your first kick, failing to rotate your hips, or dropping your hands; this way you can correct the mistakes. When done correctly, this drill will give you all the benefits of the low kicking drill previously demonstrated. It will increase your coordination, do wonders for your conditioning, and develop your hip flexor muscles, which in turn allows you to throw more powerful and accurate kicks.

1) To set up the drill, I establish my fighting stance and my training partner holds a kicking shield over his left ribs. It is important to notice how my partner is holding the shield. He has slid his left arm through both loops on the back of the shield, latched onto his right biceps with his left hand, and then placed his right hand on the back of the shield above his left arm. For both of our safety, he has tucked his elbows tightly to his sides. 2) With both of my training partner's hands tied up, he is unable to throw a cross to initiate the drill. As a result, I begin by stepping my left foot to the outside of his rear foot, rotating my hips in a counterclockwise direction, pivoting on the ball of my left foot, and throwing a rear round kick into the shield. Notice how I throw my right arm behind me to generate power in the kick and keep my left hand up to protect my face. 3) As my right leg rebounds off the kicking shield, I pull it back into my fighting stance. 4) My training partner switches his stance and moves the kicking shield over to protect the right side of his rib cage. 5) Once my partner has shifted the pad, I step my right foot toward my right side, pivot on my right foot, and throw a powerful lead round kick to my partner's midsection. This time, I throw my left arm behind me to generate power in the kick and keep my right hand up to protect my face. 6) I pull my left leg back into my fighting stance and then take a small step back to disengage. From here, I will perform another repetition.

ALTERNATING KNEES ON KICK SHIELD DRILL

This is another conditioning drill that Muay Thai practitioners have been using for centuries. With your training partner holding a kicking shield in front of his body, you wrap your arms around the back of his neck to secure the Muay Thai clinch and then alternate between throwing rear and lead straight knee strikes into his abdomen. Again, you can perform this drill on a heavy bag, but it is not nearly as effective. First, heavy bags tend to be large and unwieldy, which makes securing a proper Muay Thai clinch impossible. Second, it is very important to use your control to off-balance your opponent prior to throwing your knee strikes, and it is hard to recreate this movement on a heavy bag. If you look at the photos below, you'll notice that I constantly pull my opponent's head from side to side to shatter his base and destroy his defenses. If you fail to drill this off-balancing maneuver in practice, your knee strikes will be a lot less effective in fights.

To set up this drill, I wrap both of my hands around the back of my partner's neck, position my elbows in front of his shoulders, pinch my arms together to establish a solid Thai clinch, and then pull my partner's head downward to shatter his base. To absorb the power of my coming knee strikes, my partner holds the kicking shield in front of his abdomen.

Continuing to pull downward on my training partner's head, I shift my weight onto my left foot, lean my upper body back slightly, and drive a powerful straight rear knee into the kicking shield.

Instead of pulling my right foot back into my original stance, I drop it straight down to the mat after landing the knee strike. This will allow me to switch my stance and pull my partner off balance.

Shifting my weight onto my right leg, I step my lift leg behind me and in a counterclockwise direction. Notice how this pulls my partner in a counterclockwise direction as well and destroys his base.

I shift my weight onto my right leg, drive my hips forward, lean my upper body back slightly, and drive the tip of my left knee into the kicking shield. It is very important to notice that I am still pulling my partner's head downward to prevent him from reestablishing his base and escaping the position.

Instead of drawing my left foot back into a southpaw stance, I drop it straight down to the mat.

Shifting my weight onto my left leg, I step my right foot back and circle it in a clockwise direction. Still pulling down on my partner's head, I keep his base shattered and am free to deliver another knee strike to his abdomen. From here, I will continue throwing knee strikes for a set amount of time or repetitions.

HEAVY BAG COMBINATION DRILL

Heavy bags can be found in every boxing, Muay Thai, and MMA gym. While heavy bags respond and move differently than a real person, they have several advantages. First, they are ready to work out anytime you are. You don't need to find a willing partner to spar with or hold pads for you—you simply need to throw on your gloves and get to work. Second, you can throw your strikes at 100 percent power, which often isn't possible when training with a partner. So while it doesn't exactly mimic how an opponent will move in a fight, it better simulates the actual power you will use. Personally, there are a couple of ways in which I will use the heavy bag. If my goal is to increase the power of my strikes, I will repeat a single combination for five or ten seconds, and then take a two- to three-minute rest before performing the next repetition. This ensures that I can perform each of my sets with 100 percent power and correct form. If my goal is to work on my conditioning and stamina, I will perform constant combinations for the length of the rounds of my upcoming fight. For example, if I am preparing for a title fight, I will do five five-minute rounds with a minute break between each round. If I am preparing for a non-title fight, I will do three five-minute rounds with a minute break between sets. However you choose to use the heavy bag, just make sure to do it often. It is one of the most functional, well-rounded pieced of equipment that you can employ to develop your striking game.

NOTE: The photos below do not represent a specific drill, but rather demonstrate the type of work that can be done on the heavy bag.

Standing in my fighting stance, I initiate my bag work by rotating my hips in a clockwise direction and throwing a jab.

As I retract my jab, I take a small outward step with my left foot, rotate my hips in a counterclockwise direction, and throw a rear low round kick.

I pull my right leg back into my stance, reset my base, and then throw a cross at the bag as it swings toward me.

I pull my right arm back into my stance and then elevate my guard to block an imaginary strike. When performing heavy bag work, it is important not to forget about defense.

Having elevated my guard and with my body positioned close to the bag, I grab the bag with my left hand to mimic a lead collar tie, rotate my hips in a counterclockwise direction, and throw a rear side elbow.

Having tied up the bag in the dirty boxing clinch, I unleash some right uppercuts. Remember, even though the bag is static, do not neglect your range or defense. If you do, it is quite possible to develop bad habits.

I simulate the Muay Thai clinch by wrapping both of my arms around the bag. To capitalize on my position, I throw a rear side knee into the bag.

As I disengage from the clinch, I throw another rear side elbow. This is a very important habit to get into because many opponents will lower their guard when breaking from the clinch.

Having created distance between the bag and myself, I circle slightly toward my right, just as I would when fighting a right-handed fighter. Remember, it is important to never stand in one spot while working on a heavy bag. To get the most out of the exercise, constantly circle around the bag and practice your footwork as you throw strikes.

As I back out into punching range, I throw a rear round kick at the bag. Again, notice that I throw my right hand behind me to generate power and keep my left hand up to protect my face.

I pull my right leg back into my stance and immediately throw a quick jab.

As I retract my jab, I rotate my hips in counterclockwise direction, come up onto the ball of my right foot, and throw a right cross. It is important to mention that the techniques shown are just a small segment of my overall bag work. On any given day, I will throw hundreds of strikes in different combinations.

CATCH A JAB THROW A JAB

The jab is an extremely versatile punch. It can be used to attack, to counter your opponent's strikes, or to set up a takedown. In addition to learning how to throw a jab, you must also learn how to counter it. While it is certainly possible to move out of the way of your opponent's jab, this type of defense limits your ability to strike back. Oftentimes, a much better approach is to parry your opponent's jab using you rear hand. In addition to preventing your opponent from landing his strike, it also allows you to follow up with a jab of your own. Speed is key with this technique. The goal is to throw your jab while your opponent's arm is still outstretched, catching him off guard. By striking your opponent with your lead hand, you not only knock him off balance, but you also momentarily obscure his vision, making him susceptible to follow-up strikes or a takedown. In the sequence below, I demonstrate the "catch a jab throw a jab drill." Performing this drill on a regular basis will not only improve your ability to throw jabs and defend against your opponent's jabs, but it will also improve your timing, sense of distance, and punching stamina. Personally, I like to perform this drill for a set amount of time rather than a set number of repetitions. It is important to note that the goal is not to see how hard you can hit, but rather focus on your timing and speed.

| To set up the drill, my training partner and I stand in our fighting stances a few feet apart. | At the same time, we both throw a jab at the other's face. | As our jabs extend, we raise our rear hand to catch the other's fist and parry it away from our faces. Consistently training this drill will make it much easier for you to spot a jab coming, as well as help you learn your range for throwing a jab. With enough repetition, you will be able to land your jab with pinpoint precision while at the same time avoiding your opponent's jab. |

COUNTERING STRIKES TO TAKEDOWN DRILL

As a wrestler, my goal in many of my fights is to take my opponent to the mat and acquire the top position. However, having been in the fight game for a while, all of my opponents realize that this is my intention. In an attempt to prevent me from accomplishing my goal, they focus their training on throwing strikes from the standing position and avoiding my takedowns. When facing such a fighter, shooting blindly in for the takedown would be a horrible mistake, as I would most likely walk directly into his punches. In order to secure the takedown, I have to properly set it up using strikes or by countering his strikes. This drill is designed for developing the latter. If you look at the photos below, you'll notice that as my training partner throws a jab, I perform an outside slip to cause him to miss with his punch and then shoot into his body for the takedown. However, the most important part of this technique is timing. If you are slow to react with your shot, you give your opponent the time he needs to pull his arm back into his stance and throw another strike. In order to be effective, you must shoot forward before he can retract his punching arm. Personally, I like to perform the drill in high repetitions to ingrain the movements, so I do not complete the takedown. Instead, I shoot into my partner's body, lift him up off the mat, and then set him back down and reset for my next repetition. If you are new to situational timing drills, it's a good idea to ask your training partner to start with very light punches. After all, if you are constantly getting hit in the face, it is very difficult to develop proper form. As you get the movements down, your partner can slowly increase the speed of his punches.

To set up the drill, my training partner and I begin in our fighting stances a few feet apart. With my partner being the attacker, he assumes a more aggressive stance, and I assume a more defensive stance by positioning my hands high and my palms facing out. This will allow me to deflect his punches and shoot in for a takedown.

My training partner initiates the drill by throwing a jab at my face. Immediately I move my right hand across my body to parry his strike. At the same time, I execute an outside slip by shifting my head toward my right side.

I avoid my partner's jab by executing a parry and an outside slip. My next goal is to shoot forward into his body before he can pull his arm back into his stance and reestablish his base. Notice how with his arm still extended, he cannot hit me with a cross.

To capitalize on my dominant angle of attack, I step my right foot forward and close the distance between our bodies.

I step my left foot forward, wrap my arms around the back of my training partner's legs, and drive my head into the left side of his body. Instead of completing the takedown, I will release my control and perform another repetition.

STRIKING TO THE TAKEDOWN DRILL

The previous drill is a great way to bait, counter, and neutralize aggressive fighters who like to throw lots of strikes. However, it is a much more difficult technique to employ when up against a counterstriker like Chuck Liddell. Instead of bombarding you with punches and kicks, this type of fighter sits back and waits to counter your strikes. With some fighters it's possible to bait them into a stand-up war, but others are extremely patient and remain strong to their game plan. If you should face such a fighter and want to score a takedown, you will most likely have to do so by throwing strikes of your own. Again, learning how to properly set up your takedowns with strikes takes a lot of practice, and this drill is an excellent way to get that practice. With both you and your opponent in your fighting stances, you drop your level as you throw an overhand right to your opponent's face. While your hand is still blurring his vision, you shoot forward, sneak past his defenses, and gain control of his legs. Much like the previous drill, the intensity of this exercise can vary. Your partner can be totally compliant and allow you to perform one repetition after another without any resistance, or he can do his best to prevent you from securing control of his legs. Personally, I feel it is best to learn the general dynamics of the move first, and as you get more and more proficient with it, have your training partner slowly increase his resistance.

To set up this drill, my training partner and I assume our fighting stances a few feet apart.

To force my opponent back onto his heels and distract him from the takedown, I shift my weight onto my left leg and begin throwing an overhand punch toward the left side of his face.

Spotting the strike, my training partner shifts his weight onto his heels and elevates his guard to block the strike. Notice how the lower half of his body is currently vulnerable to attack.

As my training partner defends against my strike, I shift my weight forward and lower my elevation.

With my hips lower than my opponent's hips, I step my right foot forward and move my head to the outside of his body.

As I close the distance between us, I wrap my arms around the back of my training partner's legs, press my head into his left shoulder, and drive him laterally. Instead of finishing the takedown, I will release my control and perform another repetition.

SECTION TWO
SPORT-SPECIFIC GROUND

As you know, fighting on your feet and grappling are very different in nature, especially when it comes to the types of movement involved. When grappling, your base is dramatically increased due to a larger percentage of your body being on the ground, which unshackles your proprioceptive sense of equilibrioception and allows you to be more fluid and dynamic with your movements. In addition to this, you're also usually in very close proximity to your opponent, which often forces you to carry a portion of his body weight. For untrained athletes, the combination of these two aspects of the ground game can be extremely tiring. To prevent from gassing out, it is very important to train your body for the various types of grappling movements. While sparring is certainly a part of that training process, it can also be extremely beneficial to perform grappling drills on a regular basis.

In addition to helping improve your stamina, drills are excellent for improving your ability to maintain positional advantages. Unlike when kickboxing, once you secure a dominant position on the ground, it's possible to hold it for a long duration of time. The longer you can maintain a dominant position, the more damage you can cause with strikes and submissions. However, each of the dominant positions you can achieve are drastically different, making it important to drill specific movements for each one. To help you down this road, I have categorized the drills in this section by position.

I begin by offering a few drills that you can utilize at the beginning of your workout to not only warm up your muscles, but also develop stamina. I also demonstrate various partner warm-ups that can be done to initiate blood flow into the muscles of both practitioners.

Next, I move on to top control. Having a wrestling background, my ultimate goal in a fight is generally to end up on top of my opponent and punish him using ground and pound. This section shows some of the drills I employ to not only maintain the top position, but also advance past my opponent's guard.

Once I pass my opponent's guard and secure a dominant position such as side control or mount, I never aim to be defensive. I always advance and attack, and this section shows some of the primary drills I use in practice to sharpen that attacking mentality. Additionally, I cover the ground and pound drills that have dramatically improved my striking over the years.

Finally, I demonstrate some of the guard drills that I employ in my fighting camps. Guard is not an ideal position for me, but in any fight you must be prepared to end up on your back. Most of the time, I will immediately attempt to escape back to my feet or reverse my opponent and end up in the top position. However, you must always remember that guard is a fantastic position for catching your opponent with a submission when he makes a mistake. In order to be successful with this type of attack, however, your submissions must be second nature. To help you with this, I have included a few of my favorite guard submission drills.

Much like the standing chapter, this section is not meant to be a comprehensive list of every drill or technique you can utilize from the ground, as there are thousands of drills and techniques. The aim of this chapter is simply to demonstrate on some of the key positions that I practice to advance my grappling ability. The most important aspect of this chapter is finding which positions are necessary for your specific game plan, and then incorporating drills that allow you to become more proficient at those positions. By combining smart game planning, specific positional drilling, and ground sparring, you will sharpen your grappling technique, improve your endurance on the mat, and become much more capable of effectively mounting an offense while on the ground.

PHYSIO BALL SQUEEZE

Grappling recruits muscle groups in unique ways, and there are certain grappling movements that simply cannot be duplicated using a barbell or free weights. A perfect example is the isometric leg adduction utilized when playing the bottom guard position. Without the strength to squeeze your legs around your opponent or the stamina to hold the position for a prolonged period of time, your guard will most likely be ineffective. Training your body to perform this squeezing movement is an extremely important part of your workout, but it is difficult to accomplish using weights. In this sequence, I demonstrate a drill that allows you to train that squeezing effort. If you look at the photos below, you'll notice that I position a physio ball between my legs and then squeeze my knees together and hold the position. Although it is possible to substitute a person for the ball, it can be difficult to find a training partner who is willing to repeatedly have the life squeezed out of him. I strongly recommend adding this drill into your regimen, especially if your legs quickly fatigue when playing guard. It is an excellent sport-specific exercise to increase the strength and stamina in your legs.

1) I begin the exercise by lying on my back with a physio ball held loosely between my knees. 2)I pinch my knees together and drive my hips off the ground. This not only actives my hip adductor muscles, but my glutes and hamstrings as well. I will hold this position for a set amount of time, usually between ten and sixty seconds depending on my goals. 3) I relax, allow, my hips to drop back down to the mat, and release my inward knee pressure.

PHYSIO BALL HAMSTRING CURL

Having strength and stamina in your hamstring muscles is extremely important when grappling, especially when finishing sweeps and submissions. Although it is possible to train your hamstrings on machines and using weights, they are taxed in a different manner when grappling. Hamstring machines tend to move your legs behind your body in an arc, but when grappling, your hamstring muscles are mainly taxed by curling your feet toward your butt while your legs are in the air. Developing hamstring strength from this somewhat awkward position can make the difference between finishing a triangle choke and having your opponent rip free. If you look at the photos below, you'll notice that I again employ a physio ball. For the most gains, you want to curl your legs downward into the ball and then isometrically hold the position between ten and sixty seconds. Generally if you are squeezing with max effort, you want to be on the low side of this time span, and if you are using less than max effort, you want to be on the high side.

1) I begin the exercise by lying on my back with my legs resting on a physio ball. 2) I flex my hamstrings and curl my feet toward my butt. This pinches the physio ball between my heels and my hamstrings. At the same time, I contract my hip flexors and roll my hips back, picking the physio ball off the ground. If I do not maintain constant pressure with my hamstrings from this position, the ball will drop back to the mat. 3) I relax my abdominals, drop the ball back the mat, and then relax my hamstrings.

HEAVY BAG GROUND AND POUND

When training strikes from the standing position, it is important to spar with a training partner as well as perform heavy bag drills. The same holds true for improving your skills at striking on the ground. Sparring with a partner allows you to develop the positioning and control needed to effectively land your strikes while grappling, but it has some drawbacks. If you spar wearing the four-ounce gloves you use in a fight, and throw elbow and knee strikes as well as punches, there is a good chance that you or your opponent will get injured when going at full intensity. Shadow sparring or gearing up with protective equipment is a way to reduce the risk of injury, but they change the dynamics of your strikes. Both are excellent drills to perform because they teach you how to react and set up your striking techniques against a resisting opponent, but in order to develop the speed and power of your strikes, you must include heavy bag work into your striking training on the ground. In the sequence below, I demonstrate a hypothetical heavy bag training session where I incorporate punches and elbows into the mix. Again, performing heavy bag work alone is not enough to become a ground and pound specialist. In addition to developing your speed and power with heavy bag work, you must also develop your control and timing through sparring.

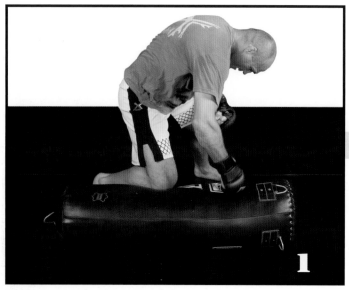

Posting up on the right side of the heavy bag, I begin the drill by delivering a powerful right punch.

Instead of retracting my right arm, I curl my right hand toward my face, rotate my hips in a counterclockwise direction, and throw a right side elbow into the heavy bag.

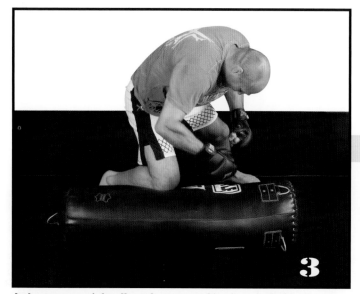

As I retract my right elbow, I rotate my hips in a clockwise direction and prepare to throw a heavy left-hand strike into the bag.

Continuing to rotate my hips in a clockwise direction, I land a left hook to the heavy bag.

Instead of retracting my left arm, I curl my left hand toward my chest and drop a left side elbow toward the heavy bag.

Having dazed my imaginary opponent with a handful of strikes, I swing my right leg over the heavy bag and move into the mount position. As soon as I secure the position, I throw a powerful straight right.

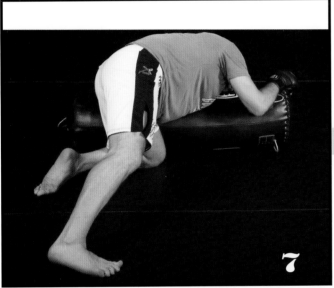

After throwing numerous strikes in the mount, I transition to the opposite side of the bag. In preparation to land a powerful knee strike to the body, I post my right leg out to the side. It is important to mention that in order to be an effective fighter, you must learn to control your opponent and execute strikes and submissions from both sides.

Controlling my imaginary opponent using my arms, I drive my right knee into the side of the heavy bag.

Posting my right foot out to my side to maintain my base, I deliver a right hook to the side of the bag. Keep in mind during this drill that the goal is to develop power and speed with your strikes.

GUARD STRIKING TO SWEEP TO MOUNT

When grappling on your back it is difficult to generate the same amount of power in your strikes as when in the top position due to your lack of leverage, but this doesn't mean strikes are useless in this scenario. Many fighters such as Kenny Florian are experts at inflicting damage while playing guard. Although it is difficult to knock your opponent out from this position, landing clean elbow strikes and punches do wonders at distracting your opponent. Instead of using his arms to land punches of his own or set up submissions, your opponent must use his arms to protect his face and body, which often creates an opportunity to initiate a sweep, reversal, or submission. In the sequence below, I demonstrate a drill that not only helps you become more efficient at striking off your back, but also flowing from strikes into a reversal. If you look at the photos below, you'll notice that I position a heavy bag between my legs to simulate an opponent in my guard. I strike the bag with an assortment of punches and elbow strikes and then immediately reverse the bag and assume the top position. Once on top of the bag, I land a few more strikes and then pull it back into my guard and continue with my strikes from the bottom. It is important to mention that due to the bag lacking limbs, the reversals you can implement will be limited. However, the goal of the drill is not to perfect your sweeps—that should be done with a training partner. The goal of the drill is to improve the speed and power of your strikes, as well as your fluidity of transitioning between those strikes and a reversal.

To set up this drill, I lie on my back, place a heavy bag between my legs, and then wrap my shins underneath the bag, just as I would when establishing the butterfly guard on an opponent. To mimic head control, I place both of my hands on top of the heavy bag.

Keeping my left hand on top of the bag to mimic a left collar tie, I rotate my hips toward my left side, curl my right hand toward my chest, and deliver a right side elbow.

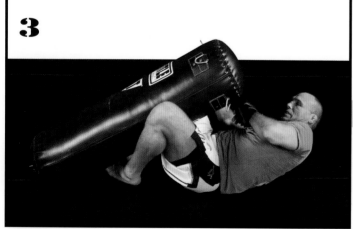

I extend my legs slightly and straighten my back, creating distance between myself and the heavy bag. This allows me to rotate my torso toward my right side and deliver a left hook.

Having created separation between the bag and my body, I throw a right cross. It is important to note that if this were a real fight, my opponent would most likely also be throwing strikes. Since he would have leverage on his side, getting into a striking war would not end in my favor. If you are not controlling his posture, you must hinder his striking by creating space using your legs.

5

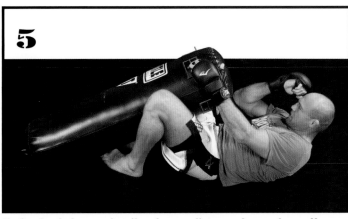

Having landed several strikes from a distance, I now close off space between myself and the punching bag by crunching my body forward and establishing a left collar tie. As I do this, I pull my right hand up by my head and then drive my elbow downward into the top of the heavy bag. It is important to note that these types of spiking elbows from the bottom position are perfectly legal.

6

Rotating my hips toward my right side, I throw a left side elbow at the top of the bag.

7

As I land the elbow, I use the momentum to execute a sweep. I accomplish this by extending my left leg and rolling onto my right hip, causing the heavy bag to roll off me and onto the mat to my right. The goal here is to stun your opponent with the elbow strike, and then use your sideways momentum to transition right into the sweep.

8

I continue to roll the bag over and establish the mount position. Immediately I squeeze my knees together to secure my position.

9

Having established the mount, I begin dropping fast, powerful punches. The goal is to land as many solid shots as possible, which is best achieved by throwing a variety of different strikes. When you land half a dozen in a row, there is a good chance the referee will intervene and stop the fight.

TURTLE BACK FLIP

In this sequence I demonstrate a partner drill that I like to perform before grappling practice to warm up my joints and muscles. As you know, the best warm-up exercises are the ones that most closely simulate the movements you will be performing while fighting. This exercise consists of arching, rolling, and sprawling, all of which you repeatedly do while grappling. By performing the turtle back flip prior to hitting the mats, you will dramatically decrease your chance of injury. The other nice part about this exercise is that both you and your training partner get a simultaneous workout. If you look at the photos below, you'll notice that as I roll over the top of my partner's back, he must stabilize his body against my weight, providing him with an isometric workout. As we switch rolls after a set number of repetitions, he gets a dynamic workout while I get an isometric workout. Overall, this is an excellent warm-up exercise that will prepare you for grappling and the more intense drills demonstrated later in this section.

To set up the drill, my partner and I both get on our hands and knees so that our bodies are perpendicular.

I begin to crawl forward, going underneath my partner's body.

I crawl completely underneath my partner's body on my hands and knees. This movement warms up my hips and shoulders.

As I come out from underneath my partner, I lean backward so that my back is resting against his left side.

I execute a backflip over my partner's back. Notice how I place my hands on the mat to prevent myself from falling on my head. Although this movement does wonders to warm up my muscles and joints, my partner also gets a workout as he isometrically flexes his body to support my weight.

I land on my hands and knees in the starting position. From here, I can execute another repetition or switch positions with my partner.

TURTLE FRONT FLIP

In this sequence I demonstrate another warm-up drill designed specifically for grappling. If you look at the photos below, you'll see that my partner assumes the turtle position and I lay my chest on his back and wrap my arms underneath his torso. This puts me into the perfect position to execute a front flip over his body. As my feet touch down on the opposite side, I use my arms to keep my back elevated off the mat, which allows me to immediately flip back over his body and return to the start position. Much like the previous exercise, this drill moves blood into your muscles and joints, but because of the opposite mechanics, it warms up all the areas of your body neglected by the turtle backflip.

To begin this drill, my partner establishes the turtle position by placing his hands and knees on the mat, and I lay my torso over his back. Next, I come up onto my feet and wrap my arms underneath his torso.

Keeping my arms hooked firmly underneath my partner's torso, I push off my legs and perform a front flip over his body. It is important to mention that if you fail to have a good grip on your partner's torso, it's possible to slip off his body and land on your head.

As my feet touch down on the mat, I keep my back arched and use nearly every muscle in my body to keep my body in the upright position.

Curling my arms, I push off my legs and flip back over my partner's body.

My feet touch down and I am back to the starting position. From here, I can execute another repetition or switch places with my partner.

GUARD PASS TO GRANBY ROLL

This is another grappling drill that simultaneously benefits both training partners. If you look at the photos below, you'll notice that I begin in my partner's guard. To begin the drill, I execute a simple guard pass. Before I can secure the position, my training partner rolls up to his knees and assumes the turtle position. Instead of backing off and letting him escape up to his feet, I wrap my arms around him and bear hug his body. This is where the drill gets tricky. The instant I secure my body lock, my partner executes an old wrestling escape known as the Granby roll. If all of my weight is pressing down on his back, his maneuver will roll me over to my back. If I am quick to back some of my weight off of the body lock, his body rolls underneath me and he ends back in guard. As you can see, this drill is beneficial to both partners. When you're on top, you get practice passing guard, securing a body lock when your partner transitions to the turtle position, and then committing just the right amount of weight to your body lock to prevent your opponent from standing up or rolling you to your back by executing the Granby roll. When you are on the bottom, you get practice escaping up to your knees when your opponent passes your guard into side control, as well as get practice escaping the turtle position by executing the Granby roll, which allows you to either roll your opponent to his back or reestablish the guard position, depending upon your opponent's pressure. Learning the delicate weight balance needed to stay on top of an opponent is not easy, but this drill will certainly send you in the right direction.

To begin the drill, I climb into my partner's guard. It is important to notice that my hands and knees are on the mat and his feet are flat on the floor. While neither position is optimal to fight from, keep in mind that the goal of this drill is to practice the Granby roll, not any specific guard pass.

I hop my lower body over my partner's legs and move into side control.

Before I can solidify my position and pin my partner's shoulders to the mat, he bucks his hips to create space between us and begins to turn away from me.

Continuing to turn away from me, my partner rolls over his left shoulder until he is on all fours. To maintain control of his body, I keep my right arm draped over his back.

As my partner assumes the all-fours position, I wrap my arms tightly around his body. Immediately he executes a Granby roll by turning back into me and rolling over his left shoulder again, this time in the opposite direction.

If I were to maintain my tight lock on my partner's body, there is a good chance that his Granby roll would force me over to my back. To prevent this, I loosen my hold and allow him to roll his body underneath me.

Due to the space I allowed my partner to create, he rolls underneath my body and pulls me into his guard.

Once my partner locks his feet together to solidify his position, we have completed one repetition. He prevented me from passing his guard by executing a Granby roll, and I prevent him from reversing me by releasing my pressure as he rolled. From here, we can execute another repetition or switch places.

HOPPING GUARD PASS

In order to be dominant when grappling from the top position, you must constantly practice neutralizing your opponent's hip movement. In the drill demonstrated below, I wrap my arms around my opponent's hips, place my head on the mat, elevate my legs into the air, and then move them off to the side. This removes my body from my opponent's guard and places me into side control. In such a scenario, the ideal goal is to immediately begin your attack from side control by pinning your opponent's back to the mat and neutralizing his hip movement. However, there are many grapplers who are absolute masters at shrimping their hips away from you, moving their legs underneath your body, and placing you back in their guard. If you should find yourself up against an opponent who has powerful and constant hip movement, sometimes floating from side to side can be an easier task than trying to pin his back to the mat. If you look at the photos below, you'll notice that as my opponent shrimps his hips away from me to place me back into his guard, I use his movement against him by once again balancing on my head, elevating my legs, and moving them to the opposite side of his body. This once again places me in side control, but with my opponent's hips turned away from me, it puts me in a much more dominant position. Aside from being a very practical drill for improving your ability to maintain dominant top control, it is a great drill for developing coordination and balance. As you hop over your opponent's legs, there is a brief moment where you balance almost all of your body weight on your head. Being able to maintain this position and land in a controlled manner on the opposite side of your opponent's body is necessary for the completion of the drill, and it will pay big dividends by increasing your athleticism on the mat.

I begin the drill in my partner's open guard.

I wrap my arms around my partner's hips, plant my head on the mat next to his left hip, and then hop my legs straight into the air. The goal is to clear his legs and move into side control.

I drop my legs down on my opponent's right side.

Before I can establish the side control position, my partner turns onto his right side, shrimps his hips, and pulls his right leg underneath my body, once again placing me in his guard.

While my partner is still turning into me, I plant my head on the mat next to his right hip and kick my legs straight up into the air.

Due to my partner's momentum, I easily hop over his legs and land in side control on his left side. Immediately he shrimps his hips toward his left side and begins pulling his left leg underneath my body.

My partner turns more onto his left side in an attempt to sneak his leg underneath my body and pull me into his guard.

To continue with the drill, I plant my head by my partner's left hip and kick my legs straight up into the air.

I drop down into side control on my partner's right side. From here, we will execute several more repetitions before switching positions.

ALTERNATING SIDE CONTROL

Much like the previous drill, this one is designed to improve your ability to move quickly from one side of your opponent's body to the other. However, rather than beginning the drill in the guard and initiating your transitions based on your partner's shrimping escapes, you begin in side control and execute your transitions at your own free will. Instead of reacting to your opponent's movement, you chose when and why to transition to the opposite side of his body. It could be to catch him unprepared and move into a submission, to achieve a more secure pin and execute some ground strikes, or simply to surprise your opponent and change the pace of the fight. While this may seem very similar to the previous drill, reacting to your opponent's movements and initiating movements yourself require different balance and coordination. When your opponent moves and you react, his ability to counter your movement diminishes greatly. When you initiate the movement, your opponent's ability to react to that movement increases. This drill will teach you how and when to make your transitions to limit your opponent's ability to counter.

To begin the drill, I establish side control on my partner's right side, establish a right underhook, and place my head on the mat to the right of his head.

Keeping my head planted firmly on the mat, I kick my legs straight up into the air and use my hands to maintain my balance. Due to the fact that I am initiating this movement, I leap extra high to avoid my partner's possible counters. If you get sloppy with this movement in a fight, your opponent could wrap his legs around your body as you relieve pressure from his chest and pull you into his guard.

I somersault over my partner's torso and land in side control on his left side.

4

To leap back in the alternate direction, I switch my head inside and place it on the ground to the left of my opponent's head. This placement is crucial. If you leap with your head on the far side in a fight, your opponent could easily roll you as your hips rise off the mat.

5

I kick my legs straight up into the air.

6

I land in side control on my partner's left side, returning to the starting position. From here, I can continue to execute more reps of the drill or switch places with my partner.

BUTTERFLY GUARD ELEVATION

Although I never develop a game plan that revolves around fighting off my back, I create strategies of escape should I find myself in this often compromising position. In MMA, one of the best tools when working off your back is the butterfly guard. To achieve this position, you position your shins to the inside of your opponent's thighs and your knees to the outside of his body. It is a good defensive position because it makes it difficult for your opponent to create the space he needs to land damaging strikes while still maintaining control of your body. It is also a good offensive position because it gives you a number of different sweeps and escapes. However, in order to be effective with these various sweeps and escapes, you must become a master at using your legs to create space. If you look at the photos below, you'll notice that I utilize a rocking motion that allows me to lift my opponent's body up off the mat using my legs. From this position, I can force his hips away from me and stand up, move him sideways and take his back, or tilt him in midair, dump him on his back, and establish the top position. Each of these techniques is highly effective, but they all require you to elevate your opponent's hips using your legs. For this reason, this is a very important drill to incorporate into your regimen. You could have the best sweeps and escapes in the world, but if you don't possess the strength or coordination to elevate the lower half of your opponent's body from the butterfly guard, you won't get a chance to put them into effect.

I begin in the sit-up butterfly guard position. Notice how my shins are to the inside of my partner's legs and my hands are positioned underneath his armpits.

To shift my partner's weight off his legs, I lean back and pull him with me using my grips underneath his armpits. It is important to notice that I keep my back curved. If you drop flat to your back, you lose all leverage and the technique will fail.

3

As my lower back hits the mat, I continue to pull my partner toward me using my hands and legs. If I allow him to rest and halt his forward momentum, he will be able to flatten me out and pass my guard.

4

To fully shatter my partner's base and balance, I rock all the way back and extend my legs and arms by contracting my quadriceps and triceps. If this were an actual grappling scenario, I would either fully extend my legs to create separation between us or execute one of the many butterfly guard sweeps. However, for the sake of the drill, I will lower my partner back to the starting position and execute another repetition.

HEAD CONTROL GET-UP

If you end up on your back, it is most likely because your opponent forced you to the mat, and your first order of business should be to prevent him from establishing side control or mount by securing him between your legs in the guard position. Once accomplished, securing the butterfly guard is an excellent option because it allows you to create space and force a change in position, but it's not always possible. If your opponent refuses to let you move your legs between his legs, sometimes you will have to fight it out from the traditional open guard. However, this does not mean that you should be content on your back. When in the bottom guard position, it's still possible to create space between you and your opponent, pull your body out from underneath him, and stand back up. One of the most effective ways to achieve this is to execute the head control get-up, which I demonstrate below. To perform this technique, you place a hand on one side of your opponent's head and force it away from your body to prevent him from pinning you to the mat. As his body moves away from you, you slip out from underneath him and climb back to your feet. While this might seem like a very basic maneuver, it can be very difficult to pull off in a fight. Chances are your opponent worked very hard to take you to the mat, and instead of letting you slip out from underneath his body, he will drive forward with all his might and try to keep your back pinned. In addition to requiring very precise timing, it can also be a very taxing movement. For these reasons, I strongly suggest practicing the drill demonstrated below as often as possible. If you look at the photos, you'll notice that I do not climb all the way up to my feet. Instead, I escape my body from underneath my opponent, come up onto one knee, and then lie back down and pull my opponent back into my guard. Next, I repeat the escape on the opposite side. By cutting the escape short, I can execute one repetition after another. When first starting out, it's best to have your partner offer minimal resistance. This allows you to learn the mechanics of the escape and ingrain the movements into your mind. However, as you get more advanced, it can be beneficial to have your partner slowly increase his resistance until it turns into a light sparring match. Your goal is to create space and escape, and his goal is to do everything in his power to keep your back pinned. As you move through the drill, you will begin to see holes that open up in your opponent's defense as he scrambles to keep you pinned to the mat. The next step is learning how to capitalize on these holes with other escapes and submissions. Remember, not every technique you execute will be successful, but as long as you string your attacks together based upon your opponent's reactions to your movements, you will eventually get the upper hand.

I begin on my back with my partner in my guard. To hinder him from posturing up or driving into me, I wrap my right hand over the back of his head.

To execute the head control get-up, I need to create space between our bodies. I accomplish this by turning onto my left hip and driving my partner's head away from me by straightening my right arm.

Having created space between my partner and me, I post my left hand on the mat behind, post my right foot on the mat to my right, and then use these points of base to sit up. It is important to notice that I still have my right arm extended, pressing into my partner's head. This prevents him from driving into me and closing off the space I created. I must maintain this grip throughout the technique or risk losing position.

Using my left hand and right foot as points of base, I lift my hips off the mat, pull my left leg out from underneath my body, and then place my left knee on the mat to solidify my position. If this were an actual fight, I would either disengage from my opponent and stand back up or move into him in an attempt to steal the top position.

5

For the purpose of the drill, I sit back into my partner and pull him into my guard.

6

I return to the bottom guard position.

7

I hook my left hand around the back of my partner's head. From here, I will escape my opposite leg out from underneath his body to get a symmetrical workout.

I extend my left arm, forcing my partner's head away from my body in an effort to create space.

I post my right hand and left foot on the mat, which allows me to sit up and begin pulling my right leg out from underneath my partner's body.

I utilize the hip heist motion once again by elevating my right leg off the mat and pulling it out from underneath my body. Once my leg is clear, I place my right knee on the mat behind me. This gives me an additional point of base and will allow me to disengage or attempt to secure top position.

SWINGING ARMBAR DRILL

In this sequence I demonstrate a classic guard drill that involves using your hips and legs to move into the armbar position. While the armbar is the destination, the real goal of the drill is to increase your ability to move your hips while on the mat. This is accomplished by swinging back and forth into alternating side armbars on a partner without using your hands. Although not using your hands might seem like a minor detail, a lot of people handicap themselves on the ground by using too much upper body and not enough lower body, and performing this drill on a regular basis is a good way to remedy that flaw. By using only your legs to move into the armbar, you become much more adept at maneuvering your hips on the ground, which leaves your hands free to tie up your opponent's arms and control his posture. However, before executing this drill it is important to learn the small details. If you look at the photos below, you'll notice that I begin with my partner in my open guard. To begin the drill, I climb my legs up my partner's body and use leg pressure on his torso to move my hips to the side. My partner's job is not to fight me, but rather stay balanced inside my guard and keep his arms extended. Partner compliancy is mandatory. However, after using the drill to warm up your legs and perfect your hip movement, you can move into sparring from the guard.

I begin lying on my back with my partner in my guard. To help me with the drill, my partner extends his arms and crossing them over my chest, positioning his hands on either side of my head. This will keep his arms properly positioned throughout the drill, despite my lack of hand control.

I contract my left hamstring and curl my left leg into my partner's back, which allows me to pivot on the mat and move my hips out to my right. At the same time, I swing my right leg toward the right side of my partner's head.

I continue to rotate my body in a clockwise direction using my legs.

Once my body is perpendicular to my partner's body, I hook my right leg over the right side of his head, pinch my knees together, and then curl both of my legs downward. If you do not apply this downward pressure in a fight, it becomes much easier for your opponent to rip his body upward and free himself from the armbar.

Having achieved the armbar position on my partner's left arm, I uncurl my legs, swing my right leg to the left side of his face, and begin rotating my body in a counterclockwise direction.

Continuing to rotate in a counterclockwise direction, I hook my right leg around my partner's left side. This provides an anchor for my body and will help me rotate.

Once my body is perpendicular to my partner's body, I hook my left leg over the left side of his head, pinch my knees together, and curl my legs downward. Notice how my partner has kept his arms crossed over my chest for the duration of the drill to help aid my movements.

Having established the armbar position on my partner's left side, I once again rotate my body in a clockwise direction to continue with the drill. The more you practice this movement, the faster you will become at alternate side armbars. It is also excellent for warming up your hip and leg muscles before practice.

HIP BUMP TO BRIDGE AND ROLL DRILL

The hip bump to bridge and roll drill is beneficial to both the top and bottom player. If you look at the photos below, you'll notice that I begin on my back with my training partner in my guard. To initiate the drill, I perform the hip bump sweep, which is an extremely effective technique against an opponent that postures up in your guard. I accomplish this by sitting up as my partner increases his elevation, obtaining control of his arm, and then bumping my hips into his hips. This causes my partner to roll over to his back, allowing me to claim the mount position. Once accomplished, it is my partner's turn to benefit from the drill. Using the momentum of his forced roll, he traps my arm, elevates his hips, and rolls me to my back, once again putting him in my guard. Without a break, I once again execute the hip bump, allowing us to go back and forth.

When these two techniques are combined into a fluid drill, both partners glean benefits. The fighter starting on the bottom learns the timing and sensitivity of a great sweep, while the partner beginning on top learns how to quickly secure control of his opponent and escape the mount position. Personally, I like to perform this drill for a set amount of time, and then switch positions so my partner and I get to practice both positions. In addition to making you more proficient at these two highly utilized techniques, the drill also increases your base, balance, and grappling stamina.

To begin the drill, my opponent postures up in my open guard.

To initiate the sweep, I sit forward so I am chest to chest with my partner and overhook his left arm with my left arm. At the same time, I post my left foot and right elbow on the mat to act as points of base.

To execute the sweep, I hook my right leg tightly around my partner's left leg, push off my left leg, and drive my hips into his body. With my right leg hooked over his left leg and my left arm hooked over his left arm, he is unable to stop the sweep by posting on the mat.

Continuing with my momentum, I put my partner on his back and establish the mount position.

Before I can settle in and firmly establish the mount, my partner immediately swims his right arm underneath my left arm.

My partner establishes a tight over-hook by wrapping his right arm around my left arm. If he secures this control quickly enough, he can use the momentum from the previous roll and drive me to the right with little resistance, forcing me to my back once again.

My partner bridges powerfully to his right by extending his legs and driving his hips into the air. To assist in moving my weight, he puts his left hand in my right armpit and pushes me further to my left. Because my left arm is over-hooked, I'm unable to post it on the mat and prevent the roll.

As I am forced to my back, my partner comes up to his knees inside my open guard.

As my partner postures up, I will sit forward and execute the hip bump sweep once again. After executing this drill for a set amount of time or repetitions, we will switch positions.

SIT-UP TO SINGLE-LEG

If you look at the first photo in the sequence below, you'll notice that I am lying on my back with my partner standing before me. This type of scenario happens all the time in mixed martial arts competition, and you must become proficient at getting back to your feet to avoid taking damage. Although there are many ways to accomplish this, quickly sitting up into your opponent and securing the single leg position is one of the most effective. In addition to escaping a compromising position, it also sets you up to put your opponent on his back and obtain a dominant top position. The reason I included this specific drill into the book is because in order to be effective with this technique, you must have explosive power. Transitioning from your back to the standing position requires a great amount of energy, and you must train your body for this movement. Although most fighters spend an ample amount of time sparring on their feet and transitioning from one ground position to the next, transitioning from their back up to their feet is often neglected. The goal with this drill is to focus on hip movement, sitting forward to secure the single-leg position, and then reversing sides. The more you practice this movement, the more it will be ingrained into your muscle memory, and the less damage you will take in a fight.

I begin in the downed guard with my partner standing over top of me. This is a common position to find yourself in when dropped with a punch or kick.

Instead of waiting for my partner to attack, I decide to make a quick escape to my feet. I begin this process by posting my right elbow on the mat, moving my hips toward my left side, and sitting up. It is important to notice that I have elevated my left arm to protect me from any strikes my partner may throw.

Continuing to move my hips toward my left side and sit up, I wrap my left arm around the outside of my partner's right leg and drive my right leg between his legs. Notice how I keep my head tight to his leg. This hinders him from throwing strikes at my head, as well as prevents him from gaining control of my head.

To obtain better control, I quickly spin my body around my partner's right leg until my left shoulder is pressing into his right hamstring. At the same time, I hook my right leg around his right foot. Once I establish this position I am not only protected from his strikes, but I can also easily twist my hips, come up onto my knees, and turn the fight into a wrestling match.

For the sake of the drill, I release my partner's leg and fall back to the downed guard position. However, if this were an actual fight, I would have executed a single-leg takedown or another attack to gain the upper hand.

I now perform the drill on the opposite side by posting my left elbow on the mat, scooting my hips out toward my right side, and shooting my left leg between my partner's legs.

I sit forward and hook my right arm around the outside of my partner's left leg. Again, I keep my head tight to his leg.

I once again obtain a dominant angle by turning the counter until my right shoulder is driving into Neil's left hamstring. From this dominant angle, I can come up to my knees and finish the single-leg. However, for sake of the drill, I will once again return to the downed guard position and execute another repetition on the opposite side.

PART THREE
TRAINING ROUTINE

Over the years I've developed a specific way of organizing my training camps that has not only allowed me to be successful in many of my fights, but also continue competing into my late forties. While most fighters understand the importance of going through some type of fight camp, the theories of how to prepare vary widely. Some do nothing but spar hard for twelve straight weeks. While this works for some, it dramatically increases the risk of injury during training. Other fighters are on the opposite end of the spectrum. They feel that light, technical training sessions of Muay Thai and Brazilian Jiu-Jitsu are adequate to prepare them for the rigors of an MMA fight. Again, this may work for some, but grappling with a gi and kicking Thai pads is no substitute for actually MMA sparring. Unfamiliar with getting punched and kicked in the face, their game plan often quickly falls apart in the cage.

Personally, I feel the most effective training camp lies somewhere between these two extremes. You train hard enough to prepare your body for the intensity of an MMA fight, but light enough to avoid serious injuries and promote longevity in your career. In this coming section, I break down my personal routine for training for fights. While my exact workout might not fit everyone's personal needs, it offers a foundation that you can alter and build upon.

TRAINING STRUCTURE

When it comes to structuring your training camp, it is very important to vary your workouts. As you know, is imperative to not only train MMA specific movements such as wrestling and kickboxing, but it is also important to incorporate general strength and conditioning sessions into your routine. This ensures that you increase your power and stamina at the same rate as your technical ability. While combining technical fight training with strength and conditioning training is a great place to start, it is also important to have variance in each of these areas. For example, some of your MMA workouts should focus more on hard sparring, while others should focus more on developing your technical ability. And when in the weight room, some of your workouts should focus on increasing power, while others should focus more on developing your conditioning.

Intensity is another aspect that should constantly vary. While hard days are essential for you to grow as a fighter, you also need light days to let your body recuperate. Most training camps consist of two training sessions per day, and if you give everything you've got every time you step into the gym, it is possible to burn out very quickly. I'm not saying that you should slack off during training—all I'm saying is that you need to be smart about your training. By structuring your hard training days and light training days ahead of time, you know just how much effort to put into your sessions.

Personally, I like to break my training sessions down by method. My morning sessions will alternate between weight lifting sessions with my strength coach and technical training sessions with my boxing or grappling coach, and my afternoon sessions will alternate between technical training and hard sparring sessions with the Xtreme Couture team.

STRENGTH AND CONDITIONING

When I step into the weight room with my strength coach Jake Bonacci, we have a multitude of different goals. As mentioned in the first chapter, our aim is always to improve upon certain areas of my athletic ability. Early in my training camp, increasing power is on the top of the list because it enhances my ability to perform all other athletic movements efficiently. We accomplish this by doing heavy, low repetition Olympic lifts (dead clean, power clean, split jerk, push press), followed by heavy, low repetition posterior chain movements (squat, front squat, deadlift), followed by high repetition upper and lower body exercises (rolling triceps, step-ups, pull-ups, lunges). While this formula works wonderfully as a whole, the most important part is the Olympic lifts because they do the most to increase power and strength. However, because I often move back and forth between fighting in the heavyweight and light-heavyweight divisions, increasing or decreasing size can be a central theme early in my training camps as well.

While the first half of the training camp is generally devoted to increasing power and size, the second half of my training camp is generally devoted to higher repetition movements designed to increase endurance and stamina in my entire body. Abandoning the heavy weights, we dive into circuit-training sessions where I move rapidly from one station to the next. At each station I do a different exercise that taxes a different area of the body, which prevents one muscle group from getting burned out. However, by performing each exercise intensely and moving from one station to the next without break, it ensures a high heart rate and breathing rate throughout the timed session.

If I'm fighting in a three round non-title fight, the eventual goal of this type of circuit training is to be able to execute three 5-minute rounds with a one minute break between each round. If I am competing in a five round title fight, then the goal is to work up to five 5-minute rounds with one minute break between each round. For a fighter, achieving the proper volume is the most important aspect of circuit training. If at the end of your training camp you can only make it through two 5-minute rounds of circuit training, and your fight goes into the third round, you'll most likely find yourself gassed out. So while training, it is important to strive to reach the same volume of work you will be required to do in your fight. Once you are able to do the proper volume, you can move on to cutting rest periods between your rounds of circuit training.

By combining heavy power-based workouts with intense conditioning-based workouts during your training camp, you can successfully increase your athletic ability.

And when done with the proper timing and volume, it allows you to peak physically the week of your fight.

TECHNICAL TRAINING

While half of my morning training sessions are dedicated to strength and conditioning, the other half is dedicated to technique. Instead of training in the weight room in these sessions, I'll split my time between my boxing coach Gil Martinez and my grappling coach Neil Melanson. The sessions are usually between one and two hours long, and their focus will depend upon my strategy for my upcoming fight. Depending upon the strengths and weakness of my opponent, I could focus on anything from working back control finishes to footwork to throwing masterful counterpunches. Personally, I feel doing this type of technical training in the morning offers a serious advantage because it keeps the moves fresh in your mind throughout the day. When you come in for your afternoon training session, you're still thinking about the moves you practiced earlier, and it allows you to apply them during sparring and work out any kinks.

MMA SPARRING SESSIONS

My afternoon training consists of some type of MMA sparring workout led by Xtreme Couture coach Ron Frazier. The entire Xtreme Couture fight team attends these sessions, and at any one time, there may be four to six of us preparing for a fight, which allows us to push each other through tough sparring sessions. The workouts begin with a long, low intensity warm-up, such as jumping rope. Next, we move on to more intense drilling and light sparring from positional advantages. Toward the end of the workout, we move into fully contested sparring situations. However, not every day is the same. Generally Monday, Wednesday, and Friday are the light days, while Tuesday and Thursdays are the hard days. The reason we include more light days than hard days is that your body needs time to recover after taking multiple shots to the head. It is important to note, however, that there is room for flexibility in this routine. During the middle of the training camp, it is possible to have additional light days or even take a few days off of sparring, depending upon how you are feeling and recovering. But as you will see when you begin studying the workout, toward the end of the training camp, days of hard sparring increase to better prepare you both physically and mentally for your upcoming battle.

OVERTRAINING

In wrestling you learn to push yourself physically in each and every workout. I took this lesson to heart and developed a very good work ethic. In fact, when wrestling in high school and college, my coaches would often use me as an example of good work ethic, which only reinforced my inclination to push it a hundred percent each and every time I stepped into the gym. When I made the transition to MMA, I brought that mindset with me and rarely took a day off, even when my body was begging for rest. While this certainly had its advantages, it often set my training back.

It is important to train hard, but it is also very important not to overtrain. I find that younger fighters are more likely to attend every training session, even when they feel awful. Instead of listening to their bodies and taking a break when they feel beat up and sluggish, they come into the gym and push their bodies past their limits. If you want to experience longevity in the sport of MMA, you've got to learn when to put on the brakes. Now if my body feels exhausted or injured, I'll force myself to take a day off. It's important not to make up excuses for yourself, but you've got to listen to what your body is telling you. Finding the delicate balance between overtraining and training enough can take many years to master, but it is important to start searching for that balance right out of the gates. If you ignore it and always have a warrior mentality when it comes to training, you could find yourself out of a job very quickly.

OVERVIEW

In the following section I provide a ten-week fight preparation workout, but due to the variables, no one workout routine can fit everyone's needs. For example, the workout provided is based on a three round fight, with each round consisting of five minutes. If you are fighting for a title fight that has five 5-minute rounds, the training camp will need more volume of work, and if you are training for a two round amateur fight, the volume of work should probably decrease. It is also important to tailor your training for your specific opponent. For example, if I am fighting a strong boxer with poor takedown defense, I'll focus less on trading punches in practice and more on striking defense and securing the takedown. The more you analyze your opponent ahead of time, the easier it is to develop a game plan and alter your training to best compliment that game plan.

The goal is to pinpoint your opponent's weaknesses, and then figure out how to use your strength to capitalize on those weaknesses.

I realize that if you are a new fighter and there is no existing video on your opponent to analyze, it can be difficult to pinpoint his weaknesses. In such a case, following a general training camp that utilizes the proper round timing (often two minutes for amateurs and five minutes for professionals) will increase your overall MMA ability and strength and conditioning. It is not ideal, but it will prepare you physically and mental for the challenge ahead of you.

If you've never been punched in the face, it is important that it happens while sparring in your training camp, not while locked in a cage with some stranger who wants to hurt you. A general training camp will also improve your power and stamina, which will have more benefit that any other activity that you can accomplish off the mats.

While the upcoming ten-week training camp might not be ideal for your specific needs, it can be used as a template. By swapping workouts and adjusting volume, you can reach your athletic potential and get into top fighting shape.

MMA SPECIFIC DRILLS

For the training camp cataloged on the coming pages, I've included some of the unique MMA drills we like to utilize at Xtreme Couture. If you are unfamiliar with these drills, here are their basic descriptions:

SHARK TANK—In this drill, you remain in the cage for five minutes straight while getting a fresh partner every minute. The constant flow of fresh opponents exhausts you physically and forces you to stay mentally tough. Shark Tank can consist exclusively of grappling or striking, or it could be a full MMA contest. However, with this drill being very demanding, it is best utilized when you are at the peak of your training camp. It is also important not to overdo Shark Tank training. As a rule of thumb, it should be utilized at most one time per week, proceeding a light day or a day off of training. It is also important to reciprocate. When one of your teammates is preparing for a fight, you should volunteer to be one of the five fresh bodies.

TOP/BOTTOM/OUT—In this drill you break off into groups of three, and each participant assumes a different position. One assumes the bottom position on the ground, one assumes the top position on the ground, and the last takes up position on the heavy bag. When the timer starts, each participant has a job for the next three minutes. The one on the bottom will use his techniques to either submit the man on top or execute a reversal. The man on top works to submit the man on the bottom, pummel him with light ground and pound, or simply keep him pined. If either is successful with his mission, they restart in their original position and continue with the drill. Over at the heavy bag, the participant executes a variety of combinations for the entire three minutes. When the buzzer sounds, indicating the end of three minutes, each participant switches spots without break. Once each participant has spent three minutes in each position, the round comes to a close and they take a break. With each round being nine minutes long, it is a very physically demanding drill. However, due to the rapid altering of positions, the participants don't get beat up too badly. For the best results, the Top/Bottom/Out drill should be utilized in the middle of your training camp when you already have a solid conditioning base.

BIG GLOVE LITTLE GLOVE— This is a great drill that allows sparring partners focus on utilizing 100% intensity in different areas of the game. The drill begins in the standing position with one of the partners wearing full sized 16 oz. boxing gloves while the other partner begins wearing only 4 oz. MMA gloves. This forces each partner into a specific game plan. The fighter wearing the big gloves is authorized to throw heavy punches to his partner's head, but because of the bulky nature of the boxing gloves, they must seek to avoid any grappling situations. Conversely, the man wearing little gloves is only allowed to throw very light strikes, but must seek to close space and execute full power takedowns in order to transition the fight to the ground. The great part about this drill is that it enables both fighters to work some aspect of their game with 100% effort, but in a safe and controlled manner. Additionally, because each partner has one specific goal, and their opponent is fully aware of that goal, it makes the fighters much more adept at seeking indirect routes to ac-

complishing their goals. This is a fantastic sparring drill that forces fighters out of their comfort zones and into a more well rounded game plan.

BURPEES— This is a great body weight conditioning drill that we often utilize at the beginning of a practice to warm-up fighters and prepare for an MMA sparring session. The movement is simple—a burpee begins in the standing position, at which point you drop your hands down to the mat and kick your legs out behind you. At this point you are in the top of a push-up position. From here you flex your arms, move your chests towards the ground, and execute a traditional push-up. As your chest ascends, you rapidly pop your feet off the ground and pull your legs forward. Now in the bottom of a full squat position, you explosively extend your legs and jump into the air. As you land, you lower your hands to the mat and repeat the drill once again. This simple body-weight movement can be extremely intense when executed even for short periods of time. As such, we often utilize it at my gym as an alternate warm-up to jumping rope just for a change of pace.

The goal of Week One is to get into a good routine and initiate your training camp successfully. Even though you begin two-a-day workouts right off the bat, it doesn't mean you have to make it to every practice. It's important to listen to your body. If your body tells you that it needs the afternoon off, take the afternoon off. At this stage in the training camp, you're just looking to develop good habits. It will do you no good to overwork yourself.

If you are a type of fighter who tends to let yourself go in the off season, the first week is when you should develop a base level of conditioning. It is also important to start your diet this first week of training. While I generally stick to a pretty healthy diet year-round, I allow myself a few treats from time to time. At the beginning of my training camp, all unhealthy food goes away and my diet becomes very regimented. The longer you wait to dial-in your diet, the longer it will take to get your training heading in the right direction.

MONDAY AM / STRENGTH AND CONDITIONING

EXERCISE	DETAILS
Dynamic Warm-up	—
Agility Hurdles	—
Core	Straight Leg Sit-Up, Oblique Crunch, Leg Scissor Crunch, Partner Med Ball Pass
Power Clean	4 Sets x 4 Repetitions
Back Squat	4 Sets x 4 Repetitions
Barbell Bench Press	3 Sets x 6 Repetitions
Bent-Over Barbell Row	3 Sets x 6 Repetitions
Single-Arm Overhead Press	2 Sets x 8 Repetitions
Rockers	2 Sets x 8 Repetitions
Alternating Dumbbell Curl	2 Sets x 8 Repetitions

MONDAY PM / MMA PRACTICE, LIGHT DAY

EXERCISE	DETAILS
Jump Rope	15 - 20 Minutes (Warm-Up)
Pummel	2 - 3 Rounds (Warm-Up, Increasing Intensity)
Drilling Guard Passes	2 - 3 Rounds (40% Resistance)
Sparring From Guard	5 x 3 Minute Rounds (MMA Gloves, 50-60% Intensity)
Cooldown	Wrestling Drills, Jogging, Dynamic Stretching

TUESDAY AM / BOXING TECHNIQUE

EXERCISE	DETAILS
Jump Rope	15 - 20 Minutes
Shadow Boxing	2 - 3 Rounds
Mitt Work	4 - 6 Rounds
Cooldown	Dynamic Stretches

TUESDAY PM / MMA PRACTICE, HARD DAY

EXERCISE	DETAILS
Jump Rope	15 - 20 Minutes (Warm-Up)
Sprints	4 - 6 Laps Across The Mat (Warm-Up, Increasing Intensity)
Shadow Sparring With Partner	3 - 4 Rounds (No Contact)
Heavy Bag Work	3 x 3 Minute Rounds
Sparring	5 x 3 Minute Rounds (16 oz. Gloves, Alternate Boxing, Kickboxing, and MMA)
Cooldown	Jogging, Dynamic Stretching

WEDNESDAY AM / STRENGTH AND CONDITIONING

EXERCISE	DETAILS
Dynamic Warm-up	—
Agility Ladder	—
Core	Ab Wheel, Russian Twist, Alternating Pikes
Circuit 1	—
Lateral Plyometric Push-Up	12 Repetitions
Depth Jump	12 Repetitions
Pull-Up	8 Repetitions
Ropes	15 Seconds
Circuit 2	—
Med Ball Punch Pass	6 Repetitions (Each Arm)
Partner Squats	12 Repetitions
Horizontal Pull-Up	8 Repetitions
Tire Sledge	16 Repetitions
Circuit 3	—
Staggered Push-Up with Med Ball	6 Repetitions (Each Arm)
Step-Up	6 Repetitions (Each Leg)
Single-Arm Flex Band Row	12 Repetitions (Each Arm)
DB Snatch	8 Repetitions

WEDNESDAY PM / MMA PRACTICE, LIGHT DAY

EXERCISE	DETAILS
Jump Rope	15 - 20 Minutes (Warm-Up)
Pummel	2 - 3 Rounds (Warm-Up, Increased Intensity)
Drilling Takedowns Against Cage	2 - 3 Rounds (40% Resistance)
Sparring Against Cage	5 x 3 Minute Rounds (MMA Gloves, 50 - 60% Resistance)
Cooldown	Wrestling Drills, Jogging, Dynamic Stretching

THURSDAY AM / GRAPPLING TECHNIQUE

EXERCISE	DETAILS
Wrestling Drills	Warm-Up
Submission Drills	40 Minutes
Live Rolling	20 Minutes
Cooldown	Dynamic Stretching

THURSDAY PM / MMA PRACTICE, HARD DAY

EXERCISE	DETAILS
Jump Rope	15 - 20 Minutes (Warm-Up)
Pummel	2 - 3 Rounds (Warm-Up, Increasing Intensity)
Shadow Sparring With Partner	3 - 4 Rounds (No Contact)
Heavy Bag Work	5 x 3 Minute Rounds (16 oz. Gloves, Alternate Boxing, Kickboxing, and MMA)
Sparring	5 x 3 Minute Rounds (16 oz. Gloves, Alternate Boxing, Kickboxing, and MMA)
Cooldown	Jogging, Dynamic Stretching

FRIDAY AM / OFF

FRIDAY PM / MMA PRACTICE, LIGHT DAY

EXERCISE	DETAILS
Jump Rope	15 - 20 Minutes (Warm-Up)
Pummel	2 - 3 Rounds (Warm-Up, Increasing Intensity)
Drill Counter Jab to Takedown	2 - 3 Rounds (40% Resistance)
Sparring Striking to Takedowns	5 x 3 Minute Rounds (MMA Gloves, 40 - 50%)
Cooldown	Wrestling Drills, Jogging, Dynamic Stretching

SATURDAY AM / STRENGTH AND CONDITIONING

EXERCISE	DETAILS
Dynamic Warm-up	—
Agility Hurdles	—
Core	Scorpion, Russian Twist, Superman, Plank On Swiss Ball
Split Jerk	4 Sets x 4 Repetitions
Front Squat	4 Sets x 3 Repetitions
Plyometric Push-Up	4 Sets x 3 Repetitions
Weighted Pull-Up	4 Sets x 3 Repetitions
Rolling Triceps	2 Sets x 8 Repetitions
Barbell Step-Up	2 Sets x 8 Repetitions

SATURDAY PM - SUNDAY PM / OFF

Week Two is very similar to Week One. The main goal should be to make it to training as often as possible without over-training, but it is also important to begin focusing on improving your strength. The stronger you become early in your training camp, the easier it will be to build your conditioning toward the end of your training camp. The second week is also an excellent time to start putting together a solid game plan for your upcoming fight. You should sit down with your various trainers and figure out what your opponent's strengths and weaknesses are. Next, assess how your strengths and weaknesses will stack up against his. Based on this knowledge, you can develop a plan of attack, ways to initiate that attack, and decide which training partners will best help you train for your opponent. During the second week, your should also spend a considerable amount of time sharpening any new techniques that you think might come in handy in the fight.

MONDAY AM / GRAPPLING TECHNIQUE

EXERCISE	DETAILS
Wrestling Drills	Warm-Up
Submission Drills	40 Minutes
Live Rolling	30 Minutes
Cooldown	Dynamic Stretching

MONDAY PM / MMA PRACTICE, LIGHT DAY

EXERCISE	DETAILS
Jump Rope	20 Minutes (Warm-Up)
Pummel	3 - 4 Rounds (Warm-Up, Increasing Intensity)
Drilling Mount Escapes	3 - 5 Rounds (40% Resistance)
Sparring Mount	6 x 4 Minute Rounds (MMA Gloves, 50-60% Resistance)
Cooldown	Wrestling Drills, Jogging, Dynamic Stretching

TUESDAY AM / STRENGTH AND CONDITIONING

EXERCISE	DETAILS
Dynamic Warm-up	—
Agility Hurdles	—
Core	Straight Leg Sit-Up, Oblique Crunch, Russian Twist, V-Up
Power Clean	4 Sets x 3 Repetitions
Back Squat	3 Sets x 3 Repetitions
Barbell Bench Press	3 Sets x 5 Repetitions
Bent-Over Barbell Row	3 Sets x 6 Repetitions
Single-Arm Overhead Press	2 Sets x 8 Repetitions
Rockers	2 Sets x 8 Repetitions
Alternating Dumbbell Curl	2 Sets x 8 Repetitions

TUESDAY PM / MMA PRACTICE, HARD DAY

EXERCISE	DETAILS
Jump Rope	20 Minutes (Warm-Up)
Sprints	6 - 8 Laps (Warm-Up, Increasing Intensity)
Shadow Sparring with Partner	3 - 4 Rounds (No Contact)
Heavy Bag Work	3 x 3 Minute Rounds
Sparring	6 x 4 Minute Rounds (16 oz. Gloves, Alternate Boxing, Kickboxing, and MMA)
Cooldown	Jogging, Dynamic Stretching

WEDNESDAY AM / BOXING TECHNIQUE

EXERCISE	DETAILS
Jump Rope	15 - 20 Minutes
Shadow Boxing	4 - 5 Rounds
Mitt Work	6 - 8 Rounds
Cooldown	Dynamic Stretching

WEDNESDAY PM / MMA PRACTICE, LIGHT DAY

EXERCISE	DETAILS
Jump Rope	20 Minutes (Warm-Up)
Pummel	3 - 4 Rounds (Warm-Up, Increasing Intensity)
Drilling Side Control Pins	2 - 3 Rounds (40% Resistance)
Sparring from Side Control	6 x 4 Minute Rounds (MMA Gloves, 50-60%)
Cooldown	Wrestling Drills, Jogging, Dynamic Stretching

THURSDAY AM / STRENGTH AND CONDITIONING

EXERCISE	DETAILS
Dynamic Warm-up	—
Agility Ladder	—
Core	Ab Wheel, Scorpion, Alternating Pikes
Circuit 1	—
Elevated Torso Plyometric Push-Up	6 Repetitions
Jump Squats	10 Repetitions
Single-Arm Horizontal Push-Up	8 Repetitions
Ropes	15 Seconds
Circuit 2	—
Dumbbell Floor Press	12 Repetitions (Each Arm)
Forward Dumbbell Lunge	12 Repetitions
Dumbbell Bent-Over Row	12 Repetitions
Band Resisted Double-Leg	8 Repetitions

Circuit 3	—
Medicine Ball Punch Pass	6 Repetitions (Each Arm)
Barbell Front Squat	12 Repetitions
Barbell Bent-Over Row	10 Repetitions
Medicine Ball Slams	12 Repetitions

THURSDAY PM / MMA PRACTICE, HARD DAY

EXERCISE	DETAILS
Jump Rope	20 Minutes (Warm-Up)
Sprints	6 - 8 Laps (Warm-Up, Increasing Intensity)
Shadow Sparring with Partner	3 - 4 Rounds (No Contact)
Heavy Bag Work	3 x 3 Minute Rounds
Sparring	6 x 4 Minute Rounds (16 oz. Gloves, Alternate Boxing, Kickboxing, and MMA)
Cooldown	Jogging, Dynamic Stretching

FRIDAY AM / GRAPPLING TECHNIQUE

EXERCISE	DETAILS
Wrestling Drills	Warm-Up
Submission Drills	40 Minutes
Live Rolling	30 Minutes
Cooldown	Dynamic Stretching

FRIDAY PM / MMA PRACTICE, LIGHT DAY

EXERCISE	DETAILS
Jump Rope	20 Minutes (Warm-Up)
Pummel	3 - 4 Rounds (Warm-Up, Increasing Intensity)
Drilling Control from Front Headlock	2 - 3 Rounds (40% Resistance)
Sparring from Front Headlock	6 x 4 Minute Rounds (MMA Gloves, 50-60%)
Cooldown	Wrestling Drills, Jogging, Dynamic Stretching

SATURDAY AM / STRENGTH AND CONDITIONING

EXERCISE	DETAILS
Dynamic Warm-Up	—
Agility Hurdles	—
Core	Crunch, Russian Twists, Bench Supported Leg lifts
Split Jerk	4 Sets x 3 Repetitions
Front Squat	4 Sets x 3 Repetitions
Plyometric Push-Up	4 Sets x 3 Repetitions
Weighted Pull-Up	4 Sets x 3 Repetitions
Rolling Triceps	2 Sets x 8 Repetitions
Barbell Step-Up	2 Sets x 8 Repetitions

SATURDAY PM / BOXING TECHNIQUE

EXERCISE	DETAILS
Jump Rope	15 - 20 Minutes
Shadow Boxing	4 - 5 Rounds
Mitt Work	6 - 8 Rounds
Cooldown	Dynamic Stretching

SUNDAY AM - SUNDAY PM / OFF

WEEK 3

By Week Three you're not at your physical peak just yet, but the two prior weeks of two-a-day training sessions should have advanced your conditioning considerably. You should be able to make it to most practices and still remain fresh for the following day. This allows you to address your weaknesses and further develop your game plan. Personally, a lot of my training sessions in the third week focus on working with specific coaches to develop specific skills. For example, I may work on perfecting my counterstrikes if my opponent is a more proficient striker or work on my submission defense if my opponent is primarily a grappler. As far as my strength and conditioning workouts, I begin lowering my repetitions and focusing on high power output. I will continue to increase my strength until the mid-point of my training camp, and then steer away from developing strength and focus solely on increasing endurance.

MONDAY AM / STRENGTH AND CONDITIONING

EXERCISE	DETAILS
Dynamic Warm-up	—
Agility Hurdles	—
Core	Leg Scissors Crunch, Horizontal Med Ball Pass, Superman
Power Clean	4 Sets x 2 Repetitions
Back Squat	2 Sets x 2 Repetitions
Barbell Bench Press	3 Sets x 4 Repetitions
Bent-Over Barbell Row	3 Sets x 6 Repetitions
Single-Arm Overhead Press	2 Sets x 8 Repetitions
Rockers	2 Sets x 8 Repetitions
Alternating Dumbbell Curl	2 Sets x 8 Repetitions

MONDAY PM / MMA PRACTICE, LIGHT DAY

EXERCISE	DETAILS
Jump Rope	20 Minutes (Warm-Up)
Pummel	3 - 4 Rounds (Warm-Up, Increasing Intensity)
Drilling Takedowns Against Cage	3 - 4 Rounds (MMA Gloves, 40% Resistance)
Sparring Against Cage	5 x 4 Minute Rounds (MMA Gloves, 50-60% Intensity)
Cool Down	Wrestling Drills, Jogging, Dynamic Stretching

TUESDAY AM / BOXING TECHNIQUE

EXERCISE	DETAILS
Jump Rope	15 - 20 Minutes
Shadow Boxing	4 - 5 Rounds
Mitt Work	8 - 10 Rounds
Cooldown	Dynamic Stretching

TUESDAY PM / MMA PRACTICE, HARD DAY

EXERCISE	DETAILS
Jump Rope	20 Minutes (Warm-Up)
Pummel	2 - 3 Rounds (Warm-Up, Increasing Intensity)
Shadow Sparring with Partner	3 - 4 Rounds (No Contact)
Heavy Bag Work	5 x 3 Minute Rounds
Sparring	6 x 4 Minute Rounds (16 oz. Gloves, Alternate Boxing, Kickboxing, and MMA)
Cooldown	Jogging, Dynamic Stretching

WEDNESDAY AM / STRENGTH AND CONDITIONING

EXERCISE	DETAILS
Dynamic Warm-Up	—
Agility Ladder	—
Core	Ab Wheel, Oblique Crunch, Alternating Pikes
Circuit 1	—
Medicine Ball Punch Pass	6 Repetitions (Each Arm)
Barbell Front Squat	12 Repetitions
Barbell Bent-Over Row	10 Repetitions
Medicine Ball Slams	12 Repetitions
Circuit 2	—
Lateral Plyometric Push-Up	12 Repetitions
Depth Jump	10 Repetitions
Ropes	15 Seconds
Circuit 3	—
Medicine Ball Punch Pass	6 Repetitions (Each Arm)
Vertical Box Jumps	8 Repetitions
Horizontal Pull-Up	8 Repetitions
Tire Sledge	16 Repetitions

WEDNESDAY PM / MMA PRACTICE, LIGHT DAY

EXERCISE	DETAILS
Jump Rope	20 Minutes (Warm-Up)
Pummel	3 - 4 Rounds (Warm-Up, Increasing Intensity)
Drilling Counter-Punches to Takedowns	3 - 4 Rounds (40% Resistance)
Sparring (Light Striking to Takedowns)	5 x 4 Minute Rounds (MMA Gloves, 40-50% Intensity)
Cooldown	Wrestling Drills, Jogging, Dynamic Stretching

THURSDAY AM / GRAPPLING TECHNIQUE

EXERCISE	DETAILS
Wrestling Drills	Warm-Up
Submission Drills	40 Minutes
Live Rolling	30 Minutes
Cooldown	Dynamic Stretching

THURSDAY PM / MMA PRACTICE, HARD DAY

EXERCISE	DETAILS
Jump Rope	20 Minutes (Warm-Up)
Sprints	8 - 10 Laps (Warm-Up, Increasing Intensity)
Shadow Sparring with Partner	3 - 4 Rounds (No Contact)
Heavy Bag Work	5 x 3 Minute Rounds
Sparring	6 x 4 Minute Rounds (16 oz. Gloves, Hands Only)
Cooldown	Jogging, Dynamic Stretching

FRIDAY AM / OFF

FRIDAY PM / MMA PRACTICE, LIGHT DAY

EXERCISE	DETAILS
Jump Rope	20 Minutes (Warm-Up)
Pummel	3 - 4 Rounds (Warm-Up, Increasing Intensity)
Drilling Side Control Escapes	3 - 4 Rounds (40% Resistance)
Sparring from Side Control	5 x 4 Minute Rounds (MMA Gloves, 40-50% Intensity)
Cooldown	Wrestling Drills, Jogging, Dynamic Stretching

SATURDAY AM / STRENGTH AND CONDITIONING

EXERCISE	DETAILS
Dynamic Warm-Up	—
Agility Hurdles	—
Core	Ab Wheel, Russian Twist, Alternating Pikes
Split Jerk	4 Sets x 2 Repetitions
Front Squat	4 Sets x 2 Repetitions
Plyometric Push-Up	4 Sets x 3 Repetitions
Weighted Pull-Up	4 Sets x 3 Repetitions
Rolling Triceps	2 Sets x 8 Repetitions
Barbell Step-Up	2 Sets x 8 Repetitions

SATURDAY PM / CONDITIONING

EXERCISE	DETAILS
Light Jog	30 Minutes

SUNDAY AM - SUNDAY PM / OFF

WEEK 4

Much like Week Three, Week Four should be dedicated to increasing work volume and practicing specific areas of your game. By this point, your body should be recovering quickly enough to allow you to make it to nearly every workout. Now getting closer to your fight, you want to add more rounds into your MMA workouts, with longer time periods than at Week One. You also still want to gear your workouts in the gym toward improving strength.

In the sample Week Four workout provided below, I switch phases, moving from one set of movement patterns to another in my strength training sessions. However, this can be done at any point in the strength development stage—it just happens to fall on Week four of this particular workout. Despite the fact that I'm changing movements, I retain my repetition scheme by staying with low reps and heavy weight. By increasing strength slowly over the beginning of the training camp, I make the transition into endurance training much easier on myself.

MONDAY AM / BOXING TECHNIQUE

EXERCISE	DETAILS
Jump Rope	15 - 20 Minutes
Shadow Boxing	4 - 5 Rounds
Mitt Work	8 - 10 Rounds
Cooldown	Dynamic Stretching

MONDAY PM / MMA PRACTICE, LIGHT DAY

EXERCISE	DETAILS
Jump Rope	20 Minutes (Warm-Up)
Pummel	3 - 4 Rounds (Warm-Up, Increasing Intensity)
Drilling Clinch Takedowns	3 - 4 Rounds (40% Resistance)
Sparring Starting in Over/Under Clinch	6 x 4 Minute Rounds (MMA Gloves, 50-60% Intensity)
Cooldown	Wrestling Drills, Jogging, Dynamic Stretching

TUESDAY AM / STRENGTH AND CONDITIONING

EXERCISE	DETAILS
Dynamic Warm-Up	—
Agility Hurdles	—
Core	Leg Scissors Crunch, Russian Twist, Plank with Load Transfer
Dead Clean	4 Sets x 3 Repetitions
Front Squat	4 Sets x 4 Repetitions
DB Bench Press with Flex Band	3 Sets x 6 Repetitions
Flex Band Row	3 Sets x 6 Repetitions
DB Front Raise	2 Sets x 8 Repetitions
Dips	2 Sets x 8 Repetitions

TUESDAY PM / MMA PRACTICE, HARD DAY

EXERCISE	DETAILS
Jump Rope	20 Minutes (Warm-Up)
Sprints / Partner Carries	8 - 10 Laps (Warm-Up, Increasing Intensity)
Shadow Sparring with Partner	3 - 4 Rounds (No Contact)
Heavy Bag Work	5 x 3 Minute Rounds
Sparring	6 x 4 Minute Rounds (16 oz. Gloves, Kickboxing)
Cooldown	Jogging, Dynamic Stretching

WEDNESDAY AM / BOXING TECHNIQUE

EXERCISE	DETAILS
Jump Rope	15 - 20 Minutes
Shadow Boxing	4 - 5 Rounds
Mitt Work	8 - 10 Rounds
Cooldown	Dynamic Stretching

WEDNESDAY PM / WRESTLING PRACTICE, LIGHT DAY

EXERCISE	DETAILS
Jogging, Dynamic Warm-Up	20 Minutes
Pummeling	10 Minutes (Warm-Up, Increasing Intensity)
Drilling Single-Leg Takedowns	40% Resistance
Wrestling from Standing & Single-Leg	70-80% Intensity
Cooldown	Wrestling Drills, Jogging, Dynamic Stretching

THURSDAY AM / STRENGTH AND CONDITIONING

EXERCISE	DETAILS
Dynamic Warm-Up	—
Agility Ladder	—
Core	Ab Wheel, Oblique Crunch, Scorpion
Circuit 1	—
Staggered Push-Up with Med Ball	6 Repetitions (Each Arm)
Barbell Step-Up	6 Repetitions (Each Arm)
Single-Arm Flex Band Row	12 Repetitions (Each Arm)
Ropes	8 Repetitions
Circuit 2	—
BOSU Ball Push-Ups	12 Repetitions (Each Arm)
Depth Jumps	6 Repetitions
Barbell Bent-Over Row	10 Repetitions
Medicine Ball Slams	12 Repetitions
Circuit 3	—
Medicine Ball Punch Pass	6 Repetitions (Each Arm)
Vertical Box Jumps	10 Repetitions
Horizontal Pull-Up	12 Repetitions
Tire Flips	12 Repetitions

THURSDAY PM / MMA PRACTICE, HARD DAY

EXERCISE	DETAILS
Jump Rope	20 Minutes (Warm-Up)
Sprints / Partner Carries	8 - 10 Laps (Warm-Up, Increasing Intensity)
Shadow Sparring with Partner	3 - 4 Rounds (No Contact)
Heavy Bag Work	5 x 3 Minute Rounds
Sparring	6 x 4 Minute Rounds (MMA gloves, MMA)
Cooldown	Jogging, Dynamic Stretching

FRIDAY AM / GRAPPLING TECHNIQUE

EXERCISE	DETAILS
Wrestling Drills	Warm-Up
Submission Drills	40 Minutes
Live Rolling	30 Minutes
Cooldown	Dynamic Stretching

FRIDAY PM / MMA PRACTICE, LIGHT DAY

EXERCISE	DETAILS
Jump Rope	20 Minutes (Warm-Up)
Top / Bottom / Out Drill	6 x 9 Minute Rounds
Cooldown	Wrestling Drills, Jogging, Dynamic Stretching

SATURDAY AM / STRENGTH AND CONDITIONING

EXERCISE	DETAILS
Dynamic Warm-Up	—
Agility Hurdles	—
Core	V-Up, Scorpion, Bench Supported Leg lifts
Push Press	4 Sets x 3 Repetitions
Overhead Squat	4 Sets x 4 Repetitions
Push-Up with Flex Band	3 Sets x 6 Repetitions
Single-Arm Dumbbell Row	3 Sets x 6 Repetitions
Rolling Triceps	2 Sets x 8 Repetitions
Dumbbell Curls	2 Sets x 8 Repetitions

SATURDAY PM / GRAPPLING TECHNIQUE

EXERCISE	DETAILS
Wrestling Drills	Warm-Up
Submission Drills	40 Minutes
Live Rolling	30 Minutes
Cooldown	Dynamic Stretching

SUNDAY AM - SUNDAY PM / OFF

Week Five is a crucial time in your fight preparation. You should be well aware of your game plan for your upcoming opponent, and dedicate more time to the specific techniques you and your coaches decided would be beneficial for your fight. Week Five is a good barometer for how your training camp is going. By this point, you should feel strong in the gym and have little problem going for multiple 5 minute rounds on the mat. You should also be having success when implementing your game plan against your training partners. However, if you are not seeing these results, you still have some time to adjust your training and get back on track. On the strength and conditioning side, this is usually my last week of strength training. After Week Five is complete, I will cease lifting heavy and focus solely on circuit training sessions to increase my stamina.

MONDAY AM / STRENGTH AND CONDITIONING

EXERCISE	DETAILS
Dynamic Warm-Up	—
Agility Hurdles	—
Core	Ab Wheel, Medicine Ball Lateral Toss, Alternating Pike, Swiss Ball Plank
Dead Clean	4 Sets x 2 Repetitions
Front Squat	4 Sets x 3 Repetitions
DB Bench Press with Flex Band	3 Sets x 6 Repetitions
Flex Band Row	3 Sets x 6 Repetitions
DB Front Raise	2 Sets x 8 Repetitions
Dips	2 Sets x 8 Repetitions

MONDAY PM / MMA PRACTICE, LIGHT DAY

EXERCISE	DETAILS
Jump Rope	20 Minutes (Warm-Up)
Pummel	3 - 4 Rounds (Warm-Up, Increasing Intensity)
Drilling Mount Escapes	3 - 4 Rounds (40% Resistance)
Sparring Starting in Mount	5 x 5 Minute Rounds (MMA Gloves, 50% Intensity)
Cooldown	Wrestling Drills, Jogging, Dynamic Stretching)

TUESDAY AM / BOXING TECHNIQUE

EXERCISE	DETAILS
Jump Rope	15 - 20 Minutes
Shadow Boxing	4 - 5 Rounds
Mitt Work	8 - 10 Rounds
Cooldown	Dynamic Stretching

TUESDAY PM / MMA PRACTICE, HARD DAY

EXERCISE	DETAILS
Jump Rope	20 Minutes, (Warm-Up)
Pummel	2 - 3 Rounds (Warm-Up, Increasing Intensity)
Shadow boxing with Partner	3 - 4 Rounds (No Contact)
Heavy Bag work	5 x 3 Minute Rounds
Sparring	5 x 5 Minute Rounds (16 oz. Gloves, Alternate Boxing, Kickboxing, MMA)
Cooldown	Jogging, Dynamic Stretching

WEDNESDAY AM / STRENGTH AND CONDITIONING

EXERCISE	DETAILS
Dynamic Warm-Up	—
Agility Ladder	—
Core	Split Crunch, Russian Twist, Swiss Ball Crunch, Superman
Circuit 1	—
Rope Climb	10 Repetitions
Medicine Ball Push-Up	12 Repetitions
Jump Squats	8 Repetitions
Tire Flips	12 Repetitions
Circuit 2	—
Medicine Ball Punch	6 Repetitions
Vertical Medicine Ball Pass	6 Repetitions
Horizontal Medicine Ball Pass	6 Repetitions
Band-Resisted Knee Strikes	6 Repetitions
Partner Assisted Band Punches	6 Repetitions
Circuit 3	—
Rope Climb	10 Repetitions
Medicine Ball Push-Up	12 Repetitions
Jump Squats	10 Repetitions
Tire Flips	12 Repetitions

WEDNESDAY PM / MMA PRACTICE, LIGHT DAY

EXERCISE	DETAILS
Jump Rope	20 Minutes (Warm-Up)
Pummel	3 - 4 Rounds (Warm-Up, Increasing Intensity)
Drilling Hip Throw Takedowns	40% Resistance
Big Glove / Little Glove Sparring	5 x 5 Minute Rounds (MMA Gloves, 16 oz. Gloves, 50% Intensity)
Cooldown	Wrestling Drills, Jogging, Dynamic Stretching

THURSDAY AM / OFF

THURSDAY PM / MMA PRACTICE, HARD DAY

EXERCISE	DETAILS
Jump Rope	20 Minutes (Warm-Up)
Sprints	8 - 10 Laps (Warm-Up, Increasing Intensity)
Shadow Sparring with Partner	3 - 4 Rounds (No Contact)
Heavy Bag Work	5 x 3 Minute Rounds
Sparring	5 x 5 Minute Rounds (16 oz. Gloves, Boxing, Kickboxing, MMA)
Cooldown	Jogging, Dynamic Stretching

FRIDAY AM / GRAPPLING TECHNIQUE

EXERCISE	DETAILS
Wrestling Drills	Warm-Up
Submission Drills	40 Minutes
Live Rolling	30 Minutes
Cooldown	Dynamic Stretching

FRIDAY PM / MMA PRACTICE, LIGHT DAY

EXERCISE	DETAILS
Jump Rope	20 Minutes (Warm-Up)
Pummel	3 - 4 Rounds (Warm-Up, Increasing Intensity)
Drilling Mount Escapes	3 - 4 Rounds (40% Resistance)
Sparring Starting in Mount	5 x 5 Minute Rounds (MMA Gloves, 50% Intensity)
Cooldown	Wrestling Drills, Jogging, Dynamic Stretching

SATURDAY AM / STRENGTH AND CONDITIONING

EXERCISE	DETAILS
Dynamic Warm-Up	—
Agility Hurdles	—
Core	Alternating Pikes, Windshield Wiper, Decline Medicine Ball Toss, Single Leg Side Bend
Push Press	4 Sets x 2 Repetitions
Overhead Squat	4 Sets x 3 Repetitions
Push-Up with Flex Band	3 Sets x 6 Repetitions
Single-Arm Dumbbell Row	3 Sets 6 Repetitions
Rolling Triceps	2 Sets x 8 Repetitions
Dumbbell Curls	2 Sets x 8 Repetitions

SATURDAY PM / BOXING TECHNIQUE

EXERCISE	DETAILS
Jump Rope	15 - 20 Minutes
Shadow Boxing	4 - 5 Rounds
Mitt Work	8 - 10 Rounds
Cooldown	Dynamic Stretching

SUNDAY AM - SUNDAY PM / OFF

WEEK 6

By Week Six you should have thoroughly tested your game plan for your upcoming fight against multiple training partners. You should be able to handle multiple 5 minute rounds. If your strategy is effective, as long as you stay on course, your should have success in your upcoming fight. On the strength and conditioning side, this is the week where I transition from strength training into conditioning training. Rather than focusing on repetitions in my circuit training sessions, my goals are time oriented. For example, I'll do as many repetitions as I can in a set amount of time rather than simply doing a set number of repetitions. The ultimate goal with this type of training is to incrementally increase the time of the rounds, until each of my rounds are the same length as the rounds of my upcoming fight. Once that goal is achieved, I then cut rest periods between circuits. However, since this is the first week of timed goals, I recommend starting easy with 3 minute rounds.

MONDAY AM / STRENGTH AND CONDITIONING

EXERCISE	DETAILS
Dynamic Warm-Up	
Core	Straight Leg Sit-Up, Oblique Crunch, Superman, Stability Ball Plank
Dumbbell Snatch	3 Sets (5 Repetitions, 4 Repetitions, 3 Repetitions)
Circuit 1	3 Minutes
Single-Arm Medicine Ball Push-Up	6 Repetitions (Each Arm)
BOSU Ball Body Weight Squat	10 Repetitions
Rope Climb	12 Repetitions
Vertical Box Jumps	10 Repetitions
Medicine Ball Slam	12 Repetitions
60 Second Break	—
Circuit 2	3 Minutes
Airdyne Bike	Build Up To Sprints
60 Second Break	
Circuit 3	3 Minutes
Plyometric Push-Up	10 Repetitions
Single-Arm Horizontal Pull-Up	8 Repetitions (Each Arm)
Standing Long Jump	8 Repetitions
Ropes	20 Seconds
Medicine Ball Lateral Toss	8 Repetitions (Each Direction)
Tire Sledges	Remaining Time

MONDAY PM / MMA PRACTICE, LIGHT DAY

EXERCISE	DETAILS
Jump Rope	20 Minutes (Warm-Up)
Pummel	3 - 4 Rounds (Warm-Up, Increasing Intensity)
Drilling Back Mount	3 - 4 Rounds (40% Resistance)
Sparring in Back Control	6 x 5 Minute Rounds (MMA Gloves, 50-60% Resistance)
Cooldown	Wrestling Drills, Jogging, Dynamic Stretching

TUESDAY AM / GRAPPLING TECHNIQUE

EXERCISE	DETAILS
Wrestling Drills	Warm-Up
Submission Drills	40 Minutes
Live Rolling	30 Minutes
Cooldown	Dynamic Stretching

TUESDAY PM / MMA PRACTICE, HARD DAY

EXERCISE	DETAILS
Jump Rope	20 Minutes (Warm-Up)
Burpess	4 x 2 Minute Rounds (Warm-Up, Increasing Intensity)
Shadow Sparring with Partner	3 - 4 Rounds (No Contact)
Heavy Bag Work	5 x 3 Minute Rounds
Sparring	5 x 5 Minute Rounds (16 oz. Gloves, Kickboxing)
Cooldown	Jogging, Dynamic Stretching

WEDNESDAY AM / STRENGTH AND CONDITIONING

EXERCISE	DETAILS
Dynamic Warm-Up	—
Core	Decline Bench Med Ball Toss, Superman, Scorpion, 2 point alternating Plank
Dead Clean	3 Sets (5 Repetitions, 5 Repetitions, 4 Repetitions)
Circuit 1	3 Minutes
Legs Elevated Plyometric Push-Up	10 Repetitions
Jump Squats	8 Repetitions
Single-Arm Upright Band Rows	8 Repetitions (Each Arm)
Single-Arm Dumbbell Row	6 Repetitions (Each Arm)
Airdyne Bike	Remaining Time
60 Second Break	—
Circuit 2	3 Minutes
Medicine Ball Push-Up	12 Repetitions

Ropes	20 Seconds
Staggered Stance Long Jump	6 Repetitions
Tire Sledges	20 Seconds
Horizontal Pull-Up	10 Repetitions
Ropes	20 Seconds
Medicine Ball Lateral Toss	8 Repetitions (Each Arm)
Medicine Ball Slam	6 Repetitions
60 Second Break	—
Circuit 3	3 Minutes
Calisthenics Round	Jumping Jacks, Body Weight Squats, Push-Ups, Lunges

WEDNESDAY PM / MMA PRACTICE, LIGHT DAY

EXERCISE	DETAILS
Jump Rope	20 Minutes
Pummel	3 - 4 Rounds (Warm-Up, Increasing Intensity)
Drilling Clinch Against Cage	3 - 4 Rounds (Warm-Up, Increasing Intensity)
Clinch Sparring Against Cage	6 x 5 Minute Rounds (MMA Gloves, 50-60% Intensity)
Cooldown	Wrestling Drills, Jogging, Dynamic Stretching

THURSDAY AM / BOXING TECHNIQUE

EXERCISE	DETAILS
Jump Rope	15 - 20 Minutes
Shadow Boxing	4 - 5 Rounds
Mitt Work	8 - 10 Rounds
Cooldown	Dynamic Stretching

THURSDAY PM / MMA PRACTICE, HARD DAY

EXERCISE	DETAILS
Jump Rope	20 Minutes (Warm-Up)
Sprints	10 - 12 Laps (Warm-Up, Increasing Intensity)
Heavy Bag Work	5 x 3 Minute Rounds
Shark Tank	5 x 5 Minute Rounds, Fresh Opponent Every Minute (MMA Gloves, 60-70%)
Cooldown	Jogging, Dynamic Stretching

FRIDAY AM / OFF

FRIDAY PM / MMA PRACTICE, LIGHT DAY

EXERCISE	DETAILS
Jump Rope	20 Minutes (Warm-Up)
Top / Bottom / Out Drill	7 x 9 Minute Rounds
Cooldown	Wrestling Drills, Jogging, Dynamic Stretching

SATURDAY AM / STRENGTH AND CONDITIONING

EXERCISE	DETAILS
Dynamic Warm-Up	—
Core	V-Up, Standing Russian Twists, Ab Wheel, Two Point Alternating Planks
Push Press	3 Sets (5 Repetitions, 5 Repetitions, 5 Repetitions)
Circuit 1	3 Minutes
Airdyne Bike	2 Minutes
Ropes	15 Seconds
Legs-Elevated Push-Ups	8 Repetitions
Tire Sledges	Remaining Time
60 Second Break	—
Circuit 2	3 Minutes
Torso-Elevated Plyometric Push-Ups	12 Repetitions
Ropes	20 Seconds
Body-Weight Lunge	6 Repetitions (Each Leg)
Horizontal Pull-Up	12 Repetitions
Tire Sledges	20 Seconds
Horizontal Medicine Ball Pass	12 Repetitions
Ropes	Remaining Time
60 Second Break	—
Circuit 3	3 Minutes
Airdyne Bike	2 Minutes
Medicine Ball Slam	30 Seconds
Vertical Medicine Ball Pass	30 Seconds

SATURDAY PM / GRAPPLING TECHNIQUE

EXERCISE	DETAILS
Wrestling Drills	Warm-Up
Submission Drills	40 Minutes
Live Rolling	30 Minutes
Cooldown	Dynamic Stretching

SUNDAY AM - SUNDAY PM / OFF

During Week Seven you're continuing your climb towards your physical and mental peak. With your conditioning trainings sessions, you want to extend the length of your rounds, while slowly decreasing the rest periods between rounds. There are just a few weeks left to go until fight time, so it is very important that your training mimics your actual fight as closely as possible. If you're training for a three-round fight, you want to do three-round circuits in your conditioning sessions. When on the mats, you want to follow your game plan and attempt to beat your training partners using the techniques you refined earlier in your training camp.

MONDAY AM / STRENGTH AND CONDITIONING

EXERCISE	DETAILS
Dynamic Warm-Up	—
Agility Ladder	—
Core	Straight Leg Sit-Up, Oblique Crunch, Partner Sit-Up, Plank
Circuit 1	3.5 Minutes
Medicine Ball Push-Up	12 Repetitions
Ropes	15 Seconds
Jumping Squat	8 Repetitions
Tire Sledges	15 Seconds
Pull-Up	12 Repetitions
Medicine Ball Lateral toss	8 Repetitions (Each Direction)
Ropes	15 Seconds
Medicine Ball Smash	8 Repetitions
Tire Sledges	Remaining Time
60 Second Break	—
Circuit 2	3.5 Minutes
Airdyne Bike	2.5 Minutes
Medicine Ball Punch	5 Repetitions (Each Arm)
Medicine Ball Punch From Knees	5 Repetitions (Each Arm)
Ropes	Remaining Time
60 Second Break	—
Circuit 3	3.5 Minutes
Airdyne Bike	2 Minutes
Band Resisted Punches	15 Seconds
Jumping Squats	8 Repetitions
Single-Arm Flex Band Row	8 Repetitions (Each Arm)
Plyometric Push-Up	6 Repetitions
Ropes	Remaining Time

MONDAY PM / MMA PRACTICE, LIGHT DAY

EXERCISE	DETAILS
Jump Rope	20 Minutes (Warm-Up)
Pummel	3 - 4 Rounds (Warm-Up, Increasing Intensity)
Drilling Front Headlock Submission	3 - 4 Rounds (40% Resistance)
Sparring From Front Headlock	6 x 5 Minute Rounds (MMA Gloves, 50-60% Intensity)
Cooldown	Wrestling Drills, Jogging, Dynamic Stretching

TUESDAY AM / GRAPPLING TECHNIQUE

EXERCISE	DETAILS
Wrestling Drills	Warm-Up
Submission Drills	40 Minutes
Live Rolling	30 Minutes
Cooldown	Dynamic Stretching

TUESDAY PM / MMA PRACTICE, HARD DAY

EXERCISE	DETAILS
Jump Rope	20 Minutes (Warm-Up)
Sprints	12 Laps (Warm-Up, Increasing Intensity)
Shadow Sparring with Partner	3 - 4 Rounds (No Contact)
Heavy Bag Work	5 x 3 Minute Rounds
Sparring	6 x 5 Minute Rounds (16 oz. Gloves, Boxing, Kickboxing, MMA)
Cooldown	Jogging, Dynamic Stretching

WEDNESDAY AM / STRENGTH AND CONDITIONING

EXERCISE	DETAILS
Dynamic Warm-Up	—
Agility Ladder	—
Core	Ab Wheel, Russian Twists, V-Up, Plank with Load Transfer
Circuit 1	4 Minutes
Airdyne Bike	2 Minutes
Single-Arm Plyometric Push-Up	6 Repetitions (Each Arm)
Ropes	15 Seconds
Single-Arm Bar Pull-Up	6 Repetitions (Each Arm)
Plyometric Hurdle Circuit	15 Seconds
Medicine Ball Smash	Remaining Time
60 Second Break	—
Circuit 2	4 Minutes
Treadmill	2 Minutes
Legs Elevated Plyometric Push-Up	15 Repetitions
Ropes	15 Seconds

Jump Squats	8 Repetitions
Single-Arm Band Row	10 Repetitions (Each Arm)
Tire Sledges	25 Seconds
Ropes	Remaining Time
60 Second Break	—
Circuit 3	4 Minutes
Airdyne Bike	2 Minutes
Band Resisted Punches	20 Seconds
Tire Flip	6 Repetitions
Ropes	20 Seconds
Medicine Ball Slam	Remaining Time

WEDNESDAY PM / OFF

THURSDAY AM / BOXING TECHNIQUE

EXERCISE	DETAILS
Jump Rope	15 - 20 Minutes
Shadow Boxing	4 - 5 Rounds
Mitt Work	8 - 10 Rounds
Cooldown	Dynamic Stretching

THURSDAY PM / MMA PRACTICE, HARD DAY

EXERCISE	DETAILS
Jump Rope	20 Minutes (Warm-Up)
Sprints	12 Laps (Warm-Up, Increasing Intensity)
Shadow Sparring with Partner	3 - 4 Rounds (No Contact)
Heavy Bag Work	5 x 3 Minute Rounds
Sparring	6 x 5 Minute Rounds (16 oz. Gloves, Boxing)
Cooldown	Jogging, Dynamic Stretching

FRIDAY AM / GRAPPLING TECHNIQUE

EXERCISE	DETAILS
Wrestling Drills	Warm-Up
Submission Drills	40 Minutes
Live Rolling	30 Minutes
Cooldown	Dynamic Stretching

FRIDAY PM / MMA PRACTICE, LIGHT DAY

EXERCISE	DETAILS
Jump Rope	20 Minutes (Warm-Up)
Drilling Front Headlock Submission	3 - 4 Rounds (40% Resistance)
Sparring From Front Headlock	5 x 5 Minute Rounds (MMA Gloves, 50-60% Intensity)
Cooldown	Wrestling Drills, Jogging, Dynamic Stretching

SATURDAY AM / STRENGTH AND CONDITIONING

EXERCISE	DETAILS
Dynamic Warm-Up	—
Agility Hurdles	—
Core	Decline Bench Med Ball Toss, Superman, Scorpion, 2 point alternating Plank
Circuit 1	4 Minutes
Legs-Elevated Plyometric Push-Up	10 Repetitions
Jump Squats	8 Repetitions
Single-Arm Upright Band Rows	8 Repetitions (Each Arm)
Single-Arm Dumbbell Row	6 Repetitions (Each Arm)
Airdyne Bike	Remaining Time
60 Second Break	—
Circuit 2	4 Minutes
Medicine Ball Push-Up	12 Repetitions
Ropes	20 Seconds
Staggered Stance Long Jump	6 Repetitions
Tire Sledges	20 Seconds
Horizontal Pull-Up	10 Repetitions
Ropes	20 Seconds
Medicine Ball Lateral Toss	8 Repetitions (Each Side)
Medicine Ball Slam	6 Repetitions
60 Second Break	—
Circuit 3	4 Minutes
Airdyne Bike	1.5 Minutes (Build Up To Sprints)
Single-Arm Medicine Ball Push-Up	6 Repetitions (Each Arm)
BOSU Ball Body Weight Squat	10 Repetitions
Rope Climb	12 Repetitions
Vertical Box Jump	10 Repetitions
Medicine Ball Slam	12 Repetitions

SATURDAY PM / BOXING TECHNIQUE

EXERCISE	DETAILS
Jump Rope	15 - 20 Minutes
Shadow Boxing	4 - 5 Rounds
Mitt Work	8 - 10 Rounds
Cooldown	Dynamic Stretching

SUNDAY AM - SUNDAY PM / OFF

By Week Eight, you should be very close to your peak. The volume of your conditioning sessions should be increasing, and when in the gym, you should be sparring close to fight level intensity to prepare for your opponent. This is an extremely hard week of training. This close to the fight, you can't afford to slack off. However, it is also no time to ignore your body. Even this late in the training camp, if I have a small nagging injury or I simply feel physically exhausted, I'll take a session off. At this point in the game, even a small injury could remove you from the fight should you neglect to treat it. Cuts are also extremely vital to avoid. An errant elbow or head butt could easily keep you from competing, so extra caution should taken. I recommend wearing the proper protective gear when sparring, as well as only training with people who possess good control and body awareness.

MONDAY AM / STRENGTH AND CONDITIONING

EXERCISE	DETAILS
Dynamic Warm-Up	—
Agility Ladder	—
Core	Straight Leg Sit-Up, V-Up, Scorpion, Superman
Circuit 1	4 Minutes
Airdyne Bike	2.5 Minutes
Lateral Plyometric Push-Up	15 Repetitions
Ropes	15 Seconds
Bent-Over Row	12 Repetitions
Overhead Squat	8 Repetitions
Dumbbell Plyometric Push-Up	12 Repetitions
60 Second Break	—
Circuit 2	4 Minutes
Treadmill	2 Minutes
Dumbbell Plyometric Push-Up	15 Repetitions
Ropes	15 Seconds
Standing Long Jump	6 Repetitions
Pull-Up	15 Repetitions
Medicine Ball Punch	6 Repetitions (Each Arm)
Tire Sledge	20 Seconds
Ropes	Remaining Time
60 Second Break	—
Circuit 3	4 Minutes
Airdyne Bike	2.5 Minutes
Medicine Ball Punch	6 Repetitions (Each Arm)
Plyometric Hurdle Circuit	15 Seconds
Legs-Elevated Plyometric Push-Up	8 Repetitions
Ropes	15 Seconds
Vertical Box Jump	6 Repetitions
Tire Sledges	Remaining Time

MONDAY PM / MMA PRACTICE, LIGHT DAY

EXERCISE	DETAILS
Jump Rope	20 Minutes (Warm-Up)
Pummel	3 - 4 Rounds (Warm-Up, Increasing Intensity)
Drilling Reversals from The Bottom	3 - 4 Rounds (40% Resistance)
Sparring from Guard	6 x 5 Minute Rounds (MMA Gloves, 50-60% Intensity)
Cooldown	Wrestling Drills, Jogging, Dynamic Stretching

TUESDAY AM / GRAPPLING TECHNIQUE

EXERCISE	DETAILS
Wrestling Drills	Warm-Up
Submission Drills	40 Minutes
Live Rolling	30 Minutes
Cooldown	Dynamic Stretching

TUESDAY PM / MMA PRACTICE, HARD DAY

EXERCISE	DETAILS
Jump Rope	20 Minutes (Warm-Up)
Pummel	3 - 4 Rounds (Warm-Up, Increasing Intensity)
Shadow Sparring with Partner	3 - 4 Rounds (No Contact)
Heavy Bag Work	5 x 3 Minute Rounds
Sparring	6 x 5 Minute Rounds (16 oz. Gloves, Kickboxing)
Cooldown	Jogging, Dynamic Stretching

WEDNESDAY AM / STRENGTH AND CONDITIONING

EXERCISE	DETAILS
Dynamic Warm-Up	—
Agility Ladder	—
Core	Leg Scissor Crunch, Horizontal Medicine Ball Pass, Russian Twists, Stability Ball Plank
Circuit 1	5 Minutes
Airdyne Bike	3 Minutes
Ropes	15 Seconds
Horizontal Bar Pull-Up	15 Repetitions
Jump Squats	8 Repetitions
Flex Band Row	15 Repetitions
60 Second Break	—
Circuit 2	5 Minutes
Treadmill	2.5 Minutes
Dumbbell Push-Up	15 Repetitions
Ropes	15 Seconds

Split-Stance Standing Long Jump	6 Repetitions
Single-Arm Band Row	10 Repetitions (Each Arm)
Medicine Ball Smash	12 Repetitions
Tire Sledges	Remaining Time
60 Second Break	—
Circuit 3	5 Minutes
Airdyne Bike	3 Minutes (Building Up To Sprints)
Medicine Ball Push-Up	6 Repetitions
BOSU Ball Squat	10 Repetitions
Legs Elevated Plyometric Push-Up	8 Repetitions
Ropes	15 Seconds
High Box Step-Ups	20 Seconds
Tire Sledges	Remaining Time

WEDNESDAY PM / MMA PRACTICE, LIGHT DAY

EXERCISE	DETAILS
Jump Rope	20 Minutes (Warm-Up)
Pummel	3 - 4 Rounds (Warm-Up, Increased Intensity)
Drilling Submissions From The Guard	3 - 4 Rounds (40% Resistance)
Sparring From Guard	6 x 5 Minute Rounds (MMA Gloves, 50-60%)
Cooldown	Wrestling Drills, Jogging, Dynamic Stretching

THURSDAY AM / GRAPPLING TECHNIQUE

EXERCISE	DETAILS
Wrestling Drills	Warm-Up
Submission Drills	40 Minutes
Live Rolling	30 Minutes
Cooldown	Dynamic Stretching

THURSDAY PM / MMA PRACTICE, HARD DAY

EXERCISE	DETAILS
Jump Rope	20 Minutes (Warm-Up)
Shadow Sparring with Partner	3-4 Rounds (No Contact)
Heavy Bag Work	5 x 3 Minute Rounds
Shark Tank	5 x 5 Minute Rounds (Fresh Opponent Each Minute, MMA Gloves, MMA)
Cooldown	Jogging, Dynamic Stretching

FRIDAY AM / OFF

FRIDAY PM / MMA PRACTICE, LIGHT DAY

EXERCISE	DETAILS
Jump Rope	20 Minutes (Warm-Up)
Top / Bottom / Out	8 x 9 Minute Rounds (MMA Gloves, 50-60% Intensity)
Cooldown	Wrestling Drills, Jogging, Dynamic Stretching

SATURDAY AM / BOXING TECHNIQUE

EXERCISE	DETAILS
Jump Rope	15 - 20 Minutes
Shadow Boxing	4 - 5 Rounds
Mitt Work	8 - 10 Rounds
Cooldown	Dynamic Stretching

SATURDAY PM - SUNDAY PM / OFF

WEEK 9

Week Nine is when your body should peak physically, as this is the last hard week of training. While it is important to be careful to avoid minor injuries or cuts, you must make every effort to have an extremely hard week of sparring in the gym. Your conditioning sessions for this week should consist of three 5 minute rounds to mimic your upcoming fight accurately. If your body handles each of these round well, then you can begin to cut the rest periods. This will train your body to recover quicker between rounds in your actual fight. With your game plan having been set for weeks now, your focus for Week Nine should be to achieve success in the last few difficult training sessions you have left.

MONDAY AM / STRENGTH AND CONDITIONING

EXERCISE	DETAILS
Dynamic Warm-Up	—
Agility Hurdles	—
Core	Pike, Two Point Planks, Lateral Ab Wheel, Standing Russian Twists
Circuit 1	5 Minutes
Treadmill	2 Minutes
Dumbbell Push-Up	15 Seconds
Jump Squats	15 Seconds
Horizontal Pull-Ups	15 Seconds
Medicine Ball Punches	15 Seconds
Ropes	15 Seconds
Airdyne Bike	Sprint For Remaining Time
60 Second Break	—
Circuit 2	5 Minutes
Treadmill	2 Minutes
Single-Arm Medicine Ball Push-Up	6 Repetitions (Each Arm)
Lateral Box Hurdles	15 Seconds
Single-Arm Horizontal Pull-Up	6 Repetitions (Each Arm)
Medicine Ball Horizontal Pass	6 Repetitions (Each Direction)
Airdyne Bike	Remaining Time
60 Second Break	—
Circuit 3	5 Minutes
Treadmill	2 Minutes
Ropes	15 Seconds
Legs-Elevated Push-Up	15 Seconds
Tire Hop	15 Seconds
Tire Sledges	15 Seconds
Pummeling	15 Seconds
Airdyne Bike	Sprint For Remaining Time

MONDAY PM / MMA PRACTICE, LIGHT DAY

EXERCISE	DETAILS
Jump Rope	20 Minutes (Warm-Up)
Pummel	3 - 4 Rounds (Warm-Up, Increasing Intensity)
Drilling Clinch Takedowns	3 - 4 Rounds (40% Resistance)
Sparring From Clinch	5 x 6 Minute Rounds (50-60% Intensity)
Cooldown	Wrestling Drills, Jogging, Dynamic Stretching

TUESDAY AM / GRAPPLING TECHNIQUE

EXERCISE	DETAILS
Wrestling Drills	Warm-Up
Submission Drills	40 Minutes
Live Rolling	30 Minutes
Cooldown	Dynamic Stretching

TUESDAY PM / MMA PRACTICE, HARD DAY

EXERCISE	DETAILS
Jump Rope	20 Minutes (Warm-Up)
Sprints with Partner Carry	10 Laps (Warm-Up, Increasing Intensity)
Shadow Sparring with Partner	3 - 4 Rounds (No Contact)
Heavy Bag Work	5 x 3 Minute Rounds
Sparring	6 x 5 Minute Rounds (16 oz. Gloves, Boxing, Kickboxing, MMA)
Cooldown	Jogging, Dynamic Stretching

WEDNESDAY AM / STRENGTH AND CONDITIONING

EXERCISE	DETAILS
Dynamic Warm-Up	—
Agility ladder	—
Core	Straight Leg Sit-Up, Two Point Planks, Lateral Ab Wheel, Superman
Circuit 1	5 Minutes
Airdyne Bike	2.5 Minutes
Plyometric Push-Up	12 Repetitions
Ropes	15 Seconds
Medicine Ball Vertical Pass	10 Repetitions
Pull-Up	12 Repetitions
Medicine Ball Punch	Remaining Time
50 Second Break	—
Circuit 2	5 Minute
Treadmill	2 Minutes
Ropes	15 Seconds

Jump Squats with medicine Ball	15 Seconds
Tire Sledges	15 Seconds
Single-Arm Band Row	10 Repetitions (Each Arm)
Ropes	15 Seconds
Horizontal Medicine Ball Pass	6 Repetitions (Each Direction)
Tire Sledges	Remaining Time
50 Second Break	5 Minutes
Circuit 3	—
Airdyne Bike	2.5 Minutes
Legs-Elevated Plyometric Push-Up	8 Repetitions
Ropes	15 Seconds
Long Jumps	6 Repetitions
Tire Sledges	15 Seconds
Upright Band Right	15 Seconds
Band Resisted Punches	Remaining Time

WEDNESDAY PM / MMA PRACTICE, LIGHT DAY

EXERCISE	DETAILS
Jump Rope	20 Minutes (Warm-Up)
Pummel	3 - 4 Rounds (Warm-Up, Increasing Intensity)
Drilling Countering Kicks to Takedowns	3 - 4 Rounds (40% Resistance)
Sparring from Standing	5 - 6 Minute Rounds (MMA Gloves, 50-60% Intensity)
Cooldown	Wrestling Drills, Jogging, Dynamic Stretching

THURSDAY AM / BOXING TECHNIQUE

EXERCISE	DETAILS
Jump Rope	15 - 20 Minutes
Shadow Boxing	4 - 5 Rounds
Mitt Work	8 - 10 Rounds
Cooldown	Dynamic Stretching

THURSDAY PM / MMA PRACTICE, HARD DAY

EXERCISE	DETAILS
Jump Rope	20 Minutes (Warm-Up)
Shadow Sparring with Partner	3 - 4 Rounds (No Contact)
Heavy Bag Work	5 x 3 Minute Rounds
Shark Tank	5 x 5 Minute Rounds (Fresh Opponent Each Minute, MMA Gloves, MMA)
Cooldown	Jogging, Dynamic Stretching

FRIDAY AM / OFF

FRIDAY PM / MMA PRACTICE, LIGHT DAY

EXERCISE	DETAILS
Jump Rope	20 Minutes (Warm-Up)
Top / Bottom / Out	8 x 9 Minute Rounds (MMA Gloves, 50-60%)
Cooldown	Wrestling Drills, Jogging, Dynamic Stretching

SATURDAY AM / GRAPPLING TECHNIQUE

EXERCISE	DETAILS
Wrestling Drills	(Warm-Up)
Submission Drills	40 Minutes
Live Rolling	30 Minutes
Cooldown	Dynamic Stretching

SATURDAY PM - SUNDAY PM / OFF

Week Ten is fight week. All of the hard work is out of the way, and now it's time to allow your body to recover, keep yourself mentally sharp, and make weight. While it is still important to go to the gym, your training sessions should be extremely light, almost like active recovery. Additionally, to help your body develop a routine, all of your training sessions this week should occur at the same time as your upcoming fight. For example, if you will be fighting at 8 p.m., all of your training sessions for this week should be at 8 p.m.. This acclimates your body to the late hours, as most people tend to workout earlier in the day during the majority of their training camps. Your strength and conditioning is also completely finished by Week Ten, as your muscles need up to a week to recover after hard weight lifting sessions.

For many fighters, it is also important to focus on cutting weight in the final week. Of course my diet stays intact for this final week, starting late Thursday, I begin to limit water intake and hit the sauna if necessary. I also begin limiting the physical weight of the food consumed for the following day's weigh-ins. After making weight, I consume food and water to re-hydrate and replenish stores of glycogen in my body. Saturday should be preparation for your fight. This means staying relaxed and clearing your mind so that you can execute the game plan you have worked so hard to develop.

MONDAY AM / OFF

MONDAY PM / GRAPPLING TECHNIQUE

EXERCISE	DETAILS
Wrestling Drills	Warm-Up
Submission Drills	20 Minutes
Light Rolling	20 Minutes
Cooldown	Stretching

TUESDAY AM / OFF

TUESDAY PM / BOXING TECHNIQUE

EXERCISE	DETAILS
Jump Rope	15 - 20 Minutes
Shadow Boxing	4 - 5 Rounds
Mitt Work	4 - 6 Rounds
Cooldown	Stretching

WEDNESDAY AM / OFF

WEDNESDAY PM / WRESTLING TECHNIQUE

EXERCISE	DETAILS
Wrestling Drills	Warm-Up
Takedown Practice	20 Minutes
Light Wrestling	20 Minutes
Cooldown	Stretching

THURSDAY AM / OFF

THURSDAY PM / GRAPPLING TECHNIQUE

EXERCISE	DETAILS
Wrestling Drills	Warm-Up
Submission Drills	20 Minutes
Light Rolling	20 Minutes
Cooldown	Stretching

FRIDAY AM - SATURDAY AM / OFF

SATURDAY PM / FIGHT NIGHT

SECTION TWO
ALTERNATE WORKOUTS

While my strength and conditioning routine has been a big part of my success, my workouts have been custom tailored over years of trial and error. When I initially began wrestling, I was much smaller and weaker than I am currently. With the level of strength and size that I possessed at the beginning of my athletic career, it would have been impossible for me to utilize my current workouts efficiently. The intensity is much too high and it would have overly taxed my body and hindered my recovery.

My workouts are tailor made for myself, an elite level athlete. However, I recognize that many people reading this book will be in the beginning stages of their athletic careers, or their goals may differ from mine. Because of this, I've decided to include additional sample workouts that stress the body in different ways and will have varying effects on your athletic development. The sample workouts I've included vary from a less demanding variation of my day-to-day routine to a full body strength training regimen. Additionally, I've added some simple beginner and intermediate routines that will allow novice fighters to increase size and strength in the weight room while still spending ample time on the mats perfecting their technique.

Again, I must stress that these are sample workouts. There are many different possible variations on exercise selection, repetition schemes, and workout order that you could utilize for the same goals. However, by using the knowledge gained throughout the book, it should be a simple process to analyze the sample workouts, determine your own personal strengths and weaknesses, and adjust each workout to suit your own demands.

NOVICE STRENGTH AND CONDITIONING WORKOUT

This workout routine is a modified version of the workouts I use during the course of my training camps. It retains the same basic features of my typical workouts, but it's been adjusted to be more accessible for the average athlete. Much like the workouts listed in the previous section, this routine begins with a dynamic warm-up (increases blood flow to the body), agility work (increases foot speed and accuracy), and core work (strengthens the mid-section of the body). The primary difference is the exercise selection. Due to the difficult nature of full Olympic lifts, this workout utilizes partial Olympic lifts, which are more manageable to learn. They develop power just like the Olympic lifts, but without the steep learning curve. In addition to altering the exercises, I have also altered the repetition scheme. As you will see, the coming workout utilizes less overall volume and less low repetition exercises. This allows beginner athletes to start with lighter weights, and then progress to heavier loaded movements once their body adequately adapts.

You will notice that the workout incorporates my circuit training routine, but I have made some modifications here as well. I've reduced the overall volume of work during each circuit, and lengthened the rest times. Circuit training can be very intense, and jumping into three 5 minute rounds can be grueling for a beginner athlete. While every athlete must challenge himself in order to advance, attempting an exercise regimen that you are unprepared for can have negative consequences. The changes to my strength and conditioning routine allows a less conditioned athlete to reap the benefits of a proven workout without over-taxing his body and jeopardizing his recovery.

DAY 1

EXERCISE	DETAILS
Dynamic Warm-Up	—
Agility Hurdles	—
Core	V-Up, Plank, Superman, Scorpions
Power Clean	3 Sets x 6 Repetitions
Front Squat	3 Sets x 8 Repetitions
Barbell Bench Press	3 Sets x 8 Repetitions
Bent-Over Barbell Row	3 Sets x 8 Repetitions
Dips	2 Sets x 10 Repetitions
Curls	2 Sets x 10 Repetitions

DAY 2

EXERCISE	DETAILS
Dynamic Warm-Up	—
Agility Hurdles	—
Core	Crunch, Ab Wheel, Windshield Wipers
Circuit 1	—
Pull-Ups	10 Repetitions
Push-Ups	10 Repetitions
Airdyne Bike	1 Minute
Medicine Ball Slams	10 Repetitions
Medicine Ball Punch Pass	10 Repetitions
Break	75 Seconds
Circuit 2	—
Dumbbell Floor Press	12 Repetitions (Each Arm)
Forward Dumbbell Lunge	12 Repetitions
Dumbbell Bent over Row	12 Repetitions
Band Resisted Double Leg	8 Repetitions
Break	75 Seconds
Circuit 3	—
Airdyne Bike	20 Seconds Sprint, 10 Seconds Rest (x 6 Sets)

DAY 3

EXERCISE	DETAILS
Dynamic Warm-Up	—
Agility Hurdles	—
Core	Oblique Crunch, Russian Twist, Plank with Load Transfer
Push Press	3 Sets x 6 Repetitions
Pull-Up	3 sets x 8 Repetitions
Floor Press with Dumbbell	3 Sets x 8 Repetitions
Single-Arm Dumbbell Row	3 Sets x 8 Repetitions (Each Arm)
Rolling Triceps	2 Sets x 10 Repetitions
Front Raises	2 Sets x 10 Repetitions

BEGINNER STRENGTH AND SIZE

This is a great workout for beginner mixed martial artists because it is tailored to increase size and strength without interfering with sports training. The core of the workout is built around three separate days, with a different emphasis on each day. Day One is an upper body workout that focuses on moving heavy weights with the arms in both pushing and pulling motions, which increases maximum strength of the arms in both movements. The goal of Day Two is to increase strength in the lower body by incorporating heavy weights with moderately low repetitions to elicit a strong response from the muscles of the posterior chain. Day Three is oriented towards utilizing high repetitions and light weight with the upper body. This increases size in the upper body and helps the athlete pack on some muscle mass.

Since the lower body is only taxed once a week in this routine, it makes it much easier for the beginner athlete to increase their strength while retaining energy for their MMA workouts. However, it is important to note that this routine excludes any type of cardio training or metabolic conditioning. This is a choice a beginner fighter must make. If your goal is to increase size and strength, forgoing a conditioning workout may be the right choice. However, if you are looking to fight in the near future, it may be necessary to taper off weight training and transition into a more condition-based routine.

DAY 1

EXERCISE	DETAILS
Dynamic Warm-Up	—
Agility Hurdles	—
Core	Plank, Sit-Up, Scorpions
Close Grip Bench Press	4 Sets x 5 Repetitions
Dumbbell Press with Flex Band	4 Sets x 10 Repetitions
Dumbbell Bent-Over Rows	4 sets x 12 Repetitions
Dumbbell Lateral Raises	3 Sets x 15 Repetitions

DAY 2

EXERCISE	DETAILS
Dynamic Warm-Up	—
Agility Hurdles	—
Core	Sit-Up, Superman, Pike

Deadlift	4 Sets x 5 Repetitions
Barbell Step-Ups	3 Sets x 10 Repetitions (Each Leg)
Band Resisted Pull-Through	4 Sets x 10 Repetitions
DB Snatch	3 Sets x 10 Repetitions (Each Arm)

DAY 3

EXERCISE	DETAILS
Dynamic Warm-Up	—
Agility Hurdles	—
Core	Alternating Pikes, Two Point Planks, Leg Raises, Lateral Ab Wheel Rollout
Dips	2 Sets x 20 Reps (or 2 x 2, 2 x 3, 2 x 5, 2 x 10)
Pull-Ups	2 sets x 20 Repetitions (or 2 x 2, 2 x 3, 2 x 5, 2 x 10)
Rolling Triceps	4 Sets x 10 Repetitions
Dumbbell Curls	3 x 10 Repetitions
Dumbbell Lateral Raises	3 Sets x 15 Repetitions

INTERMEDIATE STRENGTH AND SIZE

This routine is designed for slightly more advanced athletes. Due to the higher volume of heavy movements, it can be quite demanding on your body. However, this is exactly what intermediate athletes need. Increasing the volume and intensity of exercise are two of the most important factors in stressing the muscles, and this routine delivers both. As you will see, Day One is the most physically taxing. This is the heavy day, and the goal is to build up to new 5 repetition maxes on an exercise each week. Day Two is the light day where you decrease volume and intensity to allow your body a slight break. Day Three is a medium day. You perform the same main exercises as you did on Day One, but you use slightly lighter weight. It is important to note that due to the large amount of resistance utilized with this training program, some self-monitoring is necessary. If you find yourself extremely sore after a heavy workout, adjust the following training session by lowering volume/intensity.

DAY 1

EXERCISE	DETAILS
Dynamic Warm-Up	—
Agility Hurdles	—
Core	Two Point Plank, Leg Lift, Seated Russian Twist
Back Squats	5 Sets x 5 Repetitions
Bench Press	5 Sets x 5 Repetitions
Power Clean	5 sets x 5 Repetitions
Dumbbell Overhead Press	2 Sets x 10 Repetitions
Dumbbells Curls	2 Sets x 10 Repetitions

DAY 2

EXERCISE	DETAILS
Dynamic Warm-Up	—
Agility Hurdles	—
Core	Leg Lift, V-Up, Oblique Crunch
Front Squat	4 Sets x 5 Repetitions
Good Mornings	4 Sets x 5 Repetitions
Barbell Push Press	4 Sets x 5 Repetitions
Dips	2 Sets x 10 Repetitions
Single-Arm Flex Band Rows	2 Sets x 10 Repetitions

DAY 3

EXERCISE	DETAILS
Dynamic Warm-Up	—
Agility Hurdles	—
Core	Plank, Sit-Up, Scorpions
Back Squats	5 Sets x 5 Repetitions
Bench Press	5 Sets x 5 Repetitions
Power Clean	5 Sets x 5 Repetitions
Rolling Triceps	2 Sets x 10 Repetitions
Pull-Ups	3 Sets to Failure

ADVANCED STRENGTH BUILDING

Often fighters will use the period between training camps to focus on increasing strength, relegating cardio and sometimes even technical training. When seeking to increasing maximal strength and power, this routine is a fantastic addition to your workout regimen. Rather than a typical 3-day-a-week lifting schedule, this routine adds an additional day of strength training to increase the quantity of weight lifted, yet still allows for adequate rest between heavy exercises. Day One focuses on the development of speed with your upper body. The core of the workout is several sets of 3 reps in a heavy upper body pressing movement, such as bench press. However, this is not a 3 repetition maximum—the weight selected is only 50-65% of your maximum weight. This allows for increased bar speed, which in turn increases overall power production. Day Two focuses on maximum effort lower body movement. This day revolves around several heavy sets of 3 reps, moving up to a single rep max in either the squat or deadlift. Day Three is a maximum effort upper body day, again focusing on bench press in order to tax the upper body most efficiently. The goal is the same as Day Two, several heavy sets of 3 reps, working up to a single max effort bench press. These max effort days do an extraordinary job of challenging not only the muscles, but also the central nervous system, forcing the fighter's body to respond by increasing overall strength. Finally Day Four is a speed day focusing on the lower body. Day Four utilizes an Olympic variant to force maximal power production out of the athlete.

By varying the stresses on the body and alternating speed training and strength training, it's possible to workout with extreme intensity on a regular basis without burning out either the musculature system or the nervous system. And by improving upon both speed and strength in the same weekly routine, the ultimate result will be vastly improved power production.

DAY 1

EXERCISE	DETAILS
Dynamic Warm-Up	—
Agility Hurdles	—
Core	Sit-Up, Russian Twist
Close Grip Barbell Bench Press	6 sets x 3 Repetitions
Rolling Triceps	4 Sets x 10 Repetitions
Dumbbell Floor Press	4 Sets x 10 Repetitions
Dumbbell Overhead Press	4 Sets x 6 Repetitions
Dumbbell Front Raise	4 Sets x 6 Repetitions

DAY 2

EXERCISE	DETAILS
Dynamic Warm-Up	—
Agility Hurdles	—
Core	Sit-Up, Russian Twist
Back Squat	6 Sets x 3 Repetitions, 2 Sets x 2 Repetitions, 1 Set x 1 Repetition
Pull Through	4 Sets x 8 Repetitions
Hip Thrust	4 Sets x 10 Repetitions
Body Weight Dips	4 Sets x 10 Repetitions
Barbell Curl	4 Sets x 6 Repetitions

DAY 3

EXERCISE	DETAILS
Dynamic Warm-Up	—
Agility Hurdles	—
Core	Sit-Up, Russian Twist
Barbell Bench Press	6 Sets x 3 Repetitions, 2 Sets x 2 Repetitions, 1 Set x 1 Repetition
Dumbbell Floor Press	4 Sets x 8 Repetitions
Weighted Dips	4 Sets x 8 Repetitions
Dumbbell Front Raise	4 Sets x 8 Repetitions

DAY 4

EXERCISE	DETAILS
Dynamic Warm-Up	—
Agility Hurdles	—
Core	Sit-Up, Russian Twist
Dead Clean	6 Sets x 3 Repetitions
Good Morning	4 Sets x 8 Repetitions
Pull Through	4 Sets x 10 Repetitions
Bent-Over Barbell Row	4 Sets x 10 Repetitions
Barbell Curls	4 Sets x 10 Repetitions

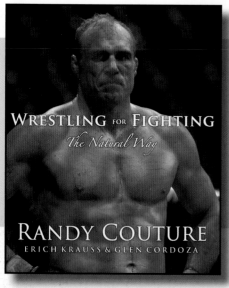

**WRESTLING FOR FIGHTING
THE NATURAL WAY**
RANDY COUTURE

**JACKSON'S
MIXED MARTIAL ARTS**
THE GROUND GAME

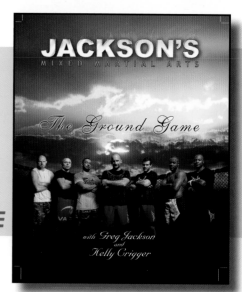

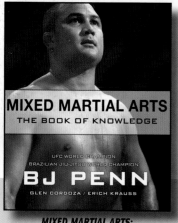

**MIXED MARTIAL ARTS:
THE BOOK OF KNOWLEDGE
BJ PENN**

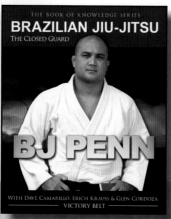

**BRAZILIAN JIU-JITSU:
THE CLOSED GUARD
BJ PENN**

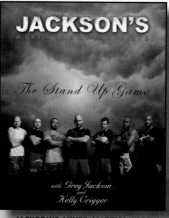

**JACKSON'S MIXED MARTIAL ARTS
THE STAND-UP GAME
GREG JACKSON**

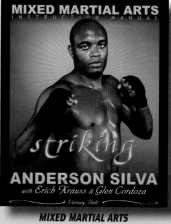

**MIXED MARTIAL ARTS
INSTRUCTION MANUAL: STRIKING
ANDERSON SILVA**

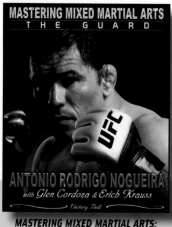

**MASTERING MIXED MARTIAL ARTS:
THE GUARD
ANTONIO NOGUEIRA**

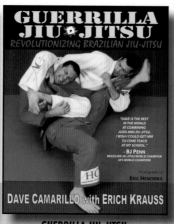

**GUERRILLA JIU-JITSU:
REVOLUTIONIZING BRAZILIAN JIU-JITSU
DAVE CAMARILLO**

**MASTERING THE RUBBER GUARD:
JIU-JITSU FOR MMA COMPETITION
EDDIE BRAVO**

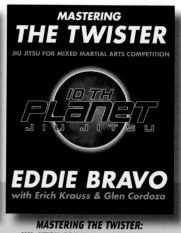

**MASTERING THE TWISTER:
JIU-JITSU FOR MMA COMPETITION
EDDIE BRAVO**

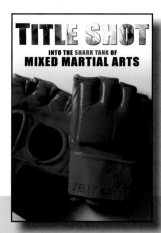

TITLE SHOT
INTO THE SHARK TANK OF MMA
KELLY CRIGGER

ADVANCED BRAZILIAN JIU-JITSU
MARCELO GARCIA

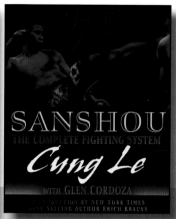

SAN SHOU
THE COMPLETE FIGHTING SYSTEM
CUNG LE

MACHIDA KARATE-DO
MIXED MARTIAL ARTS TECHNIQUES
LYOTO MACHIDA

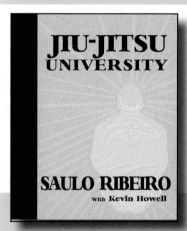

JIU-JITSU UNIVERSITY
SAULO RIBEIRO

DRILL TO WIN
12 MONTHS TO BETTER BRAZILIAN JIU-JITSU
ANDRE GALVAO

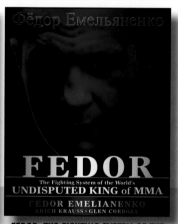

FEDOR: THE FIGHTING SYSTEM OF THE
UNDISPUTED KING OF MMA
FEDOR EMELIANENKO

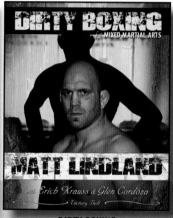

DIRTY BOXING
FOR MIXED MARTIAL ARTS
MATT LINDLAND

THE X-GUARD
GI & NO GI JIU-JITSU
MARCELO GARCIA

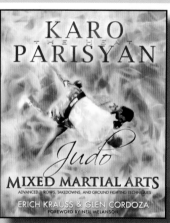

JUDO FOR MMA: ADVANCED THROWS,
TAKEDOWNS, AND GROUND FIGHTING
KARO PARISYAN

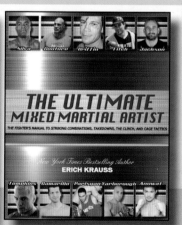

THE ULTIMATE MIXED MARTIAL ARTIST:
THE FIGHTER'S MANUAL TO STRIKING
COMBINATIONS, TAKEDOWNS,
THE CLINCH, AND CAGE TACTICS
ANDERSON SILVA
RANDY COUTURE
FORREST GRIFFIN
JON FITCH
GREG JACKSON
SHAWN THOMPKINS
DAVE CAMARILLO
KARO PARISYAN

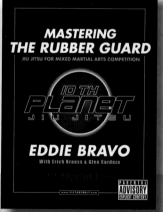

MASTERING THE RUBBER GUARD DVD:
JIU-JITSU FOR MMA COMPETITION
EDDIE BRAVO

ABOUT THE AUTHORS

Randy Couture, nicknamed "The natural," is a national-level wrestler who transformed himself into one of the most successful mixed martial arts fighters in history. He is the only UFC combatant to have claimed both the heavyweight and light heavyweight titles, and he has won more UFC title belts than anyone in the sport. He lives in Las Vegas, Nevada.

Lance Freimuth is a writer, editor, and photographer who lives in Las Vegas, NV. He also teaches grappling at Xtreme Couture, one of the most highly respected MMA gyms in the world.

Erich Krauss is the New York Times Bestselling author of Forrest Griffin's Got Fight: The Fifty Zen Principles of Hand-to-Face Combat, and he has written more than twenty five books. He is also a professional Muay Thai kickboxer who has lived and fought in Thailand. He lives in Las Vegas, Nevada.

ABOUT THE CONTRIBUTORS

Jake Bonacci grew up in Ironwood, MI. He graduated college in 2006 from the University of Wisconsin Superior after receiving his bachelor's of science degree in exercise science. In 2007 Jake earned his Master's Degree in Exercise Physiology from the College of St. Scholastica in Duluth, MN. Since earning his Master's, Jake has and continues to be the head Strength & Conditioning coach for Randy Couture and Xtreme Couture.

Neil Melanson is the head grappling coach of Xtreme Couture. Neil is the author of the much anticipated book, Triangles From The Guard.

Ron Frazier is the head MMA coach of Xtreme Couture.